RACHEL IN THE WORLD

RACHEL IN THE WORLD

A MEMOIR

JANE BERNSTEIN

University of Illinois Press

Urbana and

Chicago

Library of Congress Cataloging-in-
Publication Data
Bernstein, Jane, 1949–
Rachel in the world: a memoir /
Jane Bernstein.
p. cm.
Includes index.
ISBN-13 978-0-252-03253-0 (cloth : alk. paper)
ISBN-10 0-252-03253-5 (cloth : alk. paper)
1. Bernstein, Jane, 1949– 2. Glynn, Rachel.
3. Parents of children with disabilities—
United States—Biography. 4. Parents of
children with disabilities—Psychology. 5.
Youth with disabilities—United States—
Biography. I. Title.
HQ759.913.B46   2007
362.3092—dc22 [B]   2007005062

Photo credits: frontispiece, pp. 102,
267 by Edwin Martinez;
p. 40 by Stefi Ruben;
pp. 70, 188, 251, 264 by Charlotte Glynn;
p. 124 by Charlee Brodsky;
all others by Jane Bernstein.

Earlier versions of portions of some chapters appeared previously: chap. 1, "Taking Rachel Swimming," *Ms.*, Sept.–Oct. 1991, 40–41; chap. 2, "When She Was Small," *New York Times Magazine*, May 1994, 20; chap. 3, "Taking Care," *Creative Nonfiction* 3 (Summer 1995): 67–76; chap. 4, "On Regret," *The Sun* (Chapel Hill, N.C.), Dec. 1996, 15–18; chap. 5, "Rachel Flies Alone," *Massachusetts Review* (Summer 1999): 193–204; chap. 6, "Rachel at Seventeen," *More* (New York, N.Y.), June 2002, 60–65; chap. 7, "Rachel at Work," *Creative Nonfiction* 20 (Summer 2003): 113–30; chap. 10, "The Fourth Visit," *Maggid: A Journal of Jewish Literature* (New Milford, Conn.: Toby Press, 2005), 169–77.

Once again to Charlotte

Once again to Rachel

CONTENTS

Introduction   1

PART 1

1. Taking Rachel Swimming   15

2. When She Was Small   27

3. Taking Care   41

4. On Regret   55

5. Rachel Flies Alone   71

6. At Seventeen   87

7. Rachel at Work   103

8. Talking   125

PART 2

9. Kishorit   151

10. The Fourth Visit   163

11. Love and Death   173

12. Lifesharing   189

13. At Emilia's   211

14. Commencement   229

15. How It Happened   241

16. A Perfect Place   251

Acknowledgments   265

My love for her is not the dumb, gut love of mother for her baby rat, though that is part of it. Nor is it a sorrowful love. I love her because she is warm, charming, and responsive, because she loves in return, because she wakes up calling our names, and tells us to tickle her, because when I ask Charlotte what she wants to eat, Rachel, three rooms away, calls out, "Ummmmm cream cheese olive onion mustard fish sticks apple juice," and when I kiss her she says, "*I'm* so sweet." I love her because when I go to the bathroom, she follows behind me and says, "Excuse me, excuse me. May I come in?" and then opens the door and says, "I am in!" with great glee. She steps into the shower and says, "I am in the shower" and, "You're taking a pee-pee? I can hear it. That was good, that was very very *very* good. *Yeah!*" I love her because she is mine.

—From *Loving Rachel: A Family's Journey from Grief,* 1988

INTRODUCTION

It took me a long time to get comfortable with *Loving Rachel* as the title of my 1988 book about my daughter Rachel. It seemed a little soft and sentimental at first, not at all the way I saw myself or my own work. I simply got used to it, the way one grows accustomed to the name of a child or a dog. Fifteen years later, when I decided to write a second book about Rachel, I went back to that volume and saw for the first time how apt the title was. Like the best of titles, it captured something of the essence of the book, its most important theme—one that I had been unable to see, even though I was the author.

The story I told in that earlier work began in 1983, shortly before Rachel's birth, and ended in 1987, when she was still in preschool. The woman at the start of that story is cheerful and pregnant. She has a healthy little girl of nearly four, a husband she loves, and a house in a New Jersey suburb with a duck pond and grand white Presbyterian church in the center of town that are so picturesque they've been reproduced as a jigsaw puzzle ("Duck Pond in Spring"). Though she is far from naïve, she has no particular anxiety about this second pregnancy, an easy one, free from even the mundane discomforts that bedevil most women.

After an uneventful labor, the baby is born. She looks like an Eskimo baby, with a sweet, round face, almond-shaped eyes, and a head of black straight hair that the nurses comb into a peak. Though she's unusually quiet, it's hard to be overly alarmed by an infant who sleeps well, feeds well, and rarely cries. If anything, the new baby's placid nature makes it possible for the mother to spend more time helping her older daughter adjust to this small, wrinkled intruder. The baby's father is the one who is concerned. He's a biologist who's done work in vision, and though it's at a molecular level, on dragonfly eyes, he knows something about vision in humans. He thinks their daughter, at six weeks old, should be able to track moving objects. At a conference, he approaches a researcher who studies infant vision. She concurs.

Days later, the parents take this tiny baby to a specialist in New York, a pediatric neuro-ophthalmologist, who dilates the baby's pupils and tells them that she has optic nerve hypoplasia and is blind. As the brain matures over the next few months, some improvement in visual functioning could occur. It might allow her to see light and shadow, but they should expect nothing more than that. As for the disorder, all he can say is that something happened during the seventh or eighth week of development. Some insult, perhaps viral. It is not a progressive disease, nor is it inherited. There is no cure. They should contact the New Jersey Commission for the Blind and arrange for services to help her educationally. It's all they can do for now.

The doctor begins to dictate his notes. Stunned, the parents eventually walk out. They close the doctor's door and find themselves on terrain that is terrifying and unfamiliar, where they will become strangers to themselves and each other.

Weeks later, during some tests, this stunned couple learns that blindness is only one consequence of optic nerve hypoplasia; there is a "significant association" of such things as "intellectual impairment" and seizure disorder as well. Indeed, when the husband conducts a literature search and finds the very few papers written about ONH (which, although rare, is one of the three most common causes of blindness in babies), it seems that these related disorders are almost inevitable. It would take time for the parents to find out if their child would be blind or see only light and shadow, if she would be intellectually impaired (a term neither of them fully comprehends), and if she would have a seizure disorder.

. . . .

4   Rachel did not suffer in any way in these early months. She was not fussy or uncomfortable. We—her father, Paul; sister, Charlotte; and I—were the ones affected, first by the initial diagnosis of blindness, and then by the long and wrenching wait to find out the range and extent of her impairments.

We did not weather the beginning well. We loved this baby and were fiercely committed to her, and in this way we were united, but in our grief we became exaggerated versions of who we had been before Rachel's birth. I needed to talk and worry and read everything ever written about blindness and disability, to immerse myself in the literature, to collect facts and listen to others' stories, as if my expertise might alter Rachel's fate. Knowledge was both a balm and a curse: I did become informed, while at the same time unearthing various terrifying disorders that were similar to Rachel's but degenerative. My husband's grief traveled on different tracks. Though he brought home every paper on ONH that he could find, he did not want to read these studies, hear my concerns, or talk about the future. My moods shifted predictably after tests or reports from specialists, spurred by gloomy results or hopeful words; what triggered his ups and downs was mysterious and unpredictable, even to him. His grief was so deeply buried and so rarely expressed that whenever he broke down, it was as if he were hearing the news for the first time. Seldom were we emotionally in the same place.

For all of this, I was determined not to drown in unhappiness. When I was seventeen and my sister was murdered, I learned what could happen to a wounded family. The night after Rachel's diagnosis, I looked in on Charlotte, asleep in her room, and remembered what it was like to be the only child left, to feel that I had to be good and could never be good enough. I vowed that it would not be Charlotte's burden and tried, even in the earliest days, to make her feel that the joys and sorrows in her life mattered as much as anything that had happened to Rachel. When I look back, though, it sometimes seems as if the parties and family trips took place in the midst of a giant storm, because in truth, Rachel was like a hurricane that whipped through our house, blowing down the walls and ceilings, damaging Paul, Charlotte, and me, the relationships we had with each other, this lovely, fragile thing we called our family. That she was beloved did not lessen the chaos her birth had wrought. It's true that we worked to rebuild our family and repair the damage, but that repair work took longer than it might have if her diagnosis had been concrete. 5

The wait to find out if Rachel would have any vision, if she would be among the rare lucky ones without other disabilities, or if her impairments would be mild was long and full of dramatic events. In the summer before her first birthday, she reached for a brown kidney bean on a brown high-chair tray, proving to her father what I had begun to suspect: that she could see more than merely light and shadow. A month after that happiest incident, the infantile spasms began. First, there was a single episode in which she stiffened and bent forward; then clusters of seizures, six times a day. Words from textbook descriptions of infantile spasms came back. "Brain damage is usually evident . . . Intellectual prognosis is poor."

The treatment, with corticosteroids and adrenocorticotrophic hormone (ACTH) administered by needle, was devastating. I spent a week in a New York City hospital with her, coming back to our house in New Jersey only once, for Charlotte's first day of kindergarten. By the time I brought Rachel home, she was moonfaced and bloated; she could no longer sit or stand. We took turns holding her and listening to the unearthly hum she made, and we took turns walking away.

By her first birthday, all I wanted was for her to be free from pain.

Eventually, the drug treatments ended and over the next few months she began to regain her health. We resumed our waiting, this time from a different vantage point entirely.

Rachel's milestones over the next three years tell the story of her gains and deficits, but another story evolved over this same period that I didn't fully recognize at first. Despite all the tears and celebrations and gut-wrenching inadvertent comparisons with children her age, we had begun to accommodate to her. Without a word of discussion, we had begun to accept that there would be no miracles, medical or otherwise. What I had feared most had come to pass when she had infantile spasms. She was intellectually impaired, though I would not know the extent or full meaning of that for years, and she did have a seizure disorder. She was also cheerful and responsive and continued to make better use of her vision than anyone had expected. At twenty months she delighted us by starting to vocalize and form words, and at age two she walked at last. There were some disheartening signs of linguistic dysfunction, and scary EEGs, yet for every dream that was extinguished, another took its place. Even when I realized that her life would in no way resemble any life I'd intimately known, I kept planning and dreaming of all she could be.

It wasn't that I was particularly resilient as a mother. My constant search to find the best for Rachel, my determination to move past what she could not do, to find her strengths and abilities, was a quality of parenthood itself. I just hadn't known it. Before Rachel was born, I'd see a mother with a retarded child and wonder how that woman could go on shaking cantaloupes so blithely, how she kept up her strength to raise a child with no expectations, no future. I hadn't known that *all* children have a future, and that sometimes a parent's work is to figure out what that future is and how to attain it.

During this time I often thought about how I had searched for books about blindness and disability after Rachel was born. The only family stories I could find in the small local library felt compressed and false, too neat. The early days typically "passed in a blur," and in the end—the book's end—the family finds that they have grown because of this "special" child, this "gift from God." I had been offended by these tales, especially in the days when I was searching for some kind of reflection of what had happened to us.

I hated the treacly language people often used when writing or speaking about children with "special needs," the ruffled, fluffy packaging, the compression and tidying up of a family's disarray into neat, predictable little stages. I loved my daughter and accepted her as she was, but I didn't celebrate her disabilities or love her more because of them, or think she was put on earth to teach me something. It seemed to me that we had accommodated to Rachel in the same way I imagined a person accommodating to the loss of an arm or leg. We missed the life we'd had before her birth. We were aware of what we had lost. But we were okay about it; we were pushing forward, patching together the fragments of our family, adapting to her, incorporating her, laughing when she was funny (as she often was) or at the family we had become, and loving her without question.

I thought about these things a lot. When eventually I wrote about Rachel and my family, I hoped I'd written a compelling story for anyone who liked to read. In the back of my mind there remained the image of someone searching through book titles, desperate for a story that might lessen her sense of isolation, and I wrote the book for that person, too.

To me, *Loving Rachel* was grittier and harsher than the books I found on the library shelves. That was one of the reasons I was uncomfortable with the soft title, and the pink book jacket, as if inside was a romance novel. What I would not see for fifteen years was that, for all of turmoil I described, all the quarrels and tears and erratic behavior, there was a kind of sunniness to my narrative, a hopeful feeling, especially toward the end of the book, when I showed that this little child, partially sighted and intellectually impaired, was adored by her family. While this was—and is—still true, the surprise I felt when I reread my own work arose from my realization that I'd thought the whole story was about love. I'd thought that everything I was living and everything yet to come was about coming to terms with Rachel as she was. It was as if I had believed that our ability to love her, which took no effort at all, was proof that we were up to any challenge that might come our way.

If it wasn't easy ever, the love was simple and instinctual in those early years. She was my daughter, my flesh and blood. I did not think about loving her, or work at it; it took no courage or special effort on my part. If anything, my love was a source of sadness at times because of its depth and my inability to change things for her or change the world, which I feared would not be accepting of her. Still, I did not see that I was much different from any primate mother, except perhaps in my determination to keep my family together. I didn't want to lose my older daughter and husband; in fact, I wanted, nearly demanded, that we manage to know joy. That determination, borne out of my own complex history, was the one thing I can still say that I fought hard to have. The rest, as I've said, the love part—that was easy.

So this seemed to be the whole story. We had lived it; we had come to terms with Rachel as she was.

. . . .

"Are you going to read your mother's book?" a woman asks Charlotte at a book party in the fall of 1988, shortly after *Loving Rachel* has been released.

Charlotte's shiny hair falls nearly to her waist. Behind her wire-rimmed glasses are huge blue eyes that register every emotion—delight, impatience, scorn.

8   How awful it had been in the first months after Rachel's birth to look up from weeping and see Charlotte standing in the corner, watching mutely, those big eyes full of fear and confusion.

Now, though, she flips that long hair and says, in a dismissive way, "I don't need to read it. I *lived* it."

She is nine years old.

. . . .

"Will you write a second Rachel book?" a woman asks a few weeks later. She is in the audience at a talk I've given at the public library in Livingston, New Jersey. She has just introduced herself as the mother of a fourteen-year-old girl with developmental disabilities, and she eagerly waits for my answer.

"No!" I say, then quickly try to soften my answer by explaining that I had begun as a writer of fiction and want to return to what I love best—want, I do not say, to regain a part of my old life, my own imagination, apart from my daughter.

The look on this woman's face stops me, though I cannot tell exactly what it means.

"Oh, you will," she says. "You wait and see."

Then she vanishes.

. . . .

Over the ensuing years, I wrote a few essays about Rachel. These pieces described the years when Rachel was out of my arms, away from my constant protection. They were snapshots from when she was five or nine or fourteen, a way to mull over her experiences in school or our struggles with social services, and when she got older, my attempt to fully understand her. As the years passed and it became increasingly difficult to be Rachel's mother, that woman in the Livingston Public Library often came to mind—not her face, which I could no longer recall, or what she wore. It was her expression that I was beginning to understand, and her words: *Oh, you will. You wait and see.* I couldn't hear those words at the time, because I was in love. I was like a friend who believed that her arms around her baby were stronger than a seatbelt, that she could save her baby in a crash. How foolish my friend was to argue against the laws of physics. How foolish I had been to believe that my love would be enough. But I believed it nonetheless.

Standing in the library that day, I could never have imagined that a time would come when all my effort would be spent trying to arrange for Rachel to live apart from me. I had heard about elderly parents of grown children with mental retardation, worrying about what would happen when they died. Still, at that time, the reality of Rachel as an adult was as remote to me as imagining my own death. Inevitable, yes—but I hadn't the time or the gloomy sensibility to fret about it.

I could never have imagined standing on a street corner in Pittsburgh with two other mothers of kids with developmental disabilities. It's a March morning in 2003, the first blue-sky day in months in this gray city. Nearly fifteen years have passed since that night at the Livingston Public Library. George Bush is president; the search for weapons of mass destruction is under way. We're talking about cutbacks in services for our children when one of the women says, "I feel as if I've been handed a death sentence."

Her words shoot through my body like lightning. Suddenly I can feel my fear. I don't want a war to break out. I dread the bloodshed, the worldwide repercussions, and the effect this expense will have on state budgets. Though Rachel at twenty is not violent, like this woman's eight-year-old son, her demands are constant and unquenchable. I feel as if I will be living forever with my daughter, and that it will kill me, little by little.

Later that same week, I receive word that because of budget cuts in mental retardation services, no one under sixty is getting housing. I call an administrator at the county Office of Developmental Disabilities and Mental Retardation, as I have been advised, and hear myself confess that I am no longer a good mother and know that it is true. At the end of a long, fruitless conversation, I say, "If I can't get a placement for my daughter by June 2005, I'll leave her on your doorstep." The next day, I will send a letter, putting those same words in print. Fifteen years earlier, I could never have imagined thinking those words, much less uttering them to a stranger, as if my daughter is no more than an unwelcome package, merchandise I never ordered. I could never have imagined making such a threat.

Oh, you will. Now I can recognize the look on that woman's face.

I see the same expression on the faces of parents of disabled adolescents and adults. A kind of blunt fatigue. The parents of young children are full of tears and rage, consumed with blazing hope and a belief that their love will conquer everything. But we—parents of the older group—are tired. When we see each other, we never cry. We aren't part of support groups. No one rails about the system, though the system utterly fails our children when they grow older. Instead, on the infrequent occasions when we meet, we talk about the after-school program that's in danger of being cut. At housing meetings, we talk about how we want our children to live, though there is nothing available for any of them.

Oh, you will.

When did I change? After that street-corner discussion in March 2003, I went home and looked at myself in the mirror, as if I might be able to discover exactly what had happened to me. I could see the shadow of the young woman who had walked down a New York street in the fall of 1983, wearing the denim maternity jumper that had carried her through this, her second pregnancy. I could see her smooth face and confident walk, the sheer pleasure she felt being pregnant, could remember this woman who put all her faith in love, who would have said, without blushing, that love really did conquer all, that it was the most important thing, perhaps the only thing.

I suppose I'll never find the exact moment when the change occurred, the precise instant when that woman, that young, hopeful self, disappeared. The best I can do is arrange these stories that take place over sixteen years, from Rachel's fifth year through her twenty-first. I hope they show what happened to me—and why. I hope they also tell the story of Rachel's growing up and her determination to make a life of her own.

Loving Rachel was about us—our love, our grief, our bumpy road toward accepting her as she was. *Rachel in the World* is Rachel's own story. I'd like to imagine her thinking I got it right.

PART 1

1

Rachel is now a 4-yr., 8 mo.-old-child with evidence of multiple cognitive deficits on a central basis consistent with static encephalopathy. In addition to her visual handicap, there is evidence of difficulties with linguistic processing as well as a right hemiparesis indicating a greater degree of left hemispheric involvement. This would be consistent with her history of partial seizures arising from this hemisphere as well. The ongoing improvement exhibited would be consistent with an early prenatal insult responsible for her present problems.

—Dr. Donald J. Wight to the Department of Special
Services in Westfield, N.J., July 1988

TAKING RACHEL SWIMMING

In the summer of 1988, I bought a pair of water wings for Rachel, inflatable rings that fit around each upper arm. It took me until she was almost five years old to get them because I kept remembering my mother's advice of long ago to avoid such devices because children depend on them and then never learn to swim properly. I bought them because Rachel was getting hydrotherapy at Children's Specialized Hospital in Mountainside, New Jersey, where she was in preschool, and one day when I looked in on her, I saw her splashing wildly, laughter echoing in the pool, water wings around her arms. I was transfixed by the sight of my daughter, thrilled to the core. It was everything that I wanted for her.

Rachel looked so healthy and beautiful in the water. The months when she had been sick from the infantile spasms and the regimen of ACTH shots were behind us. She was again a cheerful child, sunny from the moment she opened her eyes and announced to everyone in the house, "I am up!" and "I am going to the bathroom!" until she went to bed. She was buoyant and happy with herself, toilet trained during the day, at last, and seizure free for long enough that we were weaning her off one of her two medications. We were doing well, too.

The time when overwhelming grief colored everything was long gone. Rachel was one of us now, a part of the family just as she was.

We weren't the only ones who enjoyed her sunny nature. Every- where I took her, people were drawn in by this tiny girl with ivory skin and brown ringlets, her big glasses (lavender wire-rims) slipping down her button nose. They were charmed when she approached them to say, "I'm Rachel. And this is my mother. Are you going to work now? Bye-bye, drive safely. Are you taking the van?" Strangers might notice the nystagmus, which made her eyes jitter, might intuit that something was different. But her speech was clear, her syntax and expression perfect, her forthright questions disarming and funny. "She's really *smart*," people often told me.

I never disagreed. Though I was well aware of her delays, I believed that something shone within my delightful, difficult child, that there was something exceptional about her, some ablity not yet fully expressed. But what? Until the day I saw her swimming, no activity engaged Rachel, no toy or game—nothing except talking.

I was sure this was because there was little she did well. Though she made excellent use of her limited vision and got around well enough to fool strangers into believing that her sight was just fine, we had seen her try to make conversation with a stone lawn ornament, and she had failed to recognize her father, ten feet away in the living room, until he spoke out. She had motor-planning problems, too; she walked and ran clumsily and often fell. She could hold a pencil but could not write. Nor could she do buttons, zippers, or laces, or play with toys that demanded much fine-motor control. Even her language—what appeared to be her greatest strength—was, paradoxically, her most serious weakness. The patter that charmed strangers was "cocktail party chatter," memorized loops she used at appropriate times, with the perfect inflection. She could not go beyond these exchanges, could not answer "why" or "when" questions, except by saying, "Hmmm. I'm *finking*," and she could not organize her thoughts to make genuine conversation.

If only I could find something she loved to do, her whole life would be different, I believed. If I could find a toy that engaged her she wouldn't stand in the kitchen and slam the refrigerator door repeatedly or bang on the cabinets with a spoon. If I could teach her a game she could play alone, she wouldn't follow me around the house, chattering nonstop. Maybe if she could *do* something, it would curtail her need to call out to locate blurry grownup shapes in the distance, reel them in with her bell-like hello, and keep them captive with her nonstop meaningless questions.

The vision specialist from the New Jersey Commission for the Blind sent us toys at regular intervals—kits with bristly, fuzzy, and soft objects; big, beautiful blocks; beeper balls; and tapes of animal sounds—and I was always searching in stores and catalogs, and in the toy library in her school, for playthings she might enjoy. I worked with letters (which she recognized) and pegs (which she could count), and I learned from her speech pathologist to cue her when she was floundering and to keep her on topic. And when I was concerned and irritated that she followed me around the house the entire time she was home, calling my name and asking "how come" questions that needed no answers, I took her to a behavioral psychologist who designed a week-by-week plan meant to modify the behavior of my "extremely disfluent" daughter. When I told him in a moment of frustration that the thought of her stuck like this in the future was devastating, he said, "It's going to be devastating."

I wept when I left the office, felt as if the world was coming to an end, then promptly and completely forgot his words. I would never have remembered the encounter at all if not for the notes I found years later, describing these visits. By then I understood why I had forgotten so quickly. I was too busy searching for toys and games—for something Rachel might love to do. A report that described her delays might fill me with despair, but then I'd witness the sheer delight she took simply waking and toddling into someone's room, or I'd hear her yawn like our dog or mumble to herself, after farting, "That was me, excuse me, I tooted," and I would be lifted from my sadness and back to work—searching for strategies that would help her and implementing plans at home. It was a job I took on eagerly. Nothing would make me stop.

· · · ·

On a humid June afternoon two weeks after I had watched Rachel swim, I went with my family to a graduation party, hosted by the parents of a boy from Rachel's preschool class at Children's Specialized Hospital. Sitting on the lawn chairs around the heated pool were Rachel's therapists, teachers, and caregivers, some of whom had known Rachel since she was six weeks old. While Paul stopped to chat with them, I slipped the water wings on Rachel's arms and took her into the water.

Seeing the group of women poolside reminded me how much I had grown used to the delight they took in Rachel's progress and the attention they lavished on Charlotte when we picked up her sister from day care each afternoon. When I let Rachel go into the pool, I knew I would be letting go in other ways, too, taking her from this small, nurturing, hospital-based program, where she could have spent another year, and enrolling her in the district's "preschool handicapped" class. This choice to place her in a less-restrictive program was my way of saying that I believed that Rachel was ready to handle more independence. But it was a scary step into a world where she would not necessarily be valued.

Watching her paddle away from me, into the deep end, my anxieties began to abate. Rachel seemed transformed by the water. Like any five-year-old in a pool, she was making bubbles, asking me to watch her kick, swimming ahead and calling for me to catch her. She was radiant, filled with energy.

My fingers were puckery and her lips blue when I tried to take her out. Rachel, my passive, uncomplaining child, yowled and fought so much that the teachers and parents at the poolside couldn't believe the fuss she made. "Is *that* Rachel?" they kept asking, amazed.

· · · ·

I packed the water wings when we left for our cottage in Maine, a knotty-pine "camp" on Quahog Bay that Paul and I bought the year we were married. From the first season, it was our sanctuary, the place where we were always happy. During the winter months, when we were mired in the complex demands of everyday life, we would pine for "Maine House" (the name Charlotte bestowed on the cottage), and when the crocuses bloomed at "Foodtown House" (her name for our New Jersey home, with its unfortunate proximity to the supermarket), we came down with "Maine Fever," a yearning to smell the pine and see the bay sparkling at the foot of the little house.

Before the kids were born, Paul and I bought a black, stitch-bound journal that became our summer diary. The first entries we made were mundane things—measurements, diagrams, and lists. Later, kids drew pictures on the unlined paper and guests left notes; newspaper clippings about notable events were taped onto the pages: a whale beached on Orr's Island; a nineteen-pound lobster pulled from a trap ("Cundy's Lobsterman Lands Whopper"). There are "journal entries" Charlotte dictated to me when she was not quite three and a "huge mad face" she drew that same summer.

There are no entries that allude to the months after Rachel's birth when we stumbled through the days, nothing about the infantile spasms she'd had at the cottage, where we thought we were immune from grief, or the months when she moaned in pain. But, like points on a map, there is a record of the road back. Her caregiver Lourie, writing, "Ray-Ray is doing great, she's almost walking," and on the next page, her grandmother listing all the words Rachel had begun to speak: "Nana, Papa, turtle, row row row your boat, mommy, daddy, and others. . . . She is a walking doll."

"Oh joy," I wrote the summer I put the water wings on Rachel and took her and Charlotte into the chilly water. Most of the time, we lowered ourselves into the bay from the granite ledge, but some afternoons we took the canoe out to one of the small nearby islands and "hand-swam" in the shallow water's edge, propelling ourselves forward in the muck—all of us, even Rachel. I saw what an equalizer the water was, and how, in the bay, we were all the same. I suppose I was just discovering what others have known for years, that because of water's natural buoyancy, people with neurological, muscular, or joint problems can do in water what is difficult or impossible for them on land.

In Maine, it was more than just the fun of seeing Rachel swim that delighted me; it was the pleasure of simply being with her—not cuing her or coaching her or working with flash cards. There was no "behavior mod" when we were in the water. There were no arguments about her right to interrupt our conversation, when her turn might consist of saying, "You know what? Windsey's coming over, and my muver says . . . Windsey's coming over, a-a-and she says, you know what? Windsey's coming over."

We were simply hanging out, and it was very nice. It made me feel as if we were just an ordinary family having what a therapist, years later, would call "a slice of just plain being together." Not special or tragic, not on some journey from grief, and Rachel, exactly as she was, could be part of it.

"Rae-Rae in water wings," I wrote. "Hand-swimming, singing, sun in my eyes. Pure joy. Oh joy. Oh wonderfulness."

By summer's end I was certain I'd made the right choice, enrolling her in the district's pre-kindergarten beginning that fall.

· · · ·

A family we slightly knew invited us to the town pool one weekday afternoon, shortly after we returned to New Jersey. I agreed to go as a favor to Charlotte, who envied the girls whose mothers took them there each day. Charlotte yearned for us to belong to the pool the way she yearned for a father whose hair was brown and not silver, for a mother who shaved under her arms, for a sister who didn't have "problems," and for a house with a family room spacious enough to fit the conventional parents and sister she ached to have, along with Barbie's own house and car. I couldn't make her father forty instead of fifty-five. And I wouldn't change my values. But I was touched by her desire to be like the other kids in our conservative New Jersey town and wanted badly for her to be comfortable in her own skin, happy about herself. I could call the solarium a family room if it pleased her, and leave my snowmobile boots in the car when I entered her school on a winter day. And I could take her to the town pool so she could swim with her friend.

Flotation devices such as water wings were not allowed at the pool, so I took Rachel to the smallest of the three pools. I watched her hand-swim in the shallow water, then watched her slide beneath the water, never struggling. She never coughed when I picked her up, and she told me, when I asked, that she was fine. But she seemed woozy and out of it.

Several minutes later, she had a series of seizures that simply would not end. *Status epilepticus,* as it is known by physicians, is the kind of event that gives seizures a bad name, for it sometimes lasted for hours or even days and can be life threatening. The lifeguards rushed over, and the gawkers gathered close. The emergency squad arrived to help Rachel, and when they dispersed the crowd they pushed Charlotte far away from me. Rachel was intubated, to make sure she did not choke, and two physicians—a husband and wife on a rare afternoon off—administered intravenous Valium. Then Rachel was rushed to a local hospital.

She spent nearly a week there while her medications were stabilized. In that time she had blood tests and EEGs. An MRI, newly approved for use on children, showed that she had septo-optic dysplasia, which was often seen with optic nerve hypoplasia, especially among the more impaired children. While this was a significant finding that foreshadowed her later pituitary problems, it was her "grossly abnormal" EEG that concerned us at the time. I was assured that the alarming seizures she'd had at the pool were the result of her being undermedicated, that the episode was inevitable and had absolutely nothing to do with the water. When her dosage was regulated and she was fully recovered, she could swim again.

And so, cautiously at first, we took her swimming again. Rachel, awkward and hesitant on land, kicked and paddled, proud and vigorous.

One Saturday in mid-winter, six seizure-free months after the *status epilepticus,* Paul decided to take both children for a swim at the Y in our town. They had been in the pool for forty-five minutes when Rachel went limp in the water, her head thrown back. Paul took her from the pool. Within a minute, she had roused and was begging to go back in. Nonetheless we were concerned.

We had her drug levels checked and found that she was within the normal range for both medications. We even arranged for her to have a twenty-four-hour EEG, in which she wore the electrodes and a small battery pack in a knapsack for a full day and night. The EEG showed no subclinical seizures.

"Take her swimming," said the neurologist, and so we did. This time I joined my family at the pool. I saw the way Rachel swam with utter abandon and joy, and then saw the sudden limpness, the peculiar way she roused, with no post-seizure grogginess, ready to go swimming again, furious that we said no.

"Was the water very cold?" the neurologist asked me.

No. She had been in the smaller pool, which was heated like her hydrotherapy pool, to nearly body temperature.

What about the temperature outside the pool. Had it been hot?

No. The chill when you stepped out of the pool was rather unpleasant.

Did she hyperventilate when she was swimming? Had she been sick? Did she swallow a great deal of water?

No to all of these questions.

What I felt then, along with the frustration of being unable to figure out what triggered these seizures, was a determination that Rachel continue to swim—a determination shared by neither the neurologist nor my husband. When the summer was upon us again, I was forced to scrutinize my feelings. Why was I unable to let go of this desire in the face of her problems? Why was I so adamant that Rachel swim?

My first argument went like this: In the water she was radiant and energetic. What did any of us gain by depriving her of the only thing that she did well?

What complicated this was the fact that Rachel never said, "Mommy, I want to swim," unless she heard others talking about it. Even then, it was easy enough to reroute her, to trick her into thinking about something else. Therefore, if she was never again in the water, she might never ask to swim, and she would never tell me that she missed swimming. Could I say, then, that I would not be depriving her of anything, that she did not really care? Or would this be like saying that pleasure is only what one is able to recall and describe?

As we packed to leave for our cottage on Quahog Bay the next summer, I wrestled with these questions, trying hard to separate my conception of pleasure from hers. I had to acknowledge that my insistence that Rachel swim was selfish, in part. I wanted her to swim because when she did, she was one of us, doing what we were able to do, equalized by the water. I only hoped that my attempt to have her live a life like ours would not risk her well-being.

I knew, though, that this issue was far bigger than that of Rachel's swimming. It had also to do with Rachel in her family's world, and beyond that, Rachel in a world set up for the unimpaired, the "typically developed." As a disinterested person, I wanted to imagine a society in which people of all abilities mixed freely in childcare centers and schools, and in the workplace. But as the mother of a child who *was* more vulnerable than most, I had the far more complicated task of figuring out how much to acknowledge her disabilities, how to protect her because of them, and how much to push her into the world.

24   Rachel was not quite six, and a child that age is still in a family's arms. I knew that I'd be grappling with these issues for years to come. The question of whether Rachel should swim was the first of many, and my adamance, with all its elements of stubbornness and denial, was my way of saying that I wanted to see how far my daughter would go before I used the word "never."

If only the answers to these larger questions were as simple as the one we settled on that summer. Rachel went swimming again, in the cold, clear water of Maine—in for fifteen glorious minutes, and out despite her complaints. And she thrived.

2

Rachel accompanied this examiner willingly to an adjoining portable classroom. She spoke spontaneously, and as we encountered a staff member sitting outside at a picnic table, Rachel responded to this staff member by saying, "How are you?" Upon entering the room which was used for this evaluation, Rachel was directed to sit in a chair, but she asserted her independence by requesting, "I prefer sitting in this chair." Rachel then went on to ask permission to kneel on the chair rather than to sit. Throughout the evaluation, it was noted that Rachel's verbal expression and syntax were excellent, though also noted was her tendency to be inappropriate at times. For example, during the evaluation she asked, "Do you mind if I make myself a cup of tea?" This examiner was not able to determine the significance of this request since there were no indications in the test room that would prompt such a request.

—Educational Evaluation, December 11, 1990, Office of
    Special Services, Westfield Public Schools

WHEN SHE WAS SMALL

Here's Rachel at eight, walking beside me in the supermarket one afternoon. One moment she's helping me push a cart, and the next, just as I've turned to check the expiration date on a gallon of milk, she is approaching another shopper, demanding to know what the woman is buying.

She is curly-haired and cute and very small, not just small for her age, but not even on the standard growth curve for a child her age. Because of her developmental problems, this particular fact, which I am reminded of mostly when she has a medical appointment, doesn't especially concern me. If anything, her smallness is a help. Small means that she fits into the toddler-sized disposable training pants she wears at night. It means she is accepted into a preschool summer program in Maine, and the childcare program at a ski resort, instead of being placed with older kids who will not play with her, or who go out to ski for part of the day—something she can never do, because of her motor-planning problems. It means that Charlotte's friends tolerate her behavior and that neighborhood babysitters aren't afraid to watch her. Her small size means that when she approaches strangers in stores, shakes their hands and introduces herself, or stands an inch away and questions them about their plans, people are still amused.

"How old are you?" the woman asks her on this particular after-noon.

"Thix," she says.

A stickler for the truth, I correct her. "How old are you, Rachel?"

"Theven."

"*How* old?"

"Eight."

The woman's face changes; she is incredulous and then uncom-fortable.

After that I start letting Rachel pass for six. It's easier that way.

Rachel's smallness lets me forget at times that in our household is an eight-year-old child who is still fully dependent on us, who cannot play by herself or walk in the street without having her hand held, who has no friends, and who has been struggling in school for the fourth straight year to master number concepts and pre-reading skills. Her smallness allows me to move away from her deficits and disabilities and the long list of things other children her age can do. Forgetting about where Rachel is in relation to other children gives me a chance to enjoy her as she is. It also lets me believe in Rachel.

I don't waste time imagining her reaching certain milestones or living a life that will be just like mine. My hope comes from the fact that there is so much I can't yet fathom about my inscrutable daugh-ter. Out of what is still unknown are possibilities, ways to unlock the glimmers of ability I often see. She is one of us without question. What I still want more than anything is to figure out how she can be who she is and still somehow fit into our family and the world outside our house.

If asked about Rachel's stature, I would say without hesitation that the effort to understand her matters far more to me than my concerns about her size, never considering the ways her small, sweet prettiness helps me hold on to my dreams for her.

• • • •

What *did* Rachel understand when she was eight? She knew that when she woke, she would get breakfast—knew and had begun to demand it. The moment she opened her eyes, she would ask, "May I have cereal?" Up on her feet, she would continue, "Where's my bowl? I need a spoon. May I have raisins?" never stopping until the food was on the table before her. She knew, too, that on weekday mornings, the little yellow bus would pull up to take her to school. If she

didn't intuit that her driver was an impatient man, she came home saying, "Stay green, baby; stay green," his words, which she tried out herself, listening for the perfect intonation. Later, when we were in the car together and I was approaching a traffic light, she'd call out, "Stay green, baby; stay green." What intrigued me was not simply that her mimicry was so good, but that she used these expressions in just the right way.

That was why, in 1991, when we were preparing to move from New Jersey to Pennsylvania, I found myself wondering what "moving" might mean to Rachel. At eight, though she needed routine—needed breakfast to be cereal served immediately and for the bus to come to take her to school—she was not otherwise sensitive to her environment. She did not mind sleeping in my old bed when she visited her grandparents, who lived forty-five minutes away, or waking in the bottom bunk of "sky crib," the bunk bed Paul built for the kids' room in Maine, with crib-siding around the top bunk for safety. As long as there was routine, she could be anywhere, it seemed, with anyone, I often thought.

Rachel seemed unaffected by the changes that occurred in the months before the move. She did not know that the department in the research lab where Paul worked had disbanded and that I had taken a job as a magazine editor in New York, waking each morning at 5:15 and returning home with just enough energy to make dinner, help Charlotte with homework, and fall into bed. She did not seem to care that I no longer worked in my attic office when she was at school, hurrying downstairs when her bus driver leaned on his horn, or that when she came home she was greeted by a mopey high-schooler named Tiffany instead of me. I cared. I didn't like this life where only urgent matters were attended to and everything else pushed aside.

· · · ·

Hope was behind my optimism for Rachel when she was eight, the expectation that her teachers and I would find strategies to unlock her abilities. Hope was also behind our decision to leave a part of the country where we'd been born and raised and where our lives were rich with family and friends. We believed we could be happier somewhere else—more comfortable, more financially secure. A move meant possibility, the chance for something better.

The upcoming move dominated family conversation in the months when I was interviewing for a tenure-track teaching position, hoping to find a job that would let me write and teach and achieve the kind of balance I found so pleasurable. Even before we knew our destination, we all had dreams. Paul hoped I'd get a job in a city where he could find a research position that wasn't too physically taxing: though he was still vibrant and full of enthusiasm, he fatigued easily because of the liver disease that had been diagnosed twelve years before. Charlotte hoped we'd buy an old house with an attic she could have for her own, and behind the door that led to this private space, a bedroom and a bathroom with a claw-foot tub. Even our feisty West Highland white terrier had dreams, or so we decided—a place where he could roll in dead mice and find girl dogs. As for Rachel, what could I imagine might be better for her? We were living in a state that, at the time, ranked at the very top in social services. The school she was attending was excellent.

In retrospect, I was right to be anxious. In our early years in New Jersey, "the system" was like an angel who flew into our house before I knew I needed her. "The system" was the sweet-faced vision specialist from the New Jersey Commission for the Blind, who showed up days after Rachel had been diagnosed, to admire her, to play with her in a cheerful, nonjudgmental way, and to refer us to the "infant stimulation" program (as early intervention was then called). She was the one who enjoyed our baby and sent us toys to stimulate her tactile senses. "The system" was the second vision specialist, who visited Rachel's classroom twice a month to give her teachers materials and train them to work with her. The system was benevolent, innovative, responsive, always there to provide appropriate adaptations.

All these things I associated with New Jersey, whereas *not New Jersey* was full of unknowns. *Not New Jersey* was the classroom I visited in Memphis, where I'd been flown for a job interview. The visit was my host's idea, his way to assure me that my daughter could fit in there, too. He had made some calls and was told about a program for children with low vision that I could observe if I liked. Shortly after I arrived, he took me with great enthusiasm to the school.

A teacher escorted me into a bare room. Four blind children sat in front of a TV while two others wandered aimlessly. There were no alternatives at that time, no approved private programs within commuting distance, nothing apart from what I'd seen.

The image of those visually impaired children sitting an inch from that TV would forever remain; it stood for everything I feared, everything that was *not New Jersey.*

· · · ·

Three years earlier, I had seen Rachel in a classroom that squelched all hope. It was the public "preschool handicapped" program where I had enrolled her so optimistically. During that school year she had gained skills, for certain. She could remove her own coat and use the bathroom without assistance, could paste and color, name parts of the body, colors, and major shapes. She'd learned to hold a pencil perfectly, too, though no one had taken the time to help her touch the point of that pencil to paper.

Rachel had also learned to sit quietly at a desk when the children were given a worksheet, though she could make out nothing on the paper before her. The vision specialist had explained to her teachers that the only images Rachel could discern were simple, bold representations an inch to an inch and a half in size. The worksheets given to my daughter had poorly reproduced pictures she could not see, of things like teepees and axes and volcanoes, items that were not part of the frame of reference for this child who could neither get enough information from picture books nor follow the flickering images on TV.

I wished that other adaptations could be made for her and that her teachers could use the kinds of therapies that had helped her in the past, so I arranged for conferences with her occupational therapist and her speech pathologist. I described the vestibular training that had been used to address Rachel's dyspraxia and her motor-planning problems, and to give her a better sense of her own body in space. "Don't come in here with words like dyspraxia," the present occupational therapist snapped. "This is a school, not a hospital. We're not going to *spin* her."

The speech pathologist wasn't hostile when we met—merely annoyed, it seemed. She explained the group activity they had done that day, how the children had washed a doll, describing each step they took, and afterward talked about what they had done. "Rachel doesn't seem to remember *anything*," she said in an exasperated way. "She can't talk about what she did a *moment* before."

Wasn't that why we were working so hard to cue her, I wondered? Wasn't that most basic strategy passed on to me years before? Questions like "What did you do in school?" or even "What did you do in speech?" were too broad, too difficult for her to answer. When I asked, "Did you play with a doll in speech?" she could say, "Yes." When I asked, "What did you do with the doll?" she could say, "Wash it." "With what?" "A washcloth."

When Rachel responded to these questions, I wasn't thinking about where she was in relation to other children her age. I was happy to see what she was able to do.

At the end of the school year, when the district decided that Rachel was a "perfect candidate" for the self-contained classroom, it was time to acknowledge that my dream that Rachel would go to the same school as her sister was not something that would benefit her. The progress she was making came through intensive therapies and in one-on-one sessions.

What made this a bump and not a disaster was that my wishes prevailed without debate. I was given a list of schools outside the district, and I visited each, trying to figure out where Rachel might best fit.

Not the county school, a chaotic place, where there were two speech pathologists for 160 children. Not the school that was well regarded for children with communication disorders, where she was cooed and fussed over, and then declared, after a half day in a classroom, "disruptive" for talking so much and rejected on the spot.

Eventually I found a school forty-five minutes from home, in a big, new prefab building that looked like a warehouse, in an area of farmland, condominium complexes, and light industry. The principal was a dynamic, thoughtful woman. After spending a few hours with Rachel and noting her many splinter skills and weak areas, she declared her "so interesting educationally." It was what I had wanted, really: someone who found her intriguing and challenging as I did and was eager to find out who she was; someone who would not merely declare her talking disruptive, but would wonder why she talked so much—perhaps she didn't get the signal to inhibit—and develop a plan for Rachel, with an agenda, and topical exchanges, and rewards for staying on topic.

The classroom reports were not always glowing. What heartened me and made me believe that Rachel was in the best possible school was the commitment her teachers had to working with her, their flexibility and willingness to adapt, and to experiment on her behalf. I saw them as realistic and hopeful—the way I might have described myself.

Now we were moving to Pittsburgh, so I could teach at Carnegie Mellon University. We were leaving family and friends, taking Charlotte from her neighborhood and Rachel from a school and teachers I trusted.

Did Rachel know where we were going or why? If I asked, "Are we moving?" she said, "Yes." If I asked, "What will you get?" she might say, "A new room." What then of the evening when she watched me scooping seeds from a cantaloupe, and then declared, "Carnegitty melon." Was "carneggity melon" a fruit to her? Or a destination? Was it something to eat or a place we would sleep? Would it make a difference to her that she was leaving so many familiar people? Would she notice?

In mid-August, the moving van came. Two giant, muscular movers took our possessions and left us in our empty house. We drove across the state, arriving early in the evening at the brick house we had bought, on a broad, curving, tree-lined boulevard in a neighborhood called Squirrel Hill. It had an enclosed back porch and a finished third floor with a bedroom for Charlotte and a bathroom with a claw-foot tub, just as she had dreamed. That first night, we wrapped ourselves in comforters and slept on the floor.

In the morning, our neighbors on one side brought us a thermos of coffee and cups. The neighbors on the other side were setting off for the Jersey shore, but not before leaving us with a bottle of wine, a loaf of bread, and a note that wished us happiness.

By the time the moving men unloaded our possessions and I began to unpack the seemingly endless number of cartons, it was with a sense of expectation, a feeling that this change would be good for us all.

PART 1

. . . .

A snapshot from my second day in Pittsburgh: I'm standing in the
midst of cartons in the kitchen of our new house when the doorbell
rings. On the porch are two little girls, pretty dark-haired sisters.
They've heard that a girl their age has moved in and want to know
if they can play with her.

These little girls, with their eager faces and shiny hair, have no
inkling of all that sweeps through my mind in the few seconds that
pass before I find my words. Yes, of course they can play with Rachel. Hasn't it been my most profound wish since her birth to see
her admitted to a world of children and adults, without a prefix, a
diagnosis, an explanation? Of course they can play with Rachel, I say,
calling upstairs to her, and knowing they never will.

I listen to her pad across the second-floor hall in her bare feet. I
know these girls won't be cruel to her, that children aren't, in my
presence, at least; it's that they don't know how to play with a child
who has no imaginative play, isn't interested in dolls or make believe;
who cannot color or cut with any comfort. Children notice what
adults often don't: that she does not really relate to people. In a social
situation, in school, or at birthday parties, adults are the ones she
engages with her questions and commands, never children. Teachers
or staff, parents, custodians, or once, at a birthday party in a fast-food
restaurant, strangers sitting in a corner. Adults are charmed by the
good manners and clear speech of this tiny girl, who looks so much
younger than she is and therefore seems oddly precocious. Adults
willingly do her bidding and ponder her questions, seeking answers
even when they make no sense to anyone, least of all to her.

Rachel walks downstairs, softer, rounder, different in ways these
girls instinctually sense but cannot articulate. It isn't that her jittering
eyes make her inaccessible; it's something else, a kind of closed-off
quality, a lack of facial expression or gesture. Standing there, I'm
struck by how much smaller and more babyish Rachel is and how
different it is from seeing the information on a growth chart. She
does not smile or step forward or make note of her visitors in any
way. It's as if she knows she cannot manipulate them and does not
even try.

WHEN SHE WAS SMALL

I'm awkward and inexperienced, fresh from a world where our friends know Rachel and strangers think she's a toddler. I try to tell the little girls about the things Rachel enjoys, like kickball and swimming, but they are wiggling with discomfort, wanting badly to leave, and it seems as if the kindest thing I can do is make that easy for them.

As soon as they are gone, I know I've bungled this introduction and failed my own daughter. I stand among the moving boxes, sadness falling over me like a heavy curtain.

When I remember this moment, another snapshot comes to mind. It's Charlotte's first day at her new school. Thinking how important it is to make a good impression, I talk her into wearing a flared powder-blue skirt with a matching T-shirt top. She arrives at her big urban middle school, twelve years old, the new girl in seventh grade. Her accent is weird, her glasses are ugly; she has frog eyes, dorky clothes; her sister is retarded. Soon enough she will dress the way she likes, grow her hair, get contact lenses, make good friends, and still she will remain *Charlotte with the retarded sister*—just as she was from the start.

• • • •

We liked our neighborhood and the families who lived on either side of us, and this softened our painful transition. All three houses had open areas in the back, decks or covered porches. When the weather was warm, we saw each other at breakfast or on weekends, and conversations and potluck dinners ensued in a natural, spontaneous way. There were six kids between us, and then eight, most of them very young. It wasn't long before we joined our three small yards to create a single play space that had grass and swings, and a flat cement pad perfect for tricycles and chalk drawings.

The little girls from around the corner never returned. The neighbors' kids didn't play with Rachel either, but they became accustomed to her. In time, Paul joined a research group at Children's Hospital. Charlotte had her own world outside the house: school, which she hated, and boys, who had begun to interest her. She made friends and had new sources of angst. She found a wart on her arm and for the next month picked at the wart, cut it, burned it, railed over the unfairness of life, wept over this small rough button on her arm, as if the wart was more complicated and tragic than anything she'd yet experienced.

Rachel became comfortable in our common yard. She liked the neighbors' swings, the tricycle, the fat colored chalk. Once, she crept outside the house before I was awake, ventured up one neighbor's back steps and into their house, wearing only a diaper. Another time I found her early in the morning, in her nightgown and helmet, riding a tricycle that was much too small. It was funny and sad seeing her on the tiny trike, and also dangerous, reminding me that it was time to lock the doors. But it was like seeing her in the swimming pool the first time, and I was thrilled by her boldness, and by the pleasure she took tooling around the cement pad.

The approved private school Rachel attended was a mile away from our house. So was the Jewish Community Center—the JCC—with an active special-needs department run by a woman who made it possible for Rachel and other children with developmental disabilities to enroll in the after-school program there. Also close to home was Rachel's Saturday morning "gym-swim," the University of Pittsburgh's adaptive physical education class, where she had an hour of swimming lessons followed by an hour playing games in the gym.

At the heart of Squirrel Hill—"upstreet"—was a busy shopping area with movie theaters, restaurants, and stores. On the streets, in the supermarket, the library, and the fast-food restaurant were more people with physical and developmental disabilities than I'd ever seen—people rolling their wheelchairs down the street, shopping for groceries, meeting friends in the atrium of JCC. It seemed like a dream made tangible, another reason to believe that I could help Rachel find a meaningful life.

These programs and activities softened the fact that Rachel had no friends; they broadened her world, introducing her to things she liked to do. They gave me valuable little blocks of time without her, time when I could read without interruption or prepare for my classes. I fell into the habit of planning exactly what I could fit into these spaces, using every second well. I took pride in my ability to use my time so efficiently I could get my work done and still grab small pleasures wherever I found them.

One of these pleasures was walking my dog with my friend and next-door neighbor, David. Every evening we left our busy households, talked feverishly about family and work for fifteen or so minutes, and then became reabsorbed in our own lives. Because David was a pediatric endocrinologist, his interest in Rachel was more than a neighborly one. I'd told him that Rachel had been seen by two different endocrinologists before our move to Pittsburgh; the first had been unconcerned by my daughter's slow growth, and the second chose to take no action, though he had stunned me with the news that Rachel's physical development was in our hands: someday we'd have to *decide* whether she went into puberty, he'd said. David continued to regard Rachel's smallness with concern.

When Rachel turned ten, David asked me to take her to his clinic at the hospital, where she underwent an X-ray of her hand to determine her bone age and tests that would tell us how much growth hormone her body was producing. One evening, about a week after this visit, David greeted me exuberantly on the sidewalk outside our houses, test results flapping in his hand. Just as he expected, Rachel was completely growth hormone deficient. It was good news, excellent news, because it was treatable. We could get her to grow! We could make her big!

· · · ·

A problem, a treatment. I understood that in many areas of medicine solutions such as this one were hard to come by. I also understood David's elation, intellectually, at least. Still, I walked beside him, sullen and miserable. For the next few evenings, Rachel's growth hormone deficiency was at the center of our conversation. David's enthusiasm never dimmed. Kids on growth hormone did so well, he kept saying. The results were fantastic. I tried to expand and stretch the word "growth," asking if there was a chance that growth might occur in *other* areas. He knew what I was really asking and cautioned me repeatedly. "Linear growth only." And when I remained unimpressed: Didn't I want her to be able to sit in a chair and have her feet touch the floor? Didn't I want people to stop treating her like a baby? "Change" was the unspoken word during these conversations. Didn't I want her to change?

There was never a question about administering growth hormone shots to Rachel. Even if I hadn't been informed of the serious medical consequences of not doing so—osteoporosis being one—neither Paul nor I would deny our daughter the opportunity of reaching a normal adult size. In my darker moments, I could not help thinking:

Miracle indeed! Before, I had a small retarded kid; now I'd have a big one! Before, I could pass as an ordinary mom with her kid in the grocery cart; now I'd be the mother of a tall, lost-looking kid, with a bell-like voice and an interest in saying hello to all things, alive and inanimate alike, a child not four or "thix" but ten. David could help her with linear growth, but what of the other changes, cognitive and emotional?

We started Rachel on the treatment. Just as David promised, the results were impressive. My daughter grew a half inch in two months— more than she had grown the entire year before. The change in her physiognomy was even more radical, muscle replacing fat, so that my tiny, chubby, babyish child, with her dimpled knuckles and knees, became more muscled and girlish. Every time I looked at her, a mix of fear and delight welled up. She was so lovely, and I was so afraid.

As I gave Rachel her nightly growth hormone shot, I was forced to ask myself for the first time: What if there was no real growth apart from the linear? How would I continue raising, with good spirits, this child of limited abilities and enormous demands? How would I keep from losing heart? Now that she was growing rapidly and soon would look her chronological age, I knew I needed to encourage her teachers to continue to prod and challenge her too, to make sure they never gave up on her.

Rachel became so sweet looking, straighter and leaner, her body filled with possibility. How could I explain to David, who was so pleased with his magic bullet, how ambivalent I was about this linear growth, this "change without change" that forced me to alter my attitude toward Rachel, to lose my complacency and plunge along with her into whatever came next?

3

John Kingery, 82, suffering from Alzheimer's disease and wearing a sweatshirt inscribed "Proud To Be An American," was abandoned outside the men's room at a dog racing track in Post Falls, Idaho. His wheelchair had been stripped of identification and his clothing labels ripped out; he couldn't remember his own name.

Pictures of him clutching his teddy bear as attendants prepared to send him home to Oregon provoked a national wince. But what turns a wince into an ache is the sudden awareness that John Kingery is no isolated case. The American College of Emergency Physicians estimates that 70,000 elderly Americans were abandoned last year by family members unable or unwilling to care for them or pay for their care.

—*New York Times,* March 26, 1992

TAKING CARE

In 1993, Rachel turned ten and my uncle Ben turned ninety—maybe. He wasn't exactly sure anymore, and no one was left to argue that his real age was eighty-nine or ninety-one, or to tell those in the next generation the actual date of his birth. Both Ben and his brother took the Fourth of July as their birth date when they emigrated from Russia or Moldava; there was even disagreement about the name of the country since borders in that region had changed so often.

Forgetting his age was the least of Ben's problems. He remembered his two daughters, but not necessarily his sister or brother, or his first wife, though they had been married for forty-six years when she died. On a more practical level, he could not remember where he put his toothpaste, or his shirts. He couldn't remember why he had been separated from his second wife, Rose. Every day, dozens of times a day, he asked, "Where's Rose?"

His daughter always said, "Rose is in Florida, Dad."

Why couldn't he see her?

Ben's younger daughter, a patient, soft-spoken woman, would say, "Rose is sick, Dad," and once again explain why Rose was in Florida and he was thousands of miles away. Ben would nod in understanding, and minutes later ask, "Where's Rose?"

Rose was the one person he never forgot—not for a moment, it seemed. It was as if her presence, her importance, had expanded to fill the mental void. The worlds of both past and present had become treacherous and unfamiliar, and the image of Rose had grown gigantic. He was obsessed.

Why wasn't he in Florida with Rose? Because Ben drove her crazy. Literally, said the daughter who lived in Chicago. The daughter in a New York suburb was doubtful, or perhaps too enraged to care about the breakdown of this wife of sixteen years, no mother to her. Rose had been complaining a lot about Ben over the last few years, about the way he hounded her with the same questions, over and over; how he forgot whatever she told him. In the summer of 1993, the calls became more frequent. Increasingly agitated, Rose began to yell at Ben's daughters. They'd better get their father, she would say. She couldn't live with him anymore.

In October the big call came. She was kicking him out. They had to get him immediately or they'd find him on the street.

Remember the story that was picked up by every wire service and the network news: old-timer abandoned outside a men's room in his wheelchair, gaunt and unshaven. And to further tug on our emotions and confuse us, the lap blanket had been arranged carefully over his knees, incontinence briefs and a teddy bear tucked alongside him.

My uncle Ben strolled off the plane, a fit, bantam-sized gent with a smile that crinkled up his eyes. He threw his arms around his daughter, happy to see her; carried his own luggage, belted himself in the car. Hello, hello. Everything seemed fine at first.

Then he asked, "Where's Rose?"

"Rose is in Florida."

And asked again. "Where's Rose?"

Without time to plan for Ben's future, the sisters made hasty, temporary arrangements. The New York son-in-law, who ran a business from his home, would look after Ben until they could think clearly about what was best for their father.

· · · ·

Imagine hearing about this for the first time: a ninety-year-old man, thrown out of his house by his wife and companion of sixteen years. Wandering in his daughter's house, a place that has become as unfamiliar as the rest of his landscape. Following whomever he sees. Down in the basement. Barging into his granddaughter's room. Wanting to know: Why were they keeping him here? Why wouldn't they let him go home and be with Rose?

Listening to this story from my kitchen in Pittsburgh, I had an image of Ben from my childhood, when he was one of two little look-alike uncles—Ben Tsion, who took the name Sidney, and Dov Baer, who became Ben. Both of them busy taking pictures at family gatherings. One was dour and busy arranging people: sit here, move left, bend your head closer, where's the smile, say cheese; the other one edging through the crowd, big smile crinkling up his face, quietly snapping photos. The second one was Ben.

I was no stranger to taking care of people, of course. In the foreground, there was Rachel. In the background, a husband whose chronic liver disease had worsened, and aging parents who had left their home of forty years and moved to the city where I now lived. Like Ben, whose move occurred the same month, my parents were in excellent physical shape, though my father was complaining with good reason that the marbles were rattling around in his head.

Even so, I was disgusted by Rose, utterly without sympathy. There were social services in Florida, local programs. Rose was not naïve; she was a woman of experience and education. All right, it was hard; I understood better than most people. But why couldn't she ask for help, instead of simply kicking him out?

My Chicago cousin had no answers, but while scrambling for solutions, she learned a number of things. In places like Florida, where there are so many elderly people, there's an abrupt loss of status when one's mate becomes senile, she read. Instead of being taken in by friends, people are dropped, left behind. Perhaps it's because old age, with its attendant ailments, looms over everyone like a plague, and as in plague days, the healthy lock their doors to ward off contagion. Or maybe, instead of seeing their own good health as the luck of the genetic draw, people consider it a mark of superiority, albeit a fragile one that must be closely protected.

To kick out her husband! What about commitment?

My cousin claimed that her father's story wasn't so uncommon.

"Apparently the commitment isn't always as great in second marriages."

. . . .

At 6:30 one December evening, my Chicago cousin called to give me an update on Uncle Ben. (Because I was getting dinner ready at 6:30, and therefore not fully engaged, it was the only time I could chat on the phone.)

Ben was miserable. They had tried letting him call Rose, but she screamed at him on the phone. So now he was writing her instead, long letters that were eloquent and clear. Love letters, filled with grief. *How could you do this to me? We were in love.* My cousin had been looking for day programs for Ben, but the only thing he wanted was to be with Rose.

Same as every night Rachel trailed beside me as I moved from counter to sink to stove, so close that I kept bumping or elbowing her accidentally. Sometimes she was stunned, but neither my words nor the memory of her bruises were strong enough to convince her to back up.

My cousin said, "When I explain that Rose is sick, he understands completely. Then ten minutes later he asks me why he can't be with her."

Rachel murmured when I murmured, spoke loud when I spoke loud. Paul thought she stood on top of us because her vision was poor. In my opinion, she lacked a sense of personal space.

Where's Rose?

My daughter said, "I'm hungry; can I have an apple?"

She'd just finished eating an apple.

We were good together, I loved her. Where's Rose?

"Can I have an apple? I'm hungry. Can we have tortellini?"

I clutched Rachel by the shoulders to steer her away from me, and thought of my own beloved father. "It must be awful," I said to my cousin. "I don't know how you can take it."

I'm hungry; can I have an apple? Are we having tortellini?

At the day programs they visited were people with Alzheimer's. When Uncle Ben saw them slumped in wheelchairs, or pacing across the room, vacant looks on their faces, he said, "They're old!" He turned away, puzzled and alarmed. Why did his daughter take him

TAKING CARE

there? These people suffered from the plague of physical disabilities, while Ben was a tough old bird. Only, as my father said about himself, the marbles were rattling in his head.

. . . .

For a long time, whenever I was asked to describe Rachel, I stressed her sweetness. How different she was from the boy at her school who bit her twice, or the girl who pulled a hank of hair out of her head and had to wear a restraining device on the bus because she was physically disinhibited. No, I always said, my daughter was good natured. Good natured and still completely dependent upon us, from the moment she woke (and she was up at the first sliver of light) until she was tucked in bed.

Total dependency meant not merely that I had to help her dress and get her meals, but that she was right beside one of us, most often me, whenever she was home. During the school week it wasn't so bad. In the morning, she was at her most alert and able, cheerful with the routine: same cereal, medication, seat at the table; same toothbrush, jacket, backpack on the hook, yellow bus outside at eight, Flo in the driver's seat, tooting the horn. She was gone until six o'clock, when one of us picked her up at the JCC after-school program and took her home, where she would chant about apples and tortellini, or whatever food she'd locked into that week.

The weekends were tough. If I was home, wherever I was, third floor to basement, she was an inch away from me, talking, repeating, firing her nonstop questions like a sniper, reminding me of my silent entreaties when she was a baby: *Please, oh, please, let her talk.* Who knew my most fervent wish would be granted in such an extravagant way?

Though Rachel's talking made Paul testy and quickly wore him out, he did not want to cue her or reinforce any behavioral strategies. He felt she deserved her turn, no matter how long she went on or how stuck she seemed to be. Charlotte began to leave the table abruptly, which angered him. It was hard for me to blame her. I too found it excruciating to be held captive while Rachel went on and on. "You know what? I have a science test and my teachers says . . . What's two plus two? You know what? . . ."

At fourteen, Charlotte had limited tolerance for us under the best of circumstances. These tense dinners made me fear that we would lose the chance to sit together, the chance to have fun.

As for time alone with Charlotte, if I wanted to take a walk with her, go shopping with her, sit and have a cookie without Rachel's continual in-your-face chant, I had three choices: pay for someone to watch Rachel, bargain with Paul, not do it. I no longer knew what other people's weekends were like. Ours always began with me negotiating for slivers of time. If you take Rachel Saturday morning, I'll take her Sunday afternoon . . . like that.

And yet, when people, knowing my situation, regarded me with mournful eyes, I always thought: Hey, it's my life, I'm used to it. I thought: Good days and bad days, same as for you. And: There were more difficult kids than Rachel, worse situations. And: Lots of teenagers can't bear their families. The fatigue I sometimes felt was natural and cyclic. True, weekends were tough and school vacations dreadful. True, Rachel seemed overwhelming at times. But so did the awesome responsibility of parenting a teenager, whose disdain for school and family had blossomed. So was the pile of manuscripts on my desk from hopeful, vulnerable students.

Around the time when Rose evicted Ben, Rachel began to scream at me and tell me she hated me, and the voice that said, "Hey, it's my life," began to be replaced by a whisper that said, "How much longer can I . . ." Sometimes she shouted a simple, straightforward "I hate you!" Though she had also shrieked, "You have no right to talk to students that way!" and once, while I was examining apples at the supermarket: "DON'T YOU DARE YELL AT ME." Another time, I was helping her down a flight of stairs, when she screamed, "You're not the boss!"

It didn't matter where my once pleasant daughter learned the expressions or whether she fully understood the words themselves. The emotion underlying her yelling was very real. I knew that her lashing out was caused by fatigue or frustration and that it was foolish to take it personally. Still, try listening to someone—to a recording, a disembodied voice—say "I hate you!" several hundred times, and the effect of these words becomes clear.

Rachel's screaming made me aware of the number of years I had taken care of her—ten. It reminded me of the number of years I had left—at least eleven. It made me feel my fatigue. In the decade since her birth, she had become more demanding, and I had started taking care of more people.

Trudging out of a doctor's office or a store with my furious child, often under the critical gaze of strangers, I was always reminded that I could not use hugs or sweet talk to jolly her out of her mood. Nor could I fall back on the usual (if regrettable) "if–then" statements that parents use as a last resort. In a world of things with the capacity to delight, it was still the case that nothing much delighted Rachel—not dolls or stuffed toys or the pictures I hung on the wall of a room decorated to please some child, but not her; not undershirts with hearts on them, or trips to the zoo, or promises that we'd swim. I could not tempt her, threaten her, get her to remember simple things. Once I saw myself as the one who knew her best: advocate, interpreter, protector, teacher, expert. Because my efforts had not come to much, there were times when it felt fruitless to keep struggling to fit her into our household. Her chatter was so incessant that my own marbles had begun to rattle. May I have an apple? *Didn't you just have an apple?* Yes. May I have an apple?

Where's Rose?

. . . .

How do we placate ourselves during hard times? *Things will change.* Isn't that what we say? I imagined my cousins thinking: *We will help him. He will get used to it here. Things will get smoother.*

It didn't work out that way. As the weeks passed, Ben became more miserable at his daughter's house. More confused, more disoriented. The only day program even vaguely appropriate for him met two days a week until three o'clock. The rest of the time he wandered through the house, barging into rooms, demanding to know why the hell he was there and Rose was not. He had become increasingly hostile. The house was a prison. They were feeding him shit. Where the hell was Rose?

I imagined my cousin switching off the bedside light, wondering how much longer she could hold out. She loved her father. (I loved my daughter.) I could imagine Richard, Ben's son-in-law, prime caregiver, afraid even to form that question. Richard, born and raised in Argentina, his own parents dead, burst into our extended family with a passionate need to be one of us. An emotional man, he was the staunchest defender of Ben, and the one who was angriest at Rose. My Chicago cousin had begun to say that Rose had a mental breakdown, and her anger had lessened. To Richard, family and responsibility were holy words, and Rose should not be excused for her actions.

I could imagine my cousin, awake at night, thinking: *He is my father.*

She is my daughter.

If she really hates me? If my parenting is irrelevant, my place in her life unimportant?

This is what you do: you take care of your children and your parents.

At the expense of our emotional needs and our professional goals?

Some would say yes.

At the expense of the others in the family?

Some—fewer, perhaps—would say: caring for those who cannot care for themselves comes first.

At the expense of our physical and mental health?

• • • •

Richard had a heart attack in January. Between trips to the hospital, his wife drove her father to LaGuardia, where he got on a flight to Chicago. He stepped off the plane at O'Hare, fit and grinning, and asking about Rose. His problems were now in the hands of his older daughter.

For most caregivers, there is heartache, but no cardiac arrest, no clear physical manifestation that allows us to say "enough" and feel certain about our decisions. This is not to say that Richard staged his heart attack as a metaphor for the occasion. No, it was real, and clearly stress related. Now Richard had to concentrate on preventing further damage to his weakened heart. There was no question that his heart attack ended his three-month stint as caregiver.

My Chicago cousin found an apartment for her father in an assisted living facility. For a fee, aides helped him with whatever he was unable to do, or, more often, what he no longer remembered to do. Ben's room was spacious and airy, and he had a private bath. For a fee, he was escorted to his meals; for a fee, someone took him for a walk. My cousin kept a list of his activities on her desk at work.

Although Uncle Ben was not interested in attending any of them, nonetheless, several times each day my cousin stopped work and called her father to remind him to go downstairs. When I asked if he might make friends, she laughed ruefully. He couldn't remember on Tuesday the person he met on Monday. "It's a hard condition for friendship."

When my cousin started Ben's phone service, she set up speed dialing for him so he could easily reach her home, fifteen minutes away. He began calling her twenty times a day, and sometimes into the night, frustrated because he couldn't find his toothpaste, or toothbrush, or shirts. There was no phone service to Rose, which was fortunate for her. He was still enraged; still beginning every conversation with questions about Rose.

• • • •

One afternoon around this time, a woman who chose to send her developmentally disabled son to an institution castigated me for shortchanging Charlotte by keeping Rachel at home. For years, doctors used this rationale with parents of babies born with a wide range of disabilities: it was best for the family to forget their damaged child. I thought about this cruel legacy that had severed relationships between thousands of children and their families, and about this woman's own son, a gentle young man I often saw with his father at Special Olympics basketball. I thought of the way people often asked me if I'd "made any decisions" about Rachel yet, a question I heard as a roundabout way of asking me how much longer she'd be living at home. The question made me feel that Rachel was something unseemly in my life, a shameful, unsightly creature. As this woman lectured me, I thought of Rachel, lovely and defenseless, and Charlotte, equally loved, and sadly shortchanged.

My heart seized with alarm. I didn't want Charlotte to struggle the way I had as a teenager, to wrestle with the impossible burden of feeling she had to be everything for us, to make up for what Rachel could not be. Maybe I'd failed. Hadn't the family therapist we saw when Charlotte was having problems in school suggested that we'd put inadvertent pressure on her to succeed? Perhaps without knowing it, she's been pushed to carry all our dreams. I knew this was true and wished more than anything I could change it. Though the word "enough" had been slipping into my head with alarming frequency, I stood with this other mother, shaking my head, thinking *no, never.* Rachel had a heart and a soul and was ours.

Two days into a holiday, after she'd stuck to me like Velcro, chanting, chattering, until I could no longer hear my own voice—death to a writer!—I found myself wondering how much longer I could hold out. (It is no accident that whenever I drove to the airport, my mind would begin to clear, and at the gate, while all around me babies yowled and adults cursed and rumbled about the delays, I found myself writing in a frenzy.)

Of course, this is the issue that most polarizes parents of children and adults with disabilities. On one side are people like the woman who accused me of expending my energy in the wrong place. On the other side are the ones who say: Tough luck if your career suffers; too bad about Charlotte, who is healthy and able. This living, breathing child is your daughter, your responsibility. I ricocheted between these sides, bouncing off these walls so regularly that when students—young women struggling with relationships and careers—said in breathless tones: You teach! You write! You have a family! How do you do it? I heard myself answer:

Badly.

This was perceived as modesty or a wry little joke, when in fact it's how I felt much of the time. I felt it when my mother said in an accusing way, "You moved us here!" because she had not seen me in a week.

I felt it when Rachel said, "I hate you."

And when Paul said, "You're always running around."

And when I realized that Charlotte thought that because I wrote more about Rachel, I also loved her more. Just when I felt that she could finally understand that it was untrue, I had a conversation with an old friend who'd grown up with a retarded sister and moved oceans and continents away from her family. This is the way it would be for Charlotte, too, she said. After she grew up it would be too hard for her to come home, too much for her to confront.

That prediction made me cry, but it still didn't bring me closer to saying "Enough."

Would anything? Sometimes I thought it would be hearing Rachel say "I hate you" for the millionth time. Sometimes the knowledge that, if I fell through a gaping hole, she wouldn't miss me much. Or perhaps circumstance would change things for me, the way it had changed things in Ben's family. Paul was ill; Charlotte couldn't stand us any longer.

Some months later, when Richard thought about the period when Ben lived with him, he said, "I don't know how Rose could stand it for so many years." A far cry from his initial rage at her abandonment. "In just *three months,* he gave me a heart attack!"

On my trip to New York, I tried to imagine a time when Rachel would be living away from home, tried to drum up a feeling of relief or contentment, to shape a dream about the simple pleasure of reading a newspaper in peace. Instead, I found myself imagining my years without her as a little fable:

Once upon a time there was a woman named Jane who took care of a lot of people. Many years passed, and soon, one by one, everyone was gone. So Jane lived all alone for the rest of her life. The End.

4

Rachel Glynn is a 10 year 7 month old white girl who appears younger than her stated age. She presents with a bright smile, very verbal and impulsive. She displays rotary nystagmus. Rachel separates easily from her mother and displays no anxiety with strangers. She is very impulsive, intrusive, and perseverative. She displays a short attention span.

The current concerns focus on inattention, distractibility, impulsivity, intrusiveness, noncompliance, and poor social skills. This is clearly a stress on the family system and Rachel's mother requests behavioral management assistance at home. In addition, an EPSDT comprehensive wrap-around treatment plan has been developed with recommendations for residential summer program, in-home therapeutic support, and additional speech and language therapy.

—Psychiatric Evaluation Form, May 6, 1994

ON REGRET

I'm sitting in a pediatrician's chilly exam room one morning a year after the crisis with Uncle Ben, shivering on the table beside Rachel. Her cheeks are flushed, and her long pale arms are bare. She is cold and I am scared. It's not her health that worries me, though for the past couple of weeks she's been sick with one thing or another, every evening seemingly better, and at daybreak, coming into our bedroom, burning with fever. Earlier on this particular morning on a day I have to teach, I'd imagined getting her dressed and putting her on the school bus, *no matter what.* It's a point of pride or an overactive sense of responsibility or maybe something I need for my sanity, but I've never missed a class because of Rachel and don't intend to now. *No matter what,* I thought. Then she began to wheeze in an alarming way and I forgot about school, called her doctor, and begged to be squeezed into his already packed schedule. Now it seems as if an hour has passed since the nurse asked me to take off Rachel's shirt. I wrap my arms around my daughter to keep her warm, and the brittle, uncaring voice I sometimes play to myself vanishes and I can feel the love and fear beneath. The ailments that have plagued Rachel these last weeks are treatable. What scares me is the news I've been reading each morning. It's the era of Newt Gingrich and the "Contract with America," and the paper is full of stories about proposed cuts in social services—deep ones, meant to save the government billions of dollars.

Some months ago, we began to access services for Rachel, and as a result, her life and ours have radically changed. Now, unable to stop her shivering, I am reminded how ineffective I am without these services and how devastating it will be if those cuts are made.

Just then a question comes into my mind, something I was asked on a TV talk show. My book *Loving Rachel* had just been published, and the host wanted to know if I regretted my daughter's birth. "If the choice were yours," she'd asked, "would you have chosen for her not to be born?"

The host was an intelligent woman, a former psychologist, if I remembered correctly. For this segment of the program, she had paired me with Josh Greenfeld, whose books about his autistic son, Noah, I admired so much. I wouldn't meet Greenfeld, as I had anticipated, because he was sitting on a pink couch in the Los Angeles television studio with the host, while I was in a grimy sound stage in New York, alone except for technicians, talking to millions and to no one at all. Though I was disappointed that we'd have no face-to-face contact, I expected to feel some rapport with him, and anticipated that our points of view would be much the same.

We were nearing the end of the segment when the question about regret was posed. I jumped at it, with the same wild passion that had prompted me to write my family's story. Rachel wasn't a holy child. She wasn't a gift from above. She was my daughter, and I loved her. "She is who she is," I said. I thought my candid answer, that I did not regret her birth, was bold. I knew if I'd been asked that question near the time of Rachel's birth, when everything around me had seemed smashed to bits, I might have said yes. But we had begun to accommodate to Rachel by then and everything seemed possible. I went on a bit about my belief that, if I worked hard with Rachel, I'd be able to help her find her place in the world.

Greenfeld answered next. He too loved and was dedicated to his son, he said. But Noah woke every day in a foreign country, a place where he did not speak the language and was "at the mercy of strangers and dependent upon their kindness." When Greenfeld thought seriously about the life that Noah had to live and the fate that was in store for him, then, no, he would not "wish to impose such a life on any individual."

At the time I did not think, *My daughter is five; his son is twenty-two.* What I thought—and said, rather defensively—was that Rachel was a happy child with some ability to get by in the world, and in that sense she was different from Noah. I could imagine her living in a group home someday and working at a simple job.

When I left that studio, it had seemed to me that Greenfeld was a curmudgeon mired in regret, while I had evolved to the point where I could see that there was room for everyone—not just those of us who were productive, but also people like Noah and Rachel. I remembered myself as enlightened.

· · · ·

I hadn't sought help because my family was strained to the point of breaking—hadn't actually known that it was something I might do. Our entry into the system came about because of a flyer Rachel brought home from school that encouraged parents to take advantage of a "loophole" in Pennsylvania law that allowed families of children with disabilities to apply for Medical Assistance without consideration of income. Though it was an official loophole, on the books, it could close at any time, we were told. Parents were encouraged to take advantage of it right away.

I did just that, spurred by the high cost of Rachel's prescriptions. Her growth hormone shots alone cost ninety dollars a day in 1993. Even with excellent health insurance, the cost of her medical care was very high.

Applying for Medical Assistance meant registering with the Allegheny County Mental Retardation/Developmental Disabilities office and getting the necessary paperwork processed, including documentation certifying that my daughter was, indeed, mentally retarded. A caseworker was assigned. Then I had to go to the Allegheny County Welfare Office.

Before I first sat in that grubby room, with its hostile signs and the molded plastic chairs that seemed designed to cause maximum discomfort, I had never really thought about social services. I paid my taxes without complaint and thought little about where my money went. Once, in my twenties, I collected unemployment insurance in a somewhat guilty way. But I'd never thought about the importance of a safety net for the less able, because I hadn't needed to think about it. I had never taken the time to consider that a fundamental respon- sibility of a civilized society, a democracy, is to make provisions for those who could not take care of themselves. I hadn't formulated the language to arrive at this position nor, since my freshman year in college, had I read the promises set out in the Constitution. The irony of my naïveté is that I'd been politically active as a young person and emboldened by the women's movement that was emerging while I was an undergraduate. I had blithely assumed my rights, without trying to understand how they had been withheld from me in the first place.

Sometime after that humbling and edifying wait in the welfare office, I was telling a neighbor (not the pediatric endocrinologist on one side, but the child psychiatry chief on the other side) how difficult it was to live with Rachel. Though I have no vivid memory of what I suspect was a casual, over-the-fence conversation, the upshot was a home visit later that week by a psychologist who evaluated Rachel, made behavioral recommendations, and completed a "Psychiatric Evaluation Form." As a result of that visit and the evaluation, in which Rachel was found to have a "dual diagnosis," with mental health and mental retardation issues, she received Wraparound Services.

The idea for Wraparound, first set out by Jane Knitzer in her 1982 book *Unclaimed Children,* came out of the recognition that children often needed different kinds of services, and that having to obtain these services from different agencies often resulted in fragmented and ineffective treatment. Knitzer's book laid the groundwork for the federal Omnibus Budget Reconciliation Act of 1989 (OBRA 89), which stated that children up to the age of twenty-one who were enrolled in Medical Assistance were entitled to all medically necessary services, including home and community-based mental health services. When Pennsylvania implemented OBRA 89, the loophole was put in place: any child with a disability could qualify for Medicaid regardless of family income.

Wraparound Services—provided by the Western Psychiatric Institute and Clinic and funded by Medicaid—designed for Rachel "highly individualized mental health interventions" to support her at home and in the community.

Parents worry about labeling their children, often with good reason. However, this label of "dual diagnosis" allowed me to access many crucial services for Rachel. She was enrolled in an after-school program that focused on helping children with behavior problems function at home and in the community. We also got funding for a behavior management program that provided us with a "trained support staff" person—a TSS—assigned to work with Rachel, and us, at home and in the community. I have much to say about the profound impact of these services, which were set up so that children with behavior problems could live at home, go to local day care or school, and be part of their community, rather than being in a more restrictive environment; but for now I want to describe something else that resulted from Rachel's dual diagnosis and the efforts of an innovative, hard-working case manager named Katie.

Again, in what I recall as a casual conversation, I was telling Katie how concerned I was about the summer. The TSS could continue working with Rachel twenty hours a week, but that left long stretches of time when my daughter had nothing to do. She was too old, too complicated, really, for local babysitters, and too big to fit into day care, solutions that had worked in the past. Nor could she regulate heat very well, perhaps a result of her septo-optic dysplasia. At a local day camp that accepted children with developmental disabilities, there was little protection from the beating sun, and she became ataxic—unsteady on her feet—and sick. It was easy enough to tell Katie that the summer was crucial for me, that I needed to write if I expected to keep my position at school. More difficult was admitting that I yearned to write, yearned, too, for the long stretches of solitude that steadied me and made it possible for me to think.

At Katie's suggestion, I looked for overnight camps that had an educational component and found one in New York that offered sessions in perceptual training and speech, held indoors. Katie found the language that enabled us to use Medicaid funds for this "therapeutic summer program."

In 1994, the first year we took Rachel to this Catskills camp, with its white bunks and leafy grounds, we were met outside the administration building by a sunburned country girl from Wales. Rachel took her hand and never looked back.

My most poignant memory from that first summer Rachel went to camp was sitting on the back porch on a Sunday afternoon with Paul and Charlotte. It had been such a stressful year for us. My father's cognitive problems had worsened and my mother hid her fear of what was happening to him behind a wall of rage. Paul's research group was moving to Boston; despite his ill health he had decided to join them. Now, though, we were just sitting on the porch, lingering over lunch, finishing our sentences, relaxed, an ordinary family doing ordinary things. Charlotte was fifteen and for the most part found it torture to be with us. That summer there were times she forgot that we were weird and annoying. I remember laughing with her over the movie *Wayne's World,* which she had rented for us one night. And I remember taking her to see Bob Dylan perform in an open-air arena on the river. As darkness fell, the city began to twinkle behind us. A tram rumbling on an elevated track stopped and the passengers opened their windows to listen to Dylan mumble and rephrase his old songs. I remember these things because I was relaxed enough to take them in.

For so long, everything had been about holding it together, about calming the volatile people in my life. I had learned forbearance, learned, too, the necessity of negotiating every move, trying to fit into the day what was most important, never walking out the front door without the obsessive, if crucial, "I'll take her till one, if you take her at three." That summer, being released from the constant bargaining was more of a relief than having a break from worrying about Rachel's medication, or whether she would pee in bed.

Charlotte had started to puzzle over her sister. Rachel didn't have a clock inside her, she decided one day when the three of us were in Maine. (We decided she had no volume control, either.) Another afternoon she said that Rachel was like a fish, only not so bad. "You know how fish swim around in a bowl, and they pass another fish and don't recognize it? It's like Rachel has to see things again and again before she realizes they're there."

Visiting day was midway through Rachel's stay at camp. On the drive from Maine, we talked about rock and roll and listened to *The Things They Carried* on tape, and I found myself wishing the summer was twice as long, so I could have more time like this, ordinary, easy time. As soon as we parked the car, I saw Rachel from a distance, in her pink camp T-shirt and her flowered shorts, her legs long and coltish. I hurried toward her, so unexpectedly happy to see her that I started to sob. Paul did too.

As for Rachel, she swam, went horseback riding, painted pictures, rehearsed songs from *Cats* for the camp show on visiting day. In this world, where she was not pressured to fit or conform, she had friends, bunkmates, and counselors from around the world. She could not tell me much about her pleasures at camp, what it felt like to ride a horse or sleep in a bunkhouse with other girls. Still, after she returned home, when she was alone in her room, she would sing the camp song in bed: "I've got the Camp Huntington feeling deep in my heart, deep in my heart."

· · · ·

When Rachel had improved, and life was more or less back to usual, I found the videotape from that TV show with Josh Greenfeld and popped it into the VCR. By then, the congressional Republicans had put forward their seven-year budget plan to reduce spending by $983 billion, cutting entitlements programs such as Medicare by $270 billion and Medicaid by $180 billion. Speaker Newt Gingrich had been quoted as saying that his real aim had been to "eliminate Medicare, not to 'save' it." Even if I had never read a newspaper, I would have been shaken by that plan. Everyone who worked in social services was concerned.

I was stunned by the way I had looked in 1988. It wasn't just that I was softer, younger, positively dreamy-eyed as I gazed into the TV camera and spoke of my unconditional love for Rachel and my acceptance of her just as she was; it was also the sight of myself from a time when my emotions were still so close to the surface. I had failed to realize that when Greenfeld spoke with bitterness about his son's life in "a care-and-support system that neither cares nor supports," he was also warning me.

Of all the things Greenfeld had said in that interview, the word that resonated most when I pondered the question of regret in 1994 was *kittenness*. "It's hard when they lose their kittenness," he said.

It brought to mind a woman I'd met at a weekend writers' conference I was able to attend because Rachel was in summer camp. The woman was a sinewy, middle-aged Ohioan with a helmet of teased hair, very blue eyes, and an insistent, blissful smile. Everyone was assembled for my workshop when she leaned across the conference table and said, "Did you see that adorable little crippled girl? You know she was adopted? Why, I think that's the most wonderful thing!"

The juxtaposition of *adorable* and *crippled* made the heat rise in my cheeks. I started thinking of the six years Rachel had spent at Children's Specialized Hospital in New Jersey, first in an early-intervention program, then in special-needs day care, and finally in preschool, where everyone doted on her. When she toddled down the hallway, people left their offices, cooed over her, knelt to hold her in their arms. At holidays, she and her classmates received so many toys from charities and businesses that I rarely bought her any playthings. Holidays also brought visits from dewy-eyed celebrities: TV stars, princesses, presidents' wives. Dandling cute "special-needs" kids on their knees, they would make pitches before the cameras, their unspoken message: *"We* love them; therefore *anyone* can love them." Although these photo opportunities irked me, the affection strangers lavished on my daughter helped me to believe that she was valued, made me feel that the world was benevolent toward my child. These were good things, at the time.

As my daughter and her peers grew older, however, I noticed that the media lost interest in them. Only the infants and preschoolers were showered with toys. The older kids, who were no longer kittenish and needed far more than toys, received nothing. So when the woman from Ohio began to croon about the "adorable little crippled girl," I wanted to say, "You like that cute girl? Take her home, please! Not just for an hour. Take her for a year. For five years! Change her diapers! Find her friends! Figure out what to do with her when the two of you are home alone!"

Actually, I wanted a lot more than that. After I convinced the woman from Ohio to take that "adorable little crippled girl" home, I wanted the visiting princess to pose for the cameras next to a teenager strapped into his wheelchair, his face chafed from saliva. I wanted, for once, to read a human-interest story in which the parents of a not-so-cute girl struggle to secure services so that the girl could reach her potential, and then struggle to secure funding to pay for those services. I wanted to tell the woman from Ohio that my regrets about

ON REGRET

Rachel had nothing to do with the effects of her birth on my family, or with the fact that she was "different"—I was over that, and had been for years. *Of course* there should be room for Rachel.

I wondered how I would have answered the TV host if she'd asked me the question about regret in 1994, when I feared what was in store for Rachel if essential programs were cut. If I had a choice . . .

In my mind, the woman from Ohio says, "You have no right to choose."

She says, "God has a way of turning bad things into good."

She says, "Trust in prayer."

All of which I'd been offered. People like this woman were not merely sentimental. Their love of God's special children was linked with a conviction that there should be less government and lower taxes. If this woman's wish came true, and deep cuts were made in social services, our special-needs babies would likely continue to receive all the toys they needed from the private sector. At the same time, the lives of our older, less photogenic children would grow empty and bleak.

As the old saying has it: "The problem with kittens is that they become cats." Since cuteness was the criterion for judging our children's worthiness, I suppose the problem with "special" babies is that they become adults who are no longer considered special, whose presence no longer inspires any message about the sanctity of life.

· · · ·

Rachel was still cute as a teenager, thanks to the costly hormone injections that gave her muscle mass and adult height. It was just that I was confronted with something I had lacked the foresight to understand years before: cute is a dreadfully short-lived and risky condition. Looking back, I see that cute allowed me to get my bearings with Rachel and to enjoy the sensual pleasures she afforded me—her softness, sweetness, loveliness. Cute paved the way, got Rachel attention and toys. Perhaps it was a mistake to lose myself for so long. Then again, she is my child, and it was nice to enjoy her.

There was no single moment when cute stopped being enough, no single event that changed things. Time passed. She got big. Her demands grew; her means did not. When I could no longer hold her in my arms, I made her walk, whether or not she wanted to be on her own feet. She would never be able to walk alone, never stroll to the house around the corner where the kids her age lived. Not that it made a difference. As the kids on either side of us grew—and Ra- chel, too, in different ways—the gap became larger. They also began to back off at the sight of her. Her only "friends" were the staff who worked with her. The best of them embedded behavior-management strategies in social events, like bitter pills stirred into applesauce.

I had begun to squirm when people told me how lucky Rachel was to have me for a mother. True, I gave her wholesome food and nice clothing, found the best medical care available, treated her with dignity and fairness, showed her the affection she deserved. *Really* lucky, I used to believe, would be having a parent who could be completely devoted to her well-being, with no other aspirations, no need for a life apart from her. Only recently had I begun to suspect that it was self-flagellation to imagine that this perfect parent existed. Someone like Rachel needed complex services in order to thrive. The small amount of county money I could use for recreation; the lump sum I could use for temporary respite services—these programs helped the way a finger plugging a leak in the dam can help. What Rachel needed was a range of reliable, complex expensive services, ones not "designed to be faded," but that would last forever.

We are not a society where "complex" sells. Simplicity is the key: quick sound bites, blurbs, one-line campaign promises.

I had a recurrent nightmare of sorts, in which a politician stands up before Congress with Rachel's thick file in his hands. He's about to use her as an example of wasteful government spending, of pork he intends to cut. Perhaps, as he skips through her medical records—the appointments with her ophthalmologist, endocrinologist, orthopedist, pediatrician, psychologist, psychiatrist, and neurologist—he resurrects the metaphor of the giant cart. Twenty million undeserving citizens are riding inside, with the rest of us pulling it. Rachel's file is the size of an urban phone book. The politician won't bother with her placement in an "approved private school," or the details of the services she gets at the school, the speech therapy, occupational therapy, adaptive physical therapy. No, he's after the paperwork authorizing the funds to send her to camp. Forget the approval for "perceptual training." (What the hell is that anyhow?) He wants to zero in on the horseback riding. He steps up to the microphone, whips out offending documents, and says, "We're spending taxpayer money to send this child *horseback* riding?" Like an American Khrushchev, he slaps her file on the podium for emphasis. *Boom!* "Horseback riding?" *Boom!* "I can't even afford to send *my own daughter* horseback riding!"

What do I have to say in Rachel's defense? In my own?

In this dream I am speechless. I know it looks bad. Although I could recite here the justification for sending Rachel horseback riding—the data showing that, for children with motor-planning problems, such activity stimulates the vestibular system and helps with balance and coordination—if I were up there on the witness stand, limited to a one-word answer, I'd have to agree that it is nonessential. She could live without horseback riding, just as any of us could live without books or music or art.

This is what I would want to say: My daughter, no longer a cuddly, adorable poster child, could not tell me who pulled that hank of hair from her head, or who bit her arm. But she knew pain, just as she knew boredom and loneliness. She could not tell me what it felt like to be up there in the saddle (though she recalled that her horse's name was Moe). But in the picture of her on horseback there is a huge smile on her face, the kind of joy she rarely displays at home.

Long ago, I accepted the job of interpreting Rachel's wants and advocating on her behalf. I accepted that for the rest of my life I would serve as her voice. It was no longer possible to be the sole provider of all that was necessary for her. I needed social services to help me, and programs I could trust that would always be in place. In the short run, I wanted these services because they made her happy. In the longer run, they helped her become more independent, not to satisfy politicians—she would never pull her weight—but for her own protection and well-being.

That year, every question I asked her psychologists and social workers was met with the same response. "It depends on the funding stream." "Cuts are being made." "We really don't know."

My imaginary politician could point out that if I died tomorrow, a system was in place to provide Rachel with shelter and food. "I know that," I would say, then ask him to look again at the photograph of Rachel on horseback, at that smile across her face. "That is my child," I would say. "She is utterly defenseless." The availability of substandard care, administered by a steady stream of impersonal caregivers paid minimum wage, offered scant comfort to me. It wasn't enough to have "a care-and-support system that neither cares nor supports . . ."

My daughter is sweet, attractive, and fearless: if Attila the Hun held out his hand, she would go off with him. What kind of life would she have when I was no longer by her side? Who would protect her and make sure she was not sexually molested? Who would feed her nourishing food, floss her teeth, make sure she got exercise? Who would train her for the sort of simple job I dreamt one day she'd have? Who would help her find activities that gave her pleasure? Since my daughter was unable to pursue her own happiness, who would help her realize this "inalienable" right? Or did the U.S. Constitution not apply to her?

• • • •

At around the same time when I was a guest on the talk show with Josh Greenfeld, I had been asked to appear on another show. A guest with multiple disabilities was suing her mother for wrongful life. My role would have been to say that all life is sacred. I declined. I had seen children, barely conscious, whose lives were filled with such agony that I'd thought it a pity they were born. Not Rachel. She liked herself. She never had a moment of sadness about her limitations. More than anything, this fact took away my despair over what she could not do. If, like Noah Greenfeld, Rachel woke every morning in a foreign country, it seemed not to trouble her at all. She laughed easily. She loved to swim, swing, sing, and ride horses. She thrived in a classroom alongside other children. Knowing that her life could be good with the necessary network of supports, I kept putting up my dukes and slugging it out for Rachel, sometimes out of love, sometimes out of fear of what was in store for her. And sometimes regretting that she was born.

• • • •

The 1995–96 budget crisis ended when President Clinton vetoed a series of bills. Weary from struggling on Rachel's behalf, I let myself dream about her future. One day I caught myself eyeing a bagger at the supermarket, sizing him up as a potential suitor, thinking: *Okay, group home, good-natured guy with mild retardation to cherish her and keep her warm in bed* . . . Even as I was working up this scenario, I knew how dangerous it would be to entrust my daughter to the good graces of any man. I didn't know what to do. If she were your child, you would not look into the future and wish for nothing more than a bed in a heated room. If she were your child, you would think, *Please, let there be someone to care for her.*

68

5

When I started film school, we learned about persistence of vision, a theory that attempts to explain why we see twenty-four frames a second as a moving image instead of individual images. Because of some glitch in our brains, we can't process each individual frame, so there's a blur. Rachel never seemed to get much from movies. So I started to wonder—could she see moving image? It made me realize that her brain doesn't work the way ours does. First I started to wonder—what could she see? That became, who is she?

—Charlotte

RACHEL FLIES ALONE

How odd it seems that after fifteen years of dreaming and planning for the time when I would be free from the everyday responsibility of Rachel, never once had I fully imagined her alone in the world, navigating without my intercession. That was the case until the night I stood in my kitchen, holding the airline ticket her father had bought for her. According to the itinerary for her return trip, Rachel was to depart from Tampa–St. Petersburg, with a layover and change of planes in Miami, before the connecting flight home to Pittsburgh. All this she was supposed to accomplish alone.

It was early in December. The house was dark except in the TV room, where Rachel was sitting on the couch, stringing beads and watching (or listening) to a snowboarding competition on ESPN, her new favorite station. Sports were the only programs she seemed to like. What she got out of sporting events—and any of them would do—I never fully understood. Maybe the breathless announcer and the cheering crowds made her feel that she had company, when in reality she was often alone unless I had "hours" with one of her caregivers. Or perhaps it was because in this house where we lived after Paul and I separated, the TV room was on the first floor, more centrally located. Sitting in a place where she could hear family *and* cheering crowds might have appealed to her.

Paul and I had not split up because of Rachel, I found myself ex-
plaining far too often, particularly to old friends who remembered the tenderness of our early love. Yes, it was true, we'd been crazy about each other, but the fault lines in the very foundation of our marriage existed long before Rachel's birth. I hated the assumption that she was to blame. It was mean-spirited and wrong. I was always rushing to her defense, setting out the reasons her father and I had separated, all of them valid, nowhere near ready to acknowledge the cost of accommodating to her demands.

So much had happened in the two years since our marriage had dissolved. Paul had moved from Boston to New York. When his health failed, he went on the waiting list for a new liver. The surgery, done in Pittsburgh, was full of complications, a wrenching mix of medical errors that nearly cost him his life and surgical advances that saved it. For a long time it was unclear if he would survive. Now, a year later, he was recuperating with his parents in Florida. When he'd first called to say he wanted to see Rachel at Christmas, I was overjoyed—for Rachel, who had not seen him in five months, and for me, because the chance to wake without anyone calling my name, and to linger over coffee and a newspaper, was the kind of simple pleasure I craved. I had known that she would have to fly alone. I even thought she would enjoy the adventure, since she was delighted by all kinds of transport, including the airport itself, with its moving sidewalk, escalators, and tram. Then I saw that she had a layover in Miami, and an awful vision clouded my head. Rachel had never been by herself in a public place. I imagined her alone in the airport, gravitating toward the escalators, which she loved, standing at the top of an "up" escalator, extending her foot, brushing it against the step as she tried to go down. Then tumbling, with no one to help her.

She simply could not be in an airport unaccompanied, not for five minutes. But after I solved that problem I was still left contemplating the reality that my daughter would, before too long, be in the world without her arm linked through mine. Without me standing beside her, coaching her, explaining to others what she wanted, what she felt, what she liked or hated. What I deemed bad for her, or good.

. . . .

74   In a way, what I had continued doing with Rachel was just an extension of what I did when she was first born, what all parents innately do. We don't simply respond to our baby's crying; we interpret the nature of the cry as well. We listen and look and say, "Oh, she's hungry," or, "she has gas pains," or, "she wants to be held." While most babies acquire language and become more or less knowable, Rachel's language, her ability to speak of what she knew or felt, remained so impaired that I never fully relinquished the job I had taken on when she was an infant. She could speak of concrete things in the absolute present, but not of intangible things like desires, emotions, experiences, and fears. These either remained locked inside her, because she had no way to give them shape, or simply vanished, dissipating like smoke. Or maybe both: she had surprised me by occasionally recalling a person or event from some months back, and she had saddened me by being unable to articulate anything about a simple event she had attended only an hour before.

    Because she was so mysterious, I remained watchful for what might be locked inside her. I continued to think of myself as her voice, her advocate and interpreter, even now that she was a teenager. I interpreted the way she followed me in the house as *anxious,* though possibly I was wrong. "Radar" was the name I'd long ago given to her habit of calling out to me dozens of times, believing that it developed because her vision was poor. I imagined her as a little tugboat, blowing her horn in the fog. *Hello! Are you there? It's me! Hello!*

    Maybe I was wrong about this, too. Maybe it had started this way and now the constant name calling, "Ma? Mom? Ma?" was nothing more than an annoying behavior.

    There were also instances when I would speak on her behalf, rather than interpreting what I thought she would actually want. I said, "Two pieces of pizza is enough," when she went to dinner without me; otherwise she ate whatever quantity was set before her, said yes to more, and sometimes vomited later. It was my call though. *I* was the one who said, "She's full."

    "She loves to walk," I told her caregivers, though she mightily resisted setting out and stopped complaining only when reminded repeatedly of what she might get at the end of her walk—a bagel and lemonade, for instance—or the repercussions of not walking: no bagel, no lemonade. I said she enjoyed walking because often, once she started out, she would trot along for miles, singing happily—especially if she had her Walkman with her.

So I speculated that she missed her father. I toted out, as evidence, the number of times she still said his name, and the fact that it made sense for her to miss the man who had been so loving with her when we all lived together.

Every night she asked to talk to him. On weekends, when we were together for long stretches, she sometimes asked about him nine or ten times a day. "Where's Daddy?" she said, as if he were asleep in another room, the way he might have been, four years ago, when we were last a family. "Can I call Daddy?" Sometimes she asked if I still loved him, and I would make a case for how sad she was, how the love he showed her was more meaningful than anyone else's affection.

Then the watch would come to mind, an inexpensive multifunction digital watch with a green mesh strap. Rachel owned it until several days before the ticket for Florida arrived. I had bought her the watch, even though it was totally inappropriate for her, since she could not tell time and could not see the numbers easily. The best I can offer as explanation for this purchase is: hope springs eternal. Also, that she wanted the watch a great deal, probably because the people she liked had watches that looked more or less the same. It made her very happy, which in turn pleased me. On the first day she wore it to school, it was confiscated by her teacher—taken, like her yo-yo, because she was fooling around with it during class. (She'd gotten sassy as a teenager, apt to test the limits.) Rachel could not seem to accept the loss of her watch. She asked me where it was ten times an hour.

If I judged my daughter's heart solely by what she said, I had to assume that she missed her watch ten times more than she missed her father. It would follow that, if I replaced the watch, I could cancel her trip to Florida. Of course, conventional wisdom was in opposition to this logic. When we lived together, her father was affectionate and undemanding, the one person who asked nothing of her. He taught her little nonsense rhymes to repeat and let her sit on his lap in the big leather chair, "thnuggling," she called it. It was a different relationship, not only because she could do as she pleased (until he had his fill) but also because he was the only one whose physical affection

RACHEL FLIES ALONE

she seemed to enjoy. She hated being touched by kids she knew, and tolerated my hugs only when she asked for them.

What made Paul's absence harder was the fact that no matter how concrete I made my language and how simple the actual words I used, I could never fully explain why I did not live with him anymore. As soon as I constructed a narrative about how sad Rachel was to be out of touch with a man who once doted on her, I would remember the watch, then come close to thinking that the watch meant more to her, then deny that it could be so.

As much as I kept trying to figure out who she was and what mattered most to her, I was reminded that no matter how closely I listened, I always ended up imposing my values and desires on her. This dynamic was at the heart of my concern about Rachel's being alone, I realized. Though the issues regarding her safety were immediate and needed to be resolved, the roots of my worry went a lot deeper. If I wasn't around, who would take the time to figure her out? Who would bother to know this child—this teenager—who was so difficult to understand?

For the first time I realized that I wanted my daughter to have freedom, while at the same time I often deprived her of it. Now I found myself wondering first what would happen if she were alone in an airport, and then what would happen if she were alone in a world where she would be expected to ask for what she wanted, to want what was good for her, and to speak out if she was poorly treated—none of which she could reliably do at present.

· · · ·

That night in my kitchen, I imagined my daughter on the plane alone, ordering a drink. Who would open her seatback tray? Who would help her put the drink in the indented circle? And the silverware, wrapped in plastic? As for the peanuts—*I* couldn't even open that little bag without chewing at the edge. Who would open it for Rachel?

I imagined a woman passenger seated beside her. What would she see when she looked at my daughter? A girl with curly hair, nicely cut. Gorgeous porcelain skin, a brush of fair freckles. Rachel's eyes wandered, though not as much as they had years before, when the nystagmus was pronounced. Her gaze was rather blank. If experience is what marks our faces with crows' feet and frown lines, maybe Rachel's face was unmarked, expressionless, because experience never fully penetrated. I could make her laugh by calling her "thunder buns" or "buffalo breath," and the expression on her face would be full of delight. Otherwise, though, it was impossible to read her, without doing something radical, like tickling her.

When she was small, her oddities were cute. Now she was five feet tall. (*A child? A teenager?* I imagined her seatmate wondering.) Her body was bulky and square, underdeveloped sexually, though not for long. (After this trip, she would be pushed through puberty with estrogen, just as I had been told seven years before. Otherwise she would be at risk for osteoporosis, memory loss, and heart problems, just like an estrogen-deficient postmenopausal woman.) In this between-stage, I couldn't tell how long it took for people to discern that she was "not right." I suspected that people sensed something different about her—the blank face—rather than thinking of her right away as "retarded." If I was correct, it was because of her uncanny talent as a mimic, her ability to catch gesture, inflection, cadence, emphasis.

I heard myself in her voice. When she answered the phone, she used my "Hey!" instead of "Hi," and copied the way I said, "So how ya doin'?" When she talked to her father, she cleared her throat the way he did and said, "How's Aunt Bea? How's Pop-Pop? Let me switch ears." Then there was the adolescent stuff: "Yeah, whatever," when I asked her to do something, and "Duh," for unmitigated scorn.

I imagined Rachel on the plane, saying, "Excuse me, I don't mean to bother you, but may I ask you a question, please?" Her graciousness was so charming, even the least friendly passenger would turn. And then it would be all over. The minute my daughter had someone close, she would begin to talk and never stop—*never*. What initially passed as conversation turned into a numbing, endless series of questions and statements. On first hearing these seemed grounded, "real." "My sister Charlotte? She finally got into college!"

And: "I saw *Aladdin*." (She hadn't.) "My sister lives in L.A." (Not anymore.) "My friend? She was going to come over? But she got confused? And it was such a riot! Last week? My mother picked me up, and actually she was going to talk to her friend, but in an hour, and we laughed so hard. You want to hear a joke? Knock knock."

RACHEL FLIES ALONE

On and on . . .

At home, when family and friends were around, I tried to nip the

meaningless loops that were so engaging at first, so seemingly coherent. Relying on old standbys that I had learned when she was in preschool, I would cue her, giving her a specific topic, and redirect her by reminding her to stick to that topic. Sometimes I simply said, "No more stories," and made her stop rattling off a stream of questions that didn't need answers, because it was annoying. Besides, I hated to see her continually reinforced for behavior that was socially unacceptable and that, ultimately, would alienate people, making her more marginalized than she already was.

If she continued undaunted, which was often the case, I rolled out the threats: "If you ask any more questions, you'll have to leave the room."

Or worse: "If you ask any more questions, I'll take away your beads!"

Rachel had been stringing beads for seven years now. (My father, in the early days of his decline into dementia, would come upon her doing this and say, "What's the point?") Stringing beads was no Sisyphean labor; it was Rachel's activity of choice, her comfort and obsession. And so she cried, "*No!*" as if I had threatened to beat her. "I promise I'll be good!"

Alas, I couldn't send her into the world with a sign around her neck that said, "Hello! Treat me with respect, but feel free to say, 'no more questions'; if I ignore you, threaten to confiscate my beads."

So I worried about her on the plane. I worried that she would somehow get the peanut bag open (or get someone to do it for her) and start to choke on a nut, and, having driven the stranger in the next seat crazy, that person would do nothing to help.

My goal at home was to treat Rachel with respect, while holding onto my sanity—two ideals that at times seemed mutually exclusive—and I was her mother, not a stranger. I demanded a certain kind of behavior that was difficult for her. There were situations when the only way for me to stop her from dominating all conversation was to physically remove her. Trying to banish my shrieking daughter from the room was awkward and embarrassing, even in the company of my closest friends. Inevitably someone would say, "Oh, just let her stay." I would not back down, though it made me feel like a witch, rigid and black-hearted. Yet in public, I was a fierce foot-stomping advocate for my daughter, intolerant of any slights. If we were out together, and she bumped into someone and got the evil eye, I was all set to say, "Listen, buddy, she's a human being with the same rights and privileges as you."

Should a stranger have to wrestle with these issues? When I imagined Rachel on the plane, this time seated next to some hapless guy trying to get ready for a meeting, the limits of what I could expect of strangers began to change. *Of course* every building in every city should be barrier-free, and every sidewalk lowered, and every means of public transport accessible. *Of course* guide dogs should be allowed into public places, and TV shows close-captioned. But should we let Rachel talk nonstop to a stranger for two and a half hours? Was that one of her inalienable rights? She would say it was.

There was more: Who would remind her to go to the bathroom? Who would show her where the toilets were, help her with the door and the latch so she would not shuffle out of the stall with her pants around her ankles? Who would say, as I did, when she was getting ready to use the toilet:

"Now what are you going to do?"

"Wipe and wash my hands."

Rachel remembered her father and her watch. She remembered that the driving age in Pennsylvania is sixteen, and that, after high school, many kids go to college—two things she claimed to badly want. These other two things—wipe and wash—she would forget to do unless she was cued, each and every time.

· · · ·

It was a busy time for the airlines. I was leaning against the kitchen counter, listening to the endless loop of an airline theme song, with its dramatic melody that made me yearn for flight, and wondering if a person would ever come on the line. Assuming one would, how might I best describe my daughter so that I could arrange for an airline employee to stay with her in the Miami airport during the entire layover? My wait was long: in the TV room, snowboarding had ended. Now it was college basketball. I could hear the squeak of sneakers, the whistles and the cheering crowd. I wondered what words would convey the most precise information about Rachel,

RACHEL FLIES ALONE

without depriving her of her humanity. For the first time I wondered whether I could let up on my constant interpretations and ask her directly: *What would you do if you were left alone in an airport?*

Just then, an actual person got on the line, and I began to explain the situation. She interrupted me, asking for the passenger's name.

Yes, she said, after she'd found the booking. It was on record that a minor was flying. Yes, someone would escort her from one gate to another in Miami. The thirty-dollar fee for this service had been paid.

Who would be in charge of Rachel once she was at the gate?

"No one is 'in charge' at that point."

"What happens during the ninety-minute layover?" I asked. "Is someone assigned to watch out for her?"

"No," said the agent, her voice full of vacant politeness.

"Will she be supervised?"

"There are agents at the gate."

Christmas break in Miami—I could just imagine the scene. Long lines, people clustered at the counter, waiting for seat assignments and boarding passes. Delays and gate changes. While my daughter sat and . . .

"She could walk off with a stranger. Someone could say, 'Come this way,' and she would. I know her. Look," I said, hesitating, "I don't know what you have in your notes, other than her being a minor. She's also retarded."

Just the week before, I'd confessed to Charlotte that I'd started using the word "retarded." Though she'd been badly bruised by the events of the last years, since leaving home that fall to start film school she'd begun to claim her complex history. We'd started talking about Rachel in a different way, often discussing issues like this.

Now she exclaimed, "Me, too!"

Partly I used it because it was concrete and to the point, I said. But I also used it in an in-your-face way. "Like gay people say *queer*," said Charlotte, knowing exactly what I meant. I had come to hate "special needs," with its ribbons and bows; it was a euphemism that isolated. "Developmentally delayed," while a mouthful, was kinder, but in crucial situations like this phone conversation, it didn't quite drive home the point. Nor did the trend toward "person-first language," which I embraced, for putting the person first, and the disability second—for getting away from such locutions as "the wheelchair-bound girl" or the "autistic boy." If I told this reservationist I had a daughter "with mental retardation" I worried that she'd think I was talking about baggage. I could imagine her saying, "Two carry-on items only."

"Retarded" was such an ugly word that it hurt to say it aloud. It was a slur, so commonly used that even Rachel had begun to say, "That is *so* retarded." As soon as I said "retarded" to the reservationist, I knew she thought "dumb" and stopped there, never imagining a teenager, a *person*, who listened to Bob Marley, slept with a bear and a penguin, and liked to position herself in my reading chair, long-abandoned glasses perched on her nose and a blanket over her lap. Exactly as I did, though her book was often upside down.

"I can't tell you that someone will be able to watch her every second," the woman said.

I knew it was all over, yet still I persisted. "She could just walk off."

"I'm sorry," said the agent, as if she was reporting on a delayed landing due to fog. "But we have no control over that."

After I hung up, I called Rachel into the kitchen. She was irritated that I was pulling her away from the basketball game. She didn't know the score or which teams were playing; even so, a game is a game. The only powerful incentive I had was chewing gum, and so I cut a deal: If she would talk to me for a few minutes and really pay attention, I'd give her a piece of gum.

· · · ·

Q: You're going to Florida with Daddy. Do you remember his name?

A: Paul.

Q: Why do you like to see him?

A: Because he's nice to me. He talks to me on the phone. He talks to me when I go see him and he walks around with me.

Q: What do you like to do with him?

A: Talk to him.

Q: What does he look like?

A: He has blue eyes like me.

Q: You're also going to see Daddy's parents in Florida. Do you remember who they are? Do you remember their names?

A: How should I know when I don't know?

Q: Nana and Papa. You'll be taking an airplane to get there. Do you know what an airplane is?

A: Whatever it is? What do you mean by that? Explain to me what that means. It's where you fly somewhere, Ma. I don't know, Ma. Just ask me the easy ones because I don't know the hard ones.

Q: Okay, here's an easy one. What will you do when you're on the plane?

A: Talk. Talk to other people. Read.

Q: What would you like to take with you?

A: Luggage. A luggage thing. Beads. Tape. Watch. What do *you* think?

Q: I'm wondering why you like your watch so much.

A: 'Cause I like it and it's really noisy.

Q: There's a change of planes in Miami. Are you going to be able to do that?

A: Ma! I have no idea. *Hel-l-o-o!* Why don't you speak clearly, Ma?

Q: Are you going to be all right by yourself?

A: I need someone to help me out there.

Q: Who is Bill Clinton?

A: A president.

Q: What is he president of?

A: Ma! I said I didn't know. *Hel-l-o-o!* You weren't paying attention!

Q: Who is Mark McGwire?

A: A baseball player.

Q: Who is Michael Jordan?

A: A basketball team.

Q: Who is Al Gore?

A: I have no idea, Ma. Whatsoever.

Q: What is a state?

A: Like right now? New York?

Q: Where do you live?

A: Pittsburgh.

Q: What's Pittsburgh?

A: What do you mean? Explain, Ma. I misunderstood what you said.

Q: What is love, Rachel?
A: It's when you love someone. Like you, Daddy, Char.

. . . .

A week passed. I went on a short trip, returning late at night. In the morning Rachel found my wheeled suitcase by the door. She took it for a spin through the hall and into the kitchen, delighted by the suitcase, perhaps because, like her watch (now forgotten), it was "really noisy."

Her request for "luggage" became her new hourly chime, so I bought her a suitcase on wheels, a slightly smaller and more manageable version of my own. The night before her trip to Florida, I packed it with clothes, beads, medications, and her stuffed penguin. In an envelope atop these things was an instruction sheet for her father, and for her grandparents, who hadn't kept in touch with either of my kids after Paul and I had separated, something that saddened me greatly. Two years had passed since they'd seen Rachel. I wanted them to know that she was capable of washing and getting dressed and undressed without help. I asked that they not overfeed her, that they make sure she had a shower each day, and to let her do everything herself except for setting the water temperature. "Rachel is a good walker and should walk each day," I wrote. I told them she could play simple card games like "War," deciding it was going too far to ask that they not let her cheat. I did suggest that they try to monitor and control her nonsense and repetitive conversation, and I shared my big secret: gum and lemonade served as powerful rewards for her compliance.

I was a little embarrassed about sending the letter, but Paul wouldn't monitor her behavior, and I wanted his family to enjoy Rachel's company and feared that they would not, because, although they were loving people, it was inevitable that their kindness would quickly run out if they didn't control her and limit her freedom. I hated imagining Rachel as the object of everyone's annoyance.

I zipped everything into her suitcase and drove Rachel to the airport. At the gate I said good-bye. She walked into the tunnel, her small suitcase rolling behind.

Maybe this—my saying good-bye—is the second part of the story, because I let Rachel go with nearly everything unresolved. I knew she

RACHEL FLIES ALONE

would be physically safe at her grandparents' house. And, because her father had agreed that she could not be left in the airport alone, I knew that he would have her return flight changed. None of the larger issues had been solved. I let her go for much the same reason that I bought her the watch: because my hope for Rachel does indeed spring eternal. I let her go because I had not yet closed the door on her abilities, and because she deserved to see her family, no matter whether the experience was lasting or ephemeral for her. And I would be lying if I did not say that I let her go out of sheer fatigue.

I said good-bye to Rachel and for the next twelve mornings awoke without anyone yelling breakfast orders in my ear. I read the newspaper. I wandered through the quiet house and went out at night, simply because I could leave at will. I had no curfew, no caregivers' fees. Missing Rachel was like a muscle ache, something my body felt. Otherwise, it was awfully nice to be without her. It occurred to me that perhaps she felt the same. Maybe it was a relief for her, not having someone monitoring her every move.

· · · ·

Paul asked the airline to accommodate our daughter, and in the end, her ticket was rewritten so that she could take a direct flight home. On the day of her return, her aunt and father put her on the plane in Tampa, and I showed up at the gate in Pittsburgh well before her scheduled arrival time. Nearly everyone had left the plane before Rachel galumphed toward me, weirdly dressed in mismatched layers, with electrified-looking hair and a tag on her sweatshirt certifying her as an unaccompanied minor. "Hi, Mom," she said casually. It was as if she had seen me an hour before. I tried to hug her, but she edged away. It was okay. I was suddenly quite happy to have her home. An exhausted-looking flight attendant asked for my picture ID, and I signed for Rachel, as if she were a piece of overnight mail. Then we linked arms and left the gate.

I asked Rachel about her vacation just as she remembered that there were escalators at the airport. The thought of them, the sheer anticipation, seemed to push all her experiences in Florida clear out of her mind. The escalators took such great hold that not even the moving walk could appease her.

So we rode the escalators down both levels, took the tram and then the long moving walkway to the parking lot. I held my questions until we reached the car. On the way home, I *cued* her and kept her *on task* and asked her the same questions five different ways. Wasn't I proud, mother who knew her best, when I got her to recall so many things?

Nearly all of them false, it turned out. I know this because when we returned home, I called her aunt to inform her of Rachel's safe arrival. Everything she told me about Rachel's stay—people, places, activities—was different from what Rachel had reported.

I asked how things had gone. She hesitated, then talked at length about my daughter's curly hair, how beautiful it was, where did she get those curls, etc. "Precious," she called Rachel, sighing. She praised me for "keeping her so nice," then heaved another sigh. "I don't know how you do it. God love her."

It was just an expression, I knew, but the sentiment scared me. I wished someone on earth besides me would do the same.

6

Rachel is a 17-year-old Caucasian female who resides with her mother in Shadyside. Her father and sister reside out of state. Her parents are divorced and her sister attends college.

Summary of problems identified by prescriber:

Noncompliance on tasks

Verbally abusive toward mother

Distractible and easily frustrated

Poorly organized and short attention span

Requires constant attention and assurances at home

Poor safety skills

Perseverative language

Current diagnoses:

Axis I—mental disorder NOS secondary to medical condition

ADHD

Other specified family circumstances

Axis II—MR, unspecified

Axis III—Partial complex seizures

Septo-optic dysplasia

Hypo-pituitarism

Hypo-thyroidism

—Wraparound/EPSDT Waiver Services report, August 2001

AT SEVENTEEN

Meryl was *staff,* and staff had been at the center of Rachel's life, and mine, for some time now. Staff worked on behavior management issues with Rachel while providing her with much of her social life. They discussed strategies they'd used with Rachel, though there was little I hadn't already tried, and made it possible for me to teach and write and have a life apart from her.

The women who worked with Rachel could be divided into three categories: "companions" I hired and paid for myself; TSS's—therapeutic support staff—that came through Wraparound, a program funded by Medicaid; and habituation aides, "hab aides," like Meryl, paid out of Rachel's Title XIX budget, which was also Medicaid money, but from a different funding stream. At its inception Title XIX was enacted as a way for people to leave institutions and still receive the services they needed. In later years, it enabled people with mental retardation—my daughter, for instance—to obtain those services in their community instead of going to an institution. Because Title XIX is a waiver, there is a limited number of slots. I was very fortunate that Rachel got one of those slots before the gate crashed down, leaving others in her cohort without a crucial source of funding. Title XIX provided me with the budget needed to pay for staff and was a prerequisite, a necessary first step before she could be considered for other services, such as housing.

When Rachel was seventeen and spending her Saturday afternoons with Meryl, I tried to count how many people had worked with her since we moved to Pittsburgh. I came up with twenty-five names. I'm pretty sure that everyone who stayed at least a month is on that list. The others, and there were dozens of them, came and went so quickly that they exist in my memory in only a shadowy way.

Hank, our first TSS, starting coming to our house when Rachel was ten. He was a short, squat guy with bright eyes, a bullet-shaped head, and an appealing, straightforward way of relating to Rachel, never babying her, never demanding more than she could handle. He was the one who introduced Rachel to Special Olympics basketball and swimming, activities that continue to be an important part of her life. He was an avid rabbit hunter, who described his hunting trips with great enthusiasm, leaving me the job of rectifying the sensitive guy who called Rachel "buddy" with the guy who blew away bunnies in his free time.

Back in 1994, when we first got Wraparound, the program was called "respite," unofficially, at least. The way I understood it, Hank's job was to work on behavior issues with Rachel and at the same time give the rest of us a break. I followed through on what I learned from him when I was with Rachel and he was not. By the time Hank left to work at a residential program, the policies had changed. For one thing, it became unheard of for a male TSS to work with a girl. After Hank there were only women, among them Ann, Jessica, Cindy, Donna, Debbie, and two Melissas. By the time Meryl came along, TSS's were no longer allowed to transport clients. Many felt that TSS service was overprescribed and misused, with families asking TSS workers to do childcare or housekeeping. Guidelines were rigorously enforced. Parents who had in-home TSS's had to be with the TSS at all times. Frankly, I would have declined a behavior management program that demanded that I trail along with the TSS and my daughter. Not that it became an issue: this was a costly mental health support service, meant "to be faded," even if the behavior issues didn't resolve. By Rachel's seventeenth birthday, her hours had been cut to fifteen a week, all of them at an after-school program at the JCC. The plan of care stressed safety and appropriate behavior in the community.

AT SEVENTEEN

Habituation aides, among them Donna, Beverly, Carolyn, Selina, and Leigh, didn't necessarily have a B.A., as was required for all TSS's; they needed a year's experience in the "mental health" field. I could tell them about some of Rachel's behavior problems and hope they would follow through on the strategies I suggested. Some did, and they were excellent. Others were essentially babysitters. Though hab aides were paid less than TSS's, they had much greater flexibility. They could take clients in their cars and go wherever they liked, without having to follow any intensive, highly structured plan. Hab aides were expensive because they came through an agency, so I used them as backups, when one of the companions I hired was unavailable or had disappeared—things that happened all the time.

"Companion" was what I had begun to write when I posted an ad in the *Pitt News* each fall. No longer was it "caregiver." Now it called for a "companion for teenager with developmental disabilities," since a companion was what Rachel needed, albeit one who would embed behavior management in ordinary activities. Everyone who answered this ad was a student at the University of Pittsburgh, except for the drama student from Point Park College, who fainted from not eating while on a bus with Rachel. I picked them both up in the emergency room and took the companion home to rest. She disappeared after that. Initially I was grateful, since she was a troubled girl, though sweet. Then I was desperate, stuck, my life on hold. It wasn't as simple as losing any semblance of a social life, though without staff, I couldn't run or take a bike ride or have dinner with the man in my life—a kind, intensely private person. I needed regular staff to be with Rachel when there were holidays and monthly in-service days at Rachel's school, when she was off and I was not. Without staff, I couldn't teach or write or hope to get tenure.

In the beginning I put great store in experience and opted to hire women who were studying physical therapy or occupational therapy, or earning degrees in special education. They got points with me for having relatives with developmental disabilities. Stella, a TSS in graduate school, had great credentials. Even so, her behavior strategies amounted to running after Rachel and crying, "Relax! Just relax!" Karen, another TSS, also had an impressive resume; she took Rachel to a bar—several times, I think—to throw back a few beers and watch some football on TV. The agency let her go before I heard the whole story.

Chrissy was in a graduate audiology program. She was a tall, toothy blonde, full of good cheer. Her cousin had Down syndrome, and she'd worked in group homes as an undergraduate. On Saturday mornings, she picked up Rachel in her tan Jeep, with her little white dog, Lenny, in the back seat and rock and roll blasting on the radio. When the weather was nice, she took Lenny and Rachel for long walks in Frick Park. She played the soundtrack to *Rent* until Rachel knew the lyrics, and then, for her birthday, drove her downtown to see the play. She was a wonderful young woman who left abruptly when her mother became critically ill. I miss her still.

Out of desperation, and sure it would never work, I hired Kelly Jane, who had a baby and a degree in art and had never known anyone with mental retardation. She learned about Rachel by spending time with her and asking me questions as they arose. At first, Kelly Jane was tentative with Rachel. Eventually, on the evenings they spent together, she simply incorporated Rachel into her own family. Their relationship was very natural.

It was the same with Jezelle, who first met Rachel at the Children's Institute in 1992. Whenever I went out of town, Rachel stayed in "her room" at Jezelle's. If they were together on a Saturday they might run errands or spend time with Jezelle's brothers or nieces or son, not as a guest or a "client," though officially, that's what she was. Mostly they did ordinary things—shopping, cooking. I often thought Rachel liked this better than trips to the zoo or the aviary or other special events. Though she loved to travel to new places—loved the noise and excitement of New York City, the subways, busses, restaurants, the carousel in Central Park—the familiar was pleasing to her. Structure comforted her and calmed her down. Mundane was fine, as long as there was a schedule that could be recited for her, over and over.

The pay for this kind of work was poor. No one earned what she deserved. I tried to pay as well as I could, given the limits of my personal budget and Rachel's Title XIX budget. I did this because I respected the work her companions did and respected the women themselves. I also hated losing someone I trusted who got along well with Rachel.

Starting all over with a stranger was like going out on a first date. I tried to describe Rachel as well as I could, stressing that she was good-natured (except with me), and that talking was her most serious behavioral issue and needed to be controlled. In the end, though, there was no predicting whether the caregiver would like Rachel or if their relationship would last. While in the beginning I suggested specific ways they might spend their hours together, it was crucial for the companion to start choosing activities that she also enjoyed.

I couldn't tell right away who would disappear and who would work out well—Kelly Jane being a case in point—except when it came to the ones who cooed over Rachel, told me she was adorable, and discounted what I said about her talking. Some, I could tell, decided I was too bossy and felt that Rachel should decide how she wanted to spend her day. Maybe among that group one or two were trying to adhere to the principles of self-determination by giving Rachel the right to make her own decisions about where to go and what to eat. Others were sentimental, fooled into thinking Rachel was a sweet little baby.

Whatever their justifications, the women who took Rachel literally ended up eating lunch at ten, buying her potato chips, pencils, and crossword puzzle books, eating dinner at three, and then watching her play Free Cell on the computer. After a visit or two, they vanished. I'd seen this happen many times. I'd seen pretty nearly everything. It was why, when someone good came along, I'd try to roll with the companion's quirks, whatever they were, to pay little mind to those who were chronically late or canceled often, who haggled over pennies, brought their kids along, who couldn't come before 6:30 or needed to be home by 9:00.

Meryl, a melancholy woman in her forties, left her better-paying job as Rachel's TSS because she was allergic to the JCC. Not literally allergic; it was just that, for whatever reason, she could no longer bring herself to walk through its door. She was always on the verge of quitting her job and leaving the city, or so she would tell me each week. In the meantime, she spent Saturday afternoons with Rachel, and some weekdays when my daughter had time off from school and I did not. They had a routine that seemed to satisfy both of them: errands first; then, if Rachel was cooperative, lunch at the bagel shop, and on to Barnes and Noble to look at books and have tea. A book I'd written had just come out in paperback. Rachel took it upon herself to police the store every Saturday to make sure it was in stock. It was like having my own local publicist.

As much as she enjoyed making sure the bookstore was devoted to my work, it was nothing compared to eating out. Going to a restaurant was without question Rachel's favorite activity. It was also a good way for Meryl to reinforce appropriate behavior in a community setting. Lunch at the bagel shop meant having to wait behind other customers, without pushing ahead. It meant being ready to place her order when it was her turn, with no unnecessary conversation, carrying the tray steadily, taking a reasonable number of napkins and straws, finding an empty table. It meant eating slowly and wiping the food off her face. While it was true that Rachel didn't consistently remember to do these things, the bigger issue was that she didn't particularly want to do them.

· · · ·

When Rachel was seventeen, Charlotte shot a short documentary about her sister for her sophomore project at film school. She claimed that Rachel was her second choice as a subject, and that her intention had originally been to make a film about lobstering in Maine but the logistics made it impossible. Shooting the documentary gave her a chance to see Rachel from a different vantage point. Charlotte wasn't just a sister responding to a complex, difficult sibling; she was a filmmaker, scrutinizing Rachel in an intense, if distanced, way. Rachel loved being a star and basked in the attention she got. She also developed a fierce crush on a handsome crew member named Mark. Whenever Charlotte tried to walk beside him, Rachel would elbow her away and wrap her arm around Mark's neck. It didn't surprise me; she wanted to be in my relationship, too, to butt between us and follow us everywhere.

When I try to describe Rachel from this period, Charlotte's words seem most apt. "Like *us*," she said of her sister. Talkative, outgoing, eager for new experiences, the type of person who liked being in the center of things. "If she was normal she'd be a real bad-ass."

This was funny and absolutely true. Wasn't it the case that there were three generations of stubborn, opinionated, bad-ass women who didn't play by all the rules? The problem was that Rachel didn't want to play by *any* of the rules.

Like us, yes; a real bad-ass, yes. A typical teenager in the way she liked to listen to her Walkman, while playing a computer game, with the TV blaring in the background. Typical in the way she cared about what she wore and had her own distinct sense of cool. Our arguments weren't about drugs or boys, sneaking out of the house, or throwing parties when I was out of town. We quarreled about hygiene, because she would often "shower" without soap or let the water run for a moment, then cheerfully call out, "All done!" We quarreled because she eschewed toilet paper and would not tell me when she had her period—despite the lessons and the monthly reminders that it was part of being a woman. I could ease her into wearing a sanitary napkin, though she was likely, on such a morning, to climb onto the school van, where her friends were sitting—Josh, Uri, and Max—and announce, "*I'm* wearing a pad!"

We quarreled because she threw her body against my bedroom door when the sun came up, demanded her breakfast, and kept demanding, no matter that she was not allowed to wake me until her alarm went off. She wanted cereal in the blue bowl and she wanted it *right now!* Every day began with Rachel's arguing, and continued through breakfast and beyond with her opposing even my most trivial requests. Like this:

"Rachel, put your bowl in the dishwasher."

"Yackety-yak."

"I mean it."

"Yak yak yak."

"If you don't do it at the count of three, no computer."

A pause, a decision; her prideful answer. "Yeah, *what*ever."

When we were apart, I often thought it thrilling the way my once passive baby, who had to be woken for feedings and coaxed to smile, had blossomed. Gone was the little girl, beautiful and curly haired, whom nothing could delight—not a stuffed bear, a noisy toy, a glittery barrette. At seventeen, Rachel was bristling with desires and demands. There were tangible things she wanted, privileges she demanded, and rules that offended her deeply.

Mostly, though, she wore me out.

· · · ·

Even the smallest outing was full of event. Take an appointment with the doctor. On the drive there, we go over the rules. "You are not going to bug people, right?" I say. "You will not take away toys from babies. You understand?"

She understands and agrees.

We reach the reception area. I take her jacket, show her where to find the magazines, then turn to sign us in.

As soon as I step away, she whips out a half-deck of Uno cards, softened and bent from being hidden in her pocket. By the time I turn back, she has coerced a man—someone's awkward, vulnerable father—to play.

"Rachel, that is *not* appropriate," I say.

Sometimes I manage to reel her in. More often, the sucker says, "Oh, it's okay." And though it really *isn't* okay, this acquiescence is all she needs to hold her ground.

At seventeen, Rachel is 5'3" and outweighs me by thirty pounds; she's capable of knocking me over while giving me a giant "hug." She cannot be budged if she does not want to go. Gone are the days when I could take her arm and move her when she failed to listen. Now she stays put. She is very strong. If I try to move her, she squeals like a pig and plants herself firmly. It gets worse if I persist.

Or we're waiting for an elevator. I'm cueing her before the doors open. Who are the people in the elevator—strangers, acquaintances, or friends? She and her companions work on these distinctions after school because it's a safety skill, a crucial one she needs to have before she moves from my house. And so I always ask:

"Are the people in the elevator your friends?"

"No."

"What are they?"

"Strangers."

"Right. Excellent. And how do you act with strangers?"

The doors part before she answers. Inside is a woman with her little boy.

"Hel-lo," Rachel says.

It's perfectly appropriate. I inhale deeply and wait.

Despite her adult height, there is something about my daughter's demeanor, her openness, her round, sweet, face, that makes people respond to her as they would to a young child. She always gets a hello in return. This time, too.

"How are you this morning?" she asks next.

Also okay, if not my style.

Then, "How old is he? Ahh, cute. Where's he going?" and before I can intercede: "This is my mom, and I'm Rachel . . ."

I'm smiling tightly, hoping the doors will open and the strangers will get out because any second she might ask us for a big group hug—more than ask, *demand* that we huddle with our arms linked, *insist.* At seventeen, she will not back down.

My daughter was so complicated—incapable of understanding that if only she complied with a request or two, I would soften up and grant her privileges, yet fully aware that I was apt to back down when we were in public. If only I could train everyone not to reinforce her inappropriate behavior. Alas, there were still 250 million Americans who did not understood that it was better to say "No thanks" when she whipped out that deck of cards.

· · · ·

If I asked Rachel later about the woman on the elevator, she could correctly say, "She was a stranger."

And the letter carrier?

"An acquaintance."

"When he brings you the mail, do you ask for a hug?"

"No."

"Why not?"

"Because he's an acquaintance."

Rachel knew the answers to these questions, because I wasn't the only one who grilled her. Her TSS's, hab aides, and companions worked on these issues. So did her teachers. Her reports from school are full of details about trips she and her classmates took, walking or rolling the few blocks from their building to the stores in Squirrel Hill to practice mobility, appropriate behavior, and "community awareness." As with Meryl, she didn't simply have lunch at a local restaurant with her peers. She practiced "using an inside voice," "eating at an appropriate rate," "decreasing impatience while waiting for food." As soon as the school day was over she went straight to her teen program at the JCC, where safety rules were again reinforced. Topics included talking to strangers, understanding signs, practicing "appropriate social distance when talking," "asking for assistance appropriately."

So many people, so many hours, so much money from so many funding streams. Sometimes it seemed that all of us were ganging up on her—family members, teachers, psychologists, TSS's, hab aides, companions—blocking her path, keeping her from doing what she wanted to do. Maybe it was cruel and dictatorial, trying to make her more like *us* so she could fit into *our* world. Maybe doing this was depriving her of a "fundamental human right" to act as she wished.

I had begun to read and hear a lot about self-determination when Rachel was seventeen. I knew that the United Nations had decreed that all persons had a right to self-determination. "All people have a right to choose how they want to spend their lives, including those with mental retardation," I read in documents attached to Rachel's paperwork from school and from the county. This was the potent argument behind the national movement meant to empower people who had developmental disabilities. Respecting people's fundamental human rights was the reason for "person-centered planning," which put choice in the hands of the individual. It was also imperfectly carried out, I was hearing. Staff had told me of cases where freedom had been handed blithely to those who hadn't the ability to make their decisions alone, as if it was nothing more than an ice cream cone.

The day I saw the words "appropriate" and "appropriately" used eight times on a single page in Rachel's behavior plan, I wasn't thinking about the downside of this important legislation. I found myself wondering instead if the whole effort we expended, this full-time behavior management, wasn't futile and mean-spirited. Maybe we were, in fact, depriving Rachel of the ability to live life the way she wanted. Maybe it was wrong of us.

Then I closed my eyes and thought about the consequences of letting Rachel loose, and a shiver ran down my spine.

I had to think that she could not—or would not—put the knowledge into play *yet* because I wanted her to live safely in my community. *Yet,* because I could see the way her behavior alienated people. *Yet,* because she was my daughter, a part of my family, but when my father died that year I did not take her to the funeral in New Jersey because

I didn't think I could manage it alone. And when I got an invitation to a party that said, "spouses, significant others, and children," I had begun to leave her home. It meant everything to me when friends specifically asked me to bring Rachel. I declined because it was exhausting to take her along. Sometimes she was fine. More often, a party offered her a chance to be in a world where people didn't manage her behavior and she could do as she pleased. She could corner people, demand they fix her yo-yo string, play Uno with a deck of fifteen cards, follow her to a distant room. It was a time when she could eat whatever she wanted.

What a problem food had become. She loved to eat and people loved to feed her—strangers, bus drivers, hab aides, teachers. Every day she came home with food in her backpack; bottles of soda, squashed cookies in cellophane, bruised apples, hairy half-wrapped candies. It was as if she were an animal in a zoo.

Her weight had begun to increase steadily. By the time she was seventeen, I had started to worry about her becoming obese. What made me sad was that, at home, she ate moderately and well. We were vegetarians. My kids had been brought up that way, and neither questioned it or complained. (When Charlotte, bad-ass older sister, rebelled, it was to be come a vegan.) At home, Rachel chose fresh fruits and vegetables and wholesome foods. She was satisfied with the portions I served her and never ate between meals. She never opened the refrigerator or cabinets on her own. Asked to name her favorite food, she said, "Salad." Indeed, she loved and anticipated salad so much that she would weep and punch herself in the head and call me "Turkey" and "Bird Brain" if I denied her a salad or dared to suggest a smaller one in the hated (smaller) brown bowl instead of the (larger) blue and yellow bowl.

Outside, where she had begun to spend more time, was where she discovered the joys of snacking. She cultivated a passion for bottled blue cheese dressing and croutons, potato chips, cheese curls, nachos, and soda. She had figured out that other people enjoyed giving her food, and that if she pocketed the coins she found in our house, someone would help her get snacks from a vending machine.

Clothes might matter to Rachel, but she was unaffected by those waifish fashion models. She felt no social pressure to maintain a reasonable weight—or to be clean. She did not understand the ramifications of weight gain on her heart, her joints, her ability to have fun. Food was easy. It was a stress-free source of pleasure for her. I knew that no amount of reinforcement would alter the fact that food was simply a more powerful force than anything else.

. . . .

By the time Rachel turned seventeen, I found myself thinking a lot about the day when she would live outside my house. I knew that beginning to plan was a responsible thing to do, that all parents of children with developmental disabilities must face their own mortality and consider who will care for their children after they are gone. Still, I was aware that my decision to find a placement for her in the next few years was powered by my own fatigue. The endless cycles of caring for her had worn me down. I knew I needed my freedom from her. What I didn't understand, until one August weekend, was how badly Rachel needed her freedom from me.

We were at the JCC summer camp in West Virginia. The regular camp season had ended, and this last weekend before Labor Day was set aside for special-needs campers and their families. Rachel was staying in a cabin with four of her cohorts, older women she knew from her Sunday "Center Folk" trips at the JCC. My cabin was down the hill in a different part of the camp. Just before bedtime, I borrowed a flashlight and trekked to her cabin to check up on her. The five bunkmates were drinking chocolate milk, listening to music, and playing cards. I started to whisper to Rachel to please use the bathroom before she went to sleep, and she told me to go away. I did.

On the cafeteria line the next afternoon, she reached for chocolate milk and potato chips. I said, "One or the other." She cast me such a withering look that again I backed off.

Five months and countless quarrels after this liberating experience, which she referenced often, we were driving home, discussing dinner (her favorite topic of conversation), when something—I don't recall exactly what—set her off. Maybe I had suggested that we have a smaller salad to accompany our dinner. Whatever it was, she exploded:

"I don't want to live here anymore! I want my own apartment. I hate this household."

"What do you hate about it?" I asked.

"It's *boring*. There's no junk."

"Like what?" As if I didn't know.

"Candy!" she stormed. "I want my own apartment!"

The next day was Martin Luther King Day. She and Meryl were supposed to have lunch at the bagel shop and then go next door to look at books. Rachel manipulated Meryl into taking her to a restaurant down the street instead, where she could order a salad (unavailable at the bagel place) and a chicken salad sandwich.

When I saw this on the receipt, I was stunned. A chicken salad sandwich? This was a girl who did not reliably know the name of the president, could not make change from a dollar, cross the street alone, or say where eggs came from. I wasn't even sure she could describe a chicken. How did she know to order a chicken salad sandwich?

I laughed. My willful, bad-ass teenage daughter was finding her way in the world, making her own decisions, seeking her own pleasures. She was peevish and hormonal, and quarreled with me about absolutely everything. At that moment, the fact that something beat inside her—love and desire—thrilled me to the core.

Rachel wanted more than chicken salad, though. She wanted to push ahead of others while waiting for that chicken salad. She wanted to engage the counter help in conversation that had nothing to do with what went on her sandwich, while the line behind her grew longer. She wanted not merely to exchange hellos with strangers but to ensnare them by asking what they were eating, where they were going, how old they were, and if they'd seen *One Hundred and One Dalmatians*. She wanted to ban all contact with toilet paper and feminine hygiene products. She wanted her own apartment.

One day she would have a place of her own, albeit with housemates and twenty-four-hour staffing, and the freedom she craved. She would be the beneficiary of person-centered planning—and the potential victim, I feared, since the law would allow her to skip her showers and eat potato chips for all three meals. No staff member had the right to impinge upon her freedom.

Rachel was unable make complex decisions based on safety or health, which was part of the reason she would always need full-time staff supervision. I wanted her to have standards so well reinforced that she would make her later choices based on what we'd done at home. She would want to take a shower every day, because she was used to it. She would choose to eat healthy foods, because those were the comfort foods from her childhood. She would enjoy getting exercise, because it had been a happy part of her life when she lived in my house.

When Rachel was an infant and her disabilities became known to me, I had to learn to accept that her life would be different from mine. Seeing her as a teenager reminded me that while I long ago acknowledged those differences, I was still struggling to shape her in my own image. I would dictate, I would reinforce, and I would quarrel with her. I would forbid her to eat chicken salad. It was my way of saying, *You are one of us, part of our family. These are the things we believe.* I knew, though, that it was time to start letting go, just as I had let go of Charlotte when she was a teenager. Rachel would not pierce her tongue when she left my house. She would not get tattoos or shave her head. She would find her own friends, her own music, her own pleasures. She would have potato chips and chocolate milk. All I could do was hope that some of what I believed was important would stick.

7

Love and work are the cornerstones of our humanness.

—Sigmund Freud

RACHEL AT WORK

      In the spring of 2002, the crocuses pushed up and the daffodils blossomed and froze, and I worried about work—not my own, which I loved, but what kind of work Rachel might be able to do when she was no longer in the shelter of school.

      On one April morning—an average morning, in fact—after quarreling with her because she would not put her bowl in the dishwasher, and threatening to take away her Uno cards if she did not brush her teeth, I asked her if she knew what *work* meant. After a few false starts—trying to make a case for computer solitaire as work, for instance—she pretty much nailed it. Work, she said, was "when you have to do stuff they ask you to do."

      Did she like to work? I asked.

"Not really."

"How come?"

"'Cause the way they talk to me is really mean. They talk harsh on me, Ma. Put it this way: When they talk to me, they tell me to be quiet and all that junk."

      Outside, a horn honked. I trailed behind Rachel as she reached for the banister and slowly edged her way down the porch steps, then into the van that took her to the Children's Institute, where on a typical day, she would sort and deliver mail, make a bed, and wipe down a table.

After the van pulled away, I stood on the sidewalk for a moment, limp with exhaustion and relief. Most of us—*us* meaning the population that designates itself "normal"—don't need prompting to use the toilet. We don't insist on wearing a sweat suit on a day when the temperature might reach 80 degrees. We don't finish breakfast with a ring of food around our mouths—or if we do, we're grateful when someone says, "Honey, you've got food on your face." Most of us don't mind touching our own faces to wipe it off. While I often found myself arguing that Rachel was one of us, deserving of the rights and privileges accorded to her by the U.S. Constitution, on this morning—during this whole season of thinking about how to make her into a working girl—I was reminded of the impediments blocking her way.

. . . .

I had always believed that Rachel would work. Even after it became obvious that she would never read books or write a single sentence, after I realized that she would never walk on the street alone or live without supervision, I held onto a vision of her having some sort of job, somewhere. When I saw a janitor or a person busing tables, I would close my eyes and try to picture Rachel doing that job, sure that despite her cognitive deficits, her poor vision, and limited fine-motor abilities, she could be trained for some job. I speculated on the challenges of making a worker out of someone like my daughter. She was unable to understand concepts like altruism and loyalty; she took no apparent pleasure from a job well done and would never fear being fired. Still, I went to sleep at night believing that some job would be found, and that the structure and routine it provided would be good for her. Away from me, she still seemed like someone with a cheerful nature. All we had to do now was help her find employment and a safe place to live, and we would be on our way.

Nearly two years had passed since I'd learned that finding a place for Rachel to live was not going to be the kind of easy transition I had imagined, so I should have known better. Still, my vague dream that Rachel would work was nourished by several factors. First, we had time to achieve that goal since Rachel would remain in school until June 2005. Second, she had been given an after-school job at Café J, a snack bar staffed by people with developmental disabilities at the JCC near our home. Though her TSS was always at her side, making sure her behavior was appropriate and keeping her on task, still it was work—a situation where she had to "do stuff they ask you to do." Third, I believed in some equally vague way that the law would protect her. In the back of my mind was the knowledge that if Rachel had been born less than a generation ago, I would have been advised—pressured, perhaps—to put her into an institution. That was where 90 percent of children with developmental disabilities languished until the 1970s. The Education of All Handicapped Children Act of 1975 (now called the Individuals with Disabilities Act, or IDEA) passed only eight years before Rachel's birth. Before Congress enacted this law guaranteeing that children with disabilities had the chance to receive a free, appropriate public education, over a million children were denied the chance to be educated and hundreds of thousands more lacked access to appropriate services. Even if I had ample funds, I would have been hard-pressed to find a nearby school she would have been able to attend. In those days a conversation with the words *school* and *Rachel* in the same sentence would have been problematic. *Work* and *Rachel* in the same sentence wouldn't have been even vaguely feasible.

I was lulled by these laws and by the fact that thus far I had not had to fight for Rachel's right to be educated—not in New Jersey, nor in Pennsylvania, where her district provided the funding for her to attend the Children's Institute, an approved private school that provided her education in accordance with the law.

A 1997 revision of IDEA stipulated that the "transition process," the time when we—parents, educators, and Rachel herself—were supposed to begin to prepare her for life beyond school, should begin no later than age sixteen. At Rachel's school, transition began at age fourteen. Each summer since then, I had filled out long questionnaires about her likes and dislikes, listed the agencies that had worked with her, the stores and restaurants she liked. I wrote down her favorite foods and games, her after-school activities and some activities I wanted to see her try. I was asked if she could be trusted with money and if she understood the passage of time. Could she accept responsibility for her actions, make appointments, talk on the phone? I answered these questions carefully, with her best interests in mind, priding myself on being realistic, believing that I had no illusions about my expectations for my daughter. When I handed in the paperwork before her 2001–2 school year began, I thought of myself as someone who could see the big picture.

In September, shortly after she had returned to school, I found Rachel's curriculum for that academic year in a manila envelope in her backpack.

Washing machine, dryer, setting the table.

I didn't think, *This is great,* or even, *This is the law.* I thought, full of utter despair, *They've given up.*

Of course, I knew that she'd been working at school—she and her classmates had tried out some lawn-maintenance jobs and had torn paper for the kennels at the Animal Rescue League. Still, her educational program in past years had included looking at pre-primers, sounding out words, learning to develop a sight vocabulary, answering verbal-comprehension questions about a story, counting by rote to thirty-five. Identifying seasonal changes, the needs of a plant, the characteristics of lions, tigers, and elephants. Though she continued to function well below grade level, the tone in the mostly boilerplate documents had always been full of strategies that would be employed and accommodations made for her, full of hope for what she might yet become.

The blunt language in the document that set out her plan for the 2001–2 academic year was different: "Due to neurological disabilities and extensive need for modification in all areas, Rachel is unable at this time to participate in the general regular education curriculum." She would be in the Life Skills Program instead. Her goals would be to learn the location of classrooms, sort mail by number up to twenty with 60 percent accuracy, count five items without verbal cues, collate four color-coded items with verbal cues. The tasks seemed so meager—so pathetically small.

First I bristled. Then I thought, *She really* is *retarded,* though for eighteen years I had known this, believed I had accepted it fully. There was something final about the plan's language that shocked me—*is and always will be* "unable to participate." Looking at this document, I was forced to see that progress for this school year was being measured by my eighteen-year-old daughter's ability to deliver mail independently to a two-room route in a building she had known for nine years.

At the October meeting to discuss her IEP—Individualized Educational Program—I said I wanted her teachers to continue working with her on some basic academic skills, since I believed it was important for Rachel to know the difference between Women's Room and Men's Room, Entrance and Exit, Cheerios and Frosted Flakes. With the spirit of cooperation I'd always felt at these meetings, a few additional goals were drafted: Rachel would "identify words related to shopping, community signs, menus and recipes" and would make change up to one dollar. I thanked her teachers and the representative from the school district for working with Rachel, and left the building alone.

I was still reeling, utterly stunned. What about the progress she'd been making at the café? Her TSS had been telling me that lately Rachel had been more cooperative about working, that she was using the cash register and closing up the café without being reminded of the sequence of required tasks. Yes, I understood that Café J was a protected environment, and that she had someone at her side prompting and cueing and redirecting. Still, two rooms without distraction—was that the most her teachers at the Children's Institute thought she could achieve?

The only way I would learn whether I was deluded or her teachers underestimated her abilities was to observe her in class. I knew this. Even so, several months would pass before I stepped into her school. And that delay, I think, had to do with the fourth reason I had held onto my some-job-somewhere dream and allowed myself to imagine that those 1975 laws would be carried out flawlessly.

I was tired. Lately, whatever didn't require my urgent attention went into an okay-for-the-present category. School had been in that category for a long time. It was *there*, except on set holidays. School didn't disappear without warning, like flaky staff. Without question, it would be part of our lives until 2005—the details of Rachel's program set out in an IEP (mandated by federal law), the quarterly progress reports sent home for my perusal. School was okay for now.

It was dangerously late to let myself hold on to any dreams that could not be substantiated, and so, that spring, I visited Rachel's school. It didn't take me long to see that I had failed to integrate all that I had actually known about Rachel. The problem was that my view of my daughter was limited. So was my understanding of "work." Here's what else I learned:

. . . .

Rachel must learn how to make toast.

She was around five when we started working with her to put on her own shoes. An occupational therapist strung elastic laces in her shoes so that tying and untying would be unnecessary. Then we re-inforced—and reinforced—the procedure, starting with "off," which was easier. First you sit in a chair. Next you bring one leg up and over the other. Cross that leg. Reach for the heel of the shoe. Pull. It was the first time I considered how complicated, and how frustrating, it might be to take off one's shoe.

I thought about teaching Rachel to put on her shoes when I ob-served her morning cooking class. The group had been doing a unit on breakfast. On this particular morning, their teacher, Bob Russell, produced a bag of bread and announced that the topic for the day was toast. Learning to make toast, like putting on one's shoes, is a multistep operation. First you had to wipe down the counter "be-cause you might drop the toast, and germs are *gross!*" Then you had to figure out what you wanted to put on the toast. After the students slowly offered suggestions for what they might choose to put on their bread—butter, peanut butter, margarine, jam—they had to figure out where they might find these things.

Butter, for instance. Where *is* it kept? The refrigerator. Right. What about the jelly?

After the kids told Bob where he might find the jelly, he scrutinized the jar and said: "So you have this purple jelly. What flavor is purple? What flavor is the red?"

He popped the bread in the toaster. "Sometimes you have to push hard on the handle to get the bread to go down. Sometimes you don't."

Back to the jelly. How do you get the jar open? Sometimes you lift the lid. Sometimes you unscrew the top.

What do you use to get the stuff out—a spoon or a knife? Can you manage a butter knife, or will you need a broad, flexible spreader?

Safety. Germs. Hand-washing. Choice. Spreading what you've chosen to go on the toast as evenly as possible. Trying to cut the toast in half.

That night at dinner, I sat across the table from my daughter and heard myself say, "Don't shove giant chunks into your mouth. . . . Chew your food—with your mouth closed, please. . . . Use a napkin. . . . Wipe your face and hands."

I thought about work not merely as a specific job or career but as "exertion" and "effort," which also are definitions. I thought of how hard Rachel worked. For her, getting dressed is work. So is clearing the breakfast table, brushing her teeth, negotiating the front steps on a sunny day. Even eating is full of lessons: You could choke. You'll gross people out. Cleanliness counts. Little is self-evident to my daughter, since she is not attuned to matters of safety or health or other people's judgment of her. These small, necessary things—cutting her food into smaller pieces, opening the napkin, wiping her fingers—were labor for her.

At the same time, she could be astoundingly lazy, capable of standing for a half hour in the shower and never once reaching for the soap. She tried to manipulate everyone she met, from staff to absolute strangers, getting anyone within earshot to lift, tote, fetch, serve, and attend to her every need.

Rachel had to learn to make her own toast. Even if she was blessed with the most accommodating friend or aide, she had to learn to choose what she wanted to eat and where she wanted to go. She had to be responsible for basic hygiene and cleanliness. The more independent she became, the better her chances for being out in the world, something my gregarious daughter craved. The domestic skills she learned would carry her beyond the kitchen into the world where things had levers, lids, and screw tops, were stored in cabinets behind opaque doors, where there were slots, stairs, escalators, revolving doors. Learning to make toast was one step toward helping her live with dignity.

Toast was more than toast.

"Life skills" didn't signal the end of the line for her. They were the skills necessary before she could be part of a community and part of the working world.

• • • •

Supported employment is not a sure thing.   111

To most people a single face embodies all individuals with mental retardation out there in the workplace: the supermarket bagger. It's the most visible job, the one we see most often. A bagger, like my pal Jimmy, an older man, balding, missing a few teeth, who bags groceries efficiently and carefully at the local supermarket, heavy stuff on the bottom, the eggs in a separate bag. (Whenever Jimmy saw me, he stopped, opened his arms wide, grunted with utter glee, and then *pronto* was back to work.) According to the Arc of the United States, the national organization for people with mental retardation, up to 7.5 million Americans have some degree of mental retardation. About 87 percent are, like Jimmy, mildly affected, a little slower than average in learning new information and skills. In the workplace they have proven to be diligent and loyal; they don't job hop or pose any additional health or safety issues.

At Rachel's school this kind of "competitive employment" was one of three categories for students in the transition program. It was possible only for those who could become independent, learn time-management skills, and use public transportation—all this before mastering the particulars of the job itself. Other students were learning skills that would enable them to seek "supported employment" in a sheltered environment. In the third group remained those with the most extreme health problems and disabilities, who would go to respite care or an adult training facility.

When I visited Bob Russell's class, I learned that making toast was more than figuring out how brown you liked your bread. After I visited Dawn Tomlin's work-production class, where students were learning specific skills, I understood that succeeding in work production meant not merely mastering specific job skills (sorting, counting, tallying), but also improving "time-on-task" skills (endurance, work rate, speed). Good workers had to be able to interact properly with each other. They had to learn to ask for supplies when they ran short and seek help if there was something they didn't understand.

Dawn's room was wonderfully familiar, on its walls a map of the world, a poster of baseball legend Roberto Clemente, a banner that read, *Understand the similarities. Celebrate the differences.* On the day of my visit, seven students sat around a long table. For several class periods, they'd been helping refurbish science kits for area schools for the "Asset Project." The plastic pieces—thousands of them—for these kits had been separated into storage bins and stacked on the shelves of a cart. That afternoon the first job was sorting two tires into a Ziploc bag.

Two students were in wheelchairs. One had partial use of one hand. The other boy, Chris, writhed continually. On the tray of his wheelchair was a state-of-the-art language board that had been programmed to say at his command the kinds of things a worker might need to say, for instance, "I need more supplies." He needed only to touch an icon on the board for it to speak. It was quite forgiving. The board "understood" Chris even when his aim was imperfect.

Five other workers were at the table—two dreamy-looking kids, and three others, including Rachel, who on this day was wearing her purple shirt and two strands of purple Mardi Gras beads. A teacher, two aides, and a student teacher were also helping out.

"Everyone will start with a yellow bin," Dawn said in a loud, clear voice. "Everyone should have what? A tire. Okay. You have to put two tires into one bag. This is the first step. Does everybody have a large tire? Everybody should have a large tire. Now, what do you need?"

"A bag!" someone eventually offered.

"Set two tires aside. You're going to have to put two—listen, Jake—*two* tires into *one* bag. Okay? This is the first step."

And so they began, each with his or her spectrum of behavioral, cognitive, and physical "differences." Each with issues. In this class, as in cooking, Rachel's were less apparent, especially on this day, when my presence put her into a bashful mode.

The boys in the wheelchairs were given plastic deli-type containers. They pushed the tires into the plastic container first. This made it easier to then slide the tires into the Ziploc bag. If the sheer effort was obvious, so too was the absence of frustration, at least on this day.

The teachers prompted and coached without stop.

"Two in a bag."

"Good job, Jake."

"Chris, you are phenomenal!"

"Nice job!"

The language board said in its sci-fi voice, "I need a bag, please."

One boy had a hard time opening the Ziploc bag.

Amy, a girl with an angelic face, was so slow it was as if she were floating underwater. Beside her, tiny Felice filled the bag without prompting or delay, then held up the bag, eyed it, placed it on the table, and very precisely, a fraction of an inch at a time, pressed down on the zip line until the bag was sealed. The whole process took a couple of minutes. Meanwhile:

"One in each container!"

"You need to *ask* if you need more supplies."

"Dawn! Dawn!" This was my kid's familiar, maddening, attention-getting chime.

Dawn was busy with Jake, asking, "How many go in a bag? How *many*, Jake?"

"Two."

"And how many are in *that* bag?"

Jake looked up, fastening his huge otherworldly eyes on her.

"I'm running out of bags!" Rachel said. Then, catching my eye, she gestured *come here* with her finger.

I ignored her. She went back to her task.

And then—here's the thing—everyone was at work. Except for the teachers' enthusiastic prompts, the room was quiet. There was no sign of discord or unhappiness, no sense that this was drudgery. These students were more focused than the kids in an average public-school class. They were working! They were engaged. And they kept at it for twenty minutes, until the first sorting job was done. The next step would be for them to put smaller tires in the same bags.

But first, break time. A chance to stretch or move about, get a drink of water, chat with their friends. One of the aides put on latex gloves, filled a huge syringe with milky-colored liquid, and squirted it into Chris's mouth. He gurgled and gagged during the messy, difficult process.

Steve showed the student teacher the vicious-looking dog on the front of his T-shirt, its white fangs glistening. "Kmart!" he told her proudly.

When Rachel found me, I asked what she was doing. "They have them putting in tires for other people," she said. "They have a lot of stuff for students to sort." Then she whipped out a bottle of purple nail polish from her pocket.

Angelic-looking Amy came toward me, stopping to sign when she was right in my face. I was embarrassed that I did not know her language, reminded, too, that I was a foreigner in this country where my daughter spent most of her time.

At last she formed a word. "Mommy?" she asked.

"Yes, I'm Rachel's mom."

"Boots?" she asked.

I lifted up my pant cuff and showed her. "Yes," I said. "I'm wearing boots."

Steve held out his T-shirt for me to admire. "That's some dog," I said.

"Kmart!" he told me.

Break was over. The students were back in their seats for a second, shorter session. Dawn reminded them with the same short, crisply delivered sentences that they would be putting two little tires into a bag that already contained two bigger tires. And then they were back to work.

When I told Dawn that I was impressed, she agreed that the kids had been working well. "We can't keep them supplied. Their rate and speed has really improved."

I *was* impressed. I was also stunned—by all the effort it took to put two tires into a plastic bag, by the sight of my daughter with her peers, by the range of ability and disability in that room, by the sheer diversity of this population that we so blithely lump together as having "special needs." Mostly what stayed with me was the diligent way the kids worked.

On the way to see Michael Stoehr, head of the career-education program at Rachel's school, I thought about how I felt when my own work went well, when I had been so absorbed by my tasks, so "in the flow" that time vanished. I thought about my sense of well-being at the end of a day like that and how much I wanted that for Rachel—not because work per se would be good for her soul, not because I was pretending her life would resemble mine, but because when she was focused (playing Free Cell or solitaire on the computer, for instance) she was at peace. When we played Uno, one of the few games that fully engaged her, she was fun to be with. Her constant talking became silenced at last.

Michael and I talked about Dawn's class and some of the other work experiences Rachel had at school—counting, sorting, house-keeping tasks. "One of her biggest difficulties is concentrating—just staying on task," he said. "She's distracted by what's going on around her." It was possible that the next year they'd try Rachel out at Good-will on a part-time basis, so she could become acclimated to what it was like in the adult service sector, but it wasn't a sure thing.

In the world outside school—even in the world of supported em-ployment—she would be expected to be "somewhat independent," he said. The job-coaching she would need was "pretty intense, pretty long-range. And at this point, the supports just aren't out there."

Supported employment isn't a sure thing.

Sometimes reality cuts like an ax.

· · · ·

Sometimes she talks so much it's hard for either of us to know what she wants.

What did Rachel want? When I left Michael Stoehr's office, I once again asked myself if it was ridiculous, the way we were pushing her to do so many things that were so difficult for her. Maybe she just didn't want to work, and our efforts to change that were futile. But if she didn't have a job, what would she do all day when she was no longer in school?

In this era of self-determination and person-centered planning, I was supposed to be asking her these kinds of questions. All the lit-erature explaining the transition process urged me to view my child as a "total person," to make sure her desires were "at the heart of decision making." The materials prepared by the Allegheny County Department of Human Services and its Office of Mental Retardation/Developmental Disabilities reminded me that people with mental retardation should have "the freedom to choose the services and supports they want, the authority to control limited resources and the responsibility for the decisions they make."

How could I respect Rachel's fundamental human right to choose what she would do after she was out of school without abandoning her to a world she could not fully understand? Again I found myself working through these issues.

Well, there was conjecture: what I thought she wanted, based on my observations. When I answered the dozens of questions about her likes and dislikes, I tried to answer as honestly as possible. Still, I couldn't deny that my own will was at work—my desires for her. Left to her own, Rachel would choose to sit in front of a trough of potato chips and eat until she fell asleep rather than go to Special Olympics basketball. I continued to say, "She likes basketball," because whenever I spied on her from the doorway, I saw she was enjoying herself. I knew I was cheating: *I* wanted her to play basketball and swim because it was good for her.

Once I told a friend that sometimes I set up my micro-cassette recorder and interviewed Rachel. "Why don't you just *talk* to her?" she asked, taken aback.

I tried to explain that interviewing Rachel had become a way of hearing her, since in everyday life she was so demanding, her non-stop talk so full of what I thought of as sheer nothingness—endless questions about each move I made, about future plans, mostly to do with food, which I'd answered dozens of times. Yes, I'll make dinner as soon as you hang up your jacket and use the bathroom. Yes (hang up your jacket). Yes (bathroom first). Yes (did you flush?) yes (did you wash your hands?) yes (with soap?) yes (you didn't flush!) yes. Her conversation was full of things that were real, overheard things that happened to someone else, things that were wrenchingly true.

If Rachel's incessant talking was both her prime means of communication and her strength—she could be funny and charming, full of personality—it was also her most profound, most unmanageable behavioral issue. She was, as one document stated, "attention seeking, with a tendency to interrupt and begin talking about a non-related topic. . . . She is difficult to redirect."

Sometimes it was so noisy when I was with her that I had to expend a great amount of energy willing myself not to shriek at her to just shut up. Sometimes she was a mountain, and I was an earthmover, up there in my little cab, yelling, "Get a move on!" and ramming her.

Whenever I interviewed her, I waited until she was out of the house before I replayed the tape. Often what I heard was how extraordinarily hard it was for her to process more than one or two simple, concrete questions before a tweeting bird or footsteps in another room set her off on a tangent. Sometimes I could sort out someone else's interests from her own. And sometimes in the silence of my room, apart from her, what I heard with great clarity was her heart's desire. Then I was close to all that made her human. I thought about her in bed, then, lost beneath a huge gorilla and a teddy bear and a dozen smaller stuffed animals. I thought about her own, very clearly defined sense of "cool"—the hooded sweatshirt and sweatpants Charlotte and I picked out for Rachel's birthday, which she sneaked out of the closet and tried to wear every day, even in summer. I thought about the books she could not read but insisted upon getting at the library every Saturday and carrying everywhere, about her purple Mardi Gras beads. I thought about her telling a friend that she wanted to drink beer when she turned twenty-one.

Listening to the tapes made me recall the day when we were preparing for her first-ever sleepover guest. When I'd asked what she wanted to do with Jennie, she said, "Thnuggle." I thought about the childish lisp that, given all the crucial therapies, all the urgent tasks she had to master, we'd never tried to correct. And I thought about this most human desire to be close to others, a desire that her incessant talking and her resistance to hygiene threatened to prevent.

I listened to the tapes and heard myself asking and asking what she wanted.

"I want to go on the bus."

"I want to be able to go out with a friend once in a while and do stuff."

"I want to see if I can get a cell phone, Ma."

"I want to look for an apartment."

Did she want a job?

"Yes. Somewhere in this area."

What kind of job? What did she like to do?

"Something me and Jennie can do together."

I cued Rachel, trying to get her to name some favorite jobs.

"Making dinner. Computer. I like to look at the newspaper once in a while."

I backed up and tried to get her back on track.

"What's my job?"

"Teaching," she said. "Writing."

"What about the JCC? What's your job there?"

"Working at the café."

I asked her to tell me what she did when she was there.

"Sell stuff to drink and eat. They have all different ice creams and all that stuff."

"What happens if a person comes and wants something?"

"They don't have any more sandwiches."

"So what happens if—"

"Listen! Listen. Just listen! They don't have any more sandwiches because they sold them all last time, and that's why we're doing this, because we don't have any more. We only have what's on the board."

Again I backed up and tried to redirect her. What did she do when the customers were gone?

"We clean up. The whole purpose is to clean up after we're done selling candy and selling drinks and locking up machines. And we're doing that because we always have power-walking, but not today. With whatever her name is. She didn't show up, so Jennie left, and then I left."

The confusion with power-walking was something that happened a few days before, I reminded her. Maybe she could tell me about cleaning up.

"There's a big problem with the machines, usually."

"What machines?"

"The yellow-and-gray machines. The Popsicle machines, Ma. The ice-cream machines. They got locked up wrong yesterday by some-one, and what happened was, after the fact that they had them locked up wrong was like a weird compliment, accomplishment, with like after this was going on it was fine, and then after that was—what are you writing down?"

Later I asked if she liked her job at the JCC.

"People talk to me too much, and I just can't stand it. It's hard for me to concentrate. It's better for me to do the dry cleaning, Mom. Better than the café."

Part of that statement was profoundly true. My daughter, with her relentless talking, was so terribly distractible that she could not concentrate where there was noise or conversation. As for the dry cleaning, which she could nicely define ("It's where you take your clothes to the laundromat, and you have to pay for it"), that was on her mind because her friend was carrying some garments on hang- ers one day. Dry cleaning was like drinking beer at twenty-one and going to college—things that others did or discussed, rather than a wish from her own heart.

A few days after my visit to Rachel's work-production class, I asked her what jobs she was doing in school.

"I'm not doing the cups anymore."

"What do you do in the mornings?"

"Only the paper towels."

"What do you do with the paper towels?" I asked.

"Put them in the holder. In the paper-towel bin."

"And what else do you do?"

"Plates. We fill plates. Although here's the big part, Ma—are you ready for it? We're selling chips and stuff like that now."

And so we had moved in time and place, from school, perhaps on that day, to her job at Café J on a nameless day in a month that fell as randomly as a snowflake.

. . . .

There is no safety net.

Café J was initially a joint project that Barbara Milch, as division director of Children, Family, and Youth at the JCC, initiated with Jewish Residential Services to employ people with a primary diagnosis of chronic mental illness. When funding from a startup grant ran out, she was able to put anyone in the job. Thus Rachel and her cohort (and their TSS's) were given shifts.

Since I had moved to Pittsburgh, I had thought of Barbara as the person who made the JCC a place where people with developmental and physical disabilities were a visible part of the community. She spearheaded the programs that made it possible for such kids to be included in after-school programs and summer camps. Nor had teens and adults been forgotten: most of what Rachel did outside of school—her chance to go to a play, see a ball game, be with friends—originated here at the JCC because of Barbara's efforts.

In my some-job-somewhere phase, I took great pleasure in seeing Rachel in her red apron, wearing her staff badge. The JCC is a busy community center with nearly fifteen thousand members. Lots of people I knew who used the athletic facilities or had kids in childcare stopped at the café and were served by Rachel. It made me feel good to think of my daughter out in the world this way, not merely some mysterious, half-grown child I was rumored to have hidden away.

When I looked beyond the gloss of relief, gratitude, and fatigue, I was forced to ask what would happen if Barbara Milch left the JCC? What would happen when Rachel had no TSS? This was not doomsday thinking, given the steady decrease in the number of hours that were funded. Rachel could not work in the café without this assistance—not for the foreseeable future, at least.

She'd learned a lot since she began working at the café. She knew the prices of everything and that the customers should check the board to see what was being offered that day. She had memorized the sequence of tasks necessary to close down the café. Skills were not enough. Before this spring I had imagined Rachel's future based merely on her strengths (she's outgoing) and deficits (low vision, limited fine-motor skills), failing to regard the rest of her. It was as if her behavior and attention issues were things that made it hard for *me* to live with her but would not affect her ability to work. I had somehow failed to integrate what I had known all along: the greatest obstacle to her working was her distractibility.

At Café J she had "difficulty balancing appropriate socialization with her peers with the need to focus and concentrate on the demands of working in the café," I read in her Comprehensive Medicaid Mental Health Services Plan from this period. "She continues to ask for assistance with skills she has mastered and can successfully manipulate various JCC staff to engage in 'over-helping.' Often she does not want to follow through with requests to complete her responsibilities for the café."

Hadn't she herself managed to tell me exactly why she was struggling? *People talk to me too much, and I just can't stand it. It's hard for me to concentrate.*

Barbara had tried to reassure me, saying, "She will always have a home at the JCC."

In the spring of 2002, I was forced to wonder: a home doing what?

Though I did not underestimate the importance of community, neither could I bear to imagine Rachel wandering the corridors of the JCC, trying to engage unwitting strangers in meaningless talk. Unwitting strangers because, if she stayed long enough, only strangers would not know to avoid her.

Wandering, following people, trying to engage them—this is what Rachel's day would look like if she could not be trained for supported employment. It was what she was like at home, that most unstructured place, where everyone else was off doing something: reading, paying bills, talking on the phone, walking up and down the stairs. When we were home for too long together, Rachel's calls for attention—her birdlike *Ma? Mommy? Ma?*—were so insistent that I chose the most distant part of the house simply to escape her.

The supports Rachel received at school were entitlements mandated by law. School districts were required to provide information on transition. Upon graduation, all of those entitlements ended. The Department of Education no longer had to provide funding for services, so the funding had to be in place while a student was still in school. Some of those on the long list of people with developmental disabilities waiting for services were twenty-one- to twenty-five-year-olds who had transitioned without having the next step in place.

The extensive job-coaching that someone like Rachel might need was costly. "Some agencies will say they're going to follow her, but the reality is they'll provide support for about a month or two," Stoehr had explained. "After that they're looking for results and turnaround, ready to pull out. . . . It's a very unfair system. There are not a lot of easy answers or nice solutions."

I knew this was true, just as I understood that distractibility was Rachel's most serious handicap. And yet I had seen her quiet down. I had watched her sit at the computer for long stretches of time. It made me wonder. In this era, adaptations were made so people could learn and travel and work. There are language boards and gigs and orthotics, bicycles that can be pedaled by hand, computers that speak, lifts to bring wheelchairs onto buses. It was hard to believe that an adaptation could never be made for Rachel, that work would be impossible for my daughter because of her extreme distractibility. To give up meant imagining her wandering aimlessly, trying to engage people, unwittingly pushing them away—a lonely, marginalized person.

• • • •

RACHEL AT WORK

Take a nap and then wake up.

So you're tired; so what, I needed to remind myself. Take a nap. While you're sleeping, dream some sweet dreams. And then wake up.

Keep doing what you're doing. Isn't that what Michael Stoehr had advised? Get Rachel as independent as possible. Push on the housing, push to get funding for a day program and for transportation.

Keep pushing. If you can't find it, look harder. If it doesn't exist, make it happen.

Exhausting to contemplate. What else could I do?

Rachel had her work, and I had mine.

8

Personal Wants/Person-Centered Principles

Rachel stated to ISC she wants to live on her own because she is an adult. She wants to live with roommates that like the same things as her. Her mother reports it is difficult to manage care for her daughter.

Individual Personal Wants

Rachel wants to be considered as an adult who is in charge of her own life. She understands she will need someone to assist her with daily living skills.

Long-Term Plan

Rachel and her family will explore a variety of options to acquire a residential placement for Rachel.

Family/Guardian Comments (Summarized by ISC)

Rachel's mother has expressed the need to have her daughter find residential placement. She can no longer provide the supports she requires.

—Plan of Care, May 28, 2003

TALKING

Two years in a row, Paul picked up Rachel from camp in mid-August and took her to Maine House, where he lived when the weather was warm. During these few days without her—glorious days, whatever the weather—a soothing voice clicked into gear. *It will be fine. Everything will be okay.* Or sometimes: *You'll live with it. You always have.*

In the meantime, there was work to do on her behalf. The transition-planning forms were due at her school before Labor Day: twenty pages of questions about her "abilities, interests and future goals" that gave me the chance to think clearly about Rachel's life before she was back home and I lost my ability to think at all. I tried to write what I believed she would answer, if she were able, what she might list as her own choices. It was a time to be blunt about her abilities, to assess the things I thought she was capable of doing and the skills it was time to concede she would never possess.

And so: What places did she like to go? By what means of transportation? Was she involved in any after-school program? What kind of group activities did she like? What about when she was alone? What did we do as a family? What were her favorite foods, TV shows and games? Could she shop wisely? Did she understand that money is needed to buy an item? Could she give change? Could she wake up independently, accept responsibility, take criticism, act appropriately in social settings? Could she communicate, and, if so, how? Could she answer the phone, get information that way, take messages? Could she apologize, express anger, talk to adults in authority? Did I want her involved in volunteer or supported employment after graduation? What was she able to do at home? Could she pick out her own clothes, get dressed without assistance, use the bathroom independently? What three or four things did I feel were most important for her to work on during the upcoming school year?

Included in the packet was a list of the goals I'd set the year before. I reviewed them, before putting down new ones for the upcoming year. It was important to be realistic. If Rachel hadn't met a goal, I had to break it down and try to figure out whether it made sense to work on it for another year.

Take the phone, which had been on the list for several years. What kept my daughter, who loved to talk on the phone, from learning how to use it herself? When I asked myself that question, I had to consider not only the mechanical issues—it was difficult for her to see the numbers on the keypad and to press each number only once—but also if she was capable of remembering phone numbers or learning to use speed dial. I didn't want to give up on this, though she had thus far been unmotivated to practice the skills she needed. There were adaptive phones yet to try. Maybe, too, I hadn't capitalized on her own love of talking, particularly to her father, who was rarely in contact but always happy to hear from her. What about learning to call for help in an emergency? This task required more than physical ability. I had to consider whether she'd be able to perceive that an emergency existed and then remember to use the phone. Though I was less sure about this one, it was such an important skill that it seemed worth keeping it on the list, along with these:

That she will behave appropriately at family events and social situations.

That she will develop skills to ensure personal safety.

That she work on controlling excess talking.

Considering her "strengths, limitations, interests and aspirations," what was my lifelong goal/aspiration for her?

That she live with peers and work in a sheltered environment.

For three years in a row I wrote this in big, bold letters, with a schoolgirl's row of exclamation points.

128   Rachel's school could not help me find Rachel a place to live. Officially, it was the role of her independent supports coordinator—the ISC—who managed her case. Jeanette, the sweet, soft-spoken woman who met with Rachel or me once a month, dutifully wrote down what I wanted for my daughter and looked at me in a sorrowful way. She didn't have to tell me that nothing was out there, because I already knew. I'd read that the Social Services Block Grant (a federal program that provided states the flexible funds to meet the needs of their most vulnerable citizens, including those with disabilities) had been steadily cut over the last few years. I'd read, too, that the Senate Appropriations Committee had approved a $1.1 billion reduction in funding in 2001, cutting available money by almost two-thirds.

I knew that in Pennsylvania, twenty-four thousand people were on the waiting list for the kinds of services Rachel needed. I knew that most of the vacancies occurred when a resident of one of the existing houses died or left the state, and that these rare vacancies were offered first to residents still in institutions, or to older people whose parents had died.

Although what I wanted for Rachel was unavailable, I had to keep pushing for her so her name and face stayed in Jeanette's mind. That way, if something did come along, if, miraculously, more money was allotted for housing and openings did occur, Rachel might be considered. There was also this: the waiting list wasn't a queue, with everyone waiting in order. Compatibility was a factor, too. When a space in a house became available, and several "clients" from the waiting list were "presented" for the opening, the chosen one would be in roughly the same age group and at a similar cognitive level—someone who was physically able, if the house was not barrier free, or someone who had physical disabilities, if the house had been adapted; someone of the same gender, who needed the same amount of staffing and had the same kind of funding. I'd been told that Rachel was a tough fit. She was young, at a time when most placements were for people in their forties and older, and she was female, in a world where there were far more men. In addition, she needed twenty-four-hour staffing, which was costly.

Though I was aware of all this, in the summers of 2002 and 2003, before Rachel returned from camp, I geared up for this impossible, necessary quest to find her a place to live. I didn't do this because I was courageous—far from it. I wasn't brave, selfless, indefatigable, or oblivious. I pushed for Rachel because I had no choice but to keep banging my head against the wall until something cracked. In the summer, my outrage was hot and pure; that was when I imagined her in a bright little apartment in Squirrel Hill, with friends and caring staff, when I thought how easy it would be for her to be happy. That was when I said, to anyone who would listen: How is it that the richest country on earth, so proud of its democracy, fails to support and protect its less able citizens? It wasn't that Rachel herself was sweet, simple, and mild-mannered, qualities people ascribed to those with mental retardation, as if they were all part of one big, cute group. It's that she had no existential worries, no career aspirations, no vanity, no anxieties about money, mortality, or disease. It really shouldn't be all that hard, I thought.

129

This was when she was gone—this outrage on her behalf, this tender scrutiny. When she was gone I painstakingly interpreted her words, attempting to solve the puzzle of her identity, searching for a way in, a method, an answer. When she was gone I thought of her soft skin with its pale freckles, heard her laughter, saw her long, slender fingers, gesturing the way mine did. It was only when she was gone. Because as soon as she was home, it was over.

· · · ·

It starts the first morning. "Ma!" Her voice in the dark: "Ma! Can I have cereal? Ma, I'm up! Can I put on my robe? Can I have cereal? Ma, I'm hungry."

Still cushioned from our time apart, I am civil when I respond. "Go back to sleep. The alarm didn't go off."

She is like a bird. No matter how dark her room, when she is up, she is up. And when she is up, she starts and does not stop. "Can I pick my cereal? Can I have a hug? Can I put on my robe? Will you make me lunch, Ma? Am I taking the bus to school? How will I get there, Ma? I have my robe on, Ma, can I come out? I'm hungry, Ma. Can I have cereal?"

Early in the season, I can find the soothing voice inside me. *Okay, okay, get up, just do it.* "Can I have oatmeal, Ma? In the blue bowl? Are

TALKING

there bananas, Ma? Can I come down without getting dressed? Ma, can I have cereal, Ma?"

I crawl out of bed, the "Ma!" like a needle in my skull.

"Ma! Will you make me tea, Ma? Do I have Goodwill today? Ma, I'm hungry. Can I have Cream of Wheat, Ma? Can I get the milk?"

I slip on the clothes I've thrown over a chair—shirt, jeans, sandals.

"Ma, I'm hungry. Can I wear a dress? Is the pink bra okay? Will you make me tea? Can I wear my boots? Am I taking the bus to school? Can you make me tea? Can I have oatmeal?"

Paul did it better. He was an early riser, more alert than I was, more together. She drove him crazy, too, but he was quicker to get her breakfast and medication and start the morning rolling. I am not quick. All my life, I have been slow to rouse in the mornings, slow to think and move and enter full consciousness. It's the way I'm made, not something that I can alter, no matter how much sleep I get or what time I rise.

"Ma! Can I have the blue bowl? Can I have more? Can I have a plum? Can you make the tea? Can I have the spoon, please? Can you pour the milk?"

I put the food in front of her, count out the meds and place them in the little yellow dish, grind the coffee beans and step outside to retrieve the papers. The light is lovely. In the summer, without her, when I can wake slowly, I am a different person, not irritable and headachy. The birds cheep. *In an hour,* I think. It's my own song. *In an hour, she'll be gone. Hold on until the bus comes and it will be all right. Just hold on.*

Inside the house. "Ma! Can you make me tea? Can you please pour the milk please? Ma, can I have tea? Can I have a spoon please? Can I have a bagel for lunch? Can I have Cheez-Its? Can I do computer before I leave? Can I have tea? Can you toast the bread for my sandwich? Can I have a pickle . . . "

· · · ·

I tried making her breakfast the night before. I set out the cereal in a covered bowl (the blue one), next to a banana and her meds, leaving a small container of milk inside the fridge. I tried this. The first morning she found the milk, assembled her breakfast, and ate it peacefully. When I woke without the sound of her hectoring voice, I felt as if I had been resurrected. The second morning, she got up very early, ate her breakfast, and watched ESPN on TV in her nightgown—water skiing without skis or extreme skateboarding. That was fine, too. The third morning, she got up at 4:00 A.M. and ate her breakfast. At 7:00 she demanded another one and was outraged and inconsolable when she didn't get it. The fourth day she rose like a sleepwalker while I was reading in bed: it was just after 11:00 P.M. By the time I made it downstairs, her breakfast was half gone, which was not okay at all.

I stopped the experiment for a few days and tried again. The whole cycle was repeated. Clearly, Rachel's anticipation of breakfast was so profound that she could barely sleep—evidence that her memory (for some things, at least) was perfectly intact. Breakfast! You'd think it was a loved one returning home from a sea voyage. *Darling breakfast, I couldn't sleep just thinking of you.*

So we were back to breakfast in the morning, and water to wash down the assortment of pills, including Concerta, the time-released Ritalin, which did not stop the talking but sometimes cooled her out a bit for the next phase, in which I needed her to put her shoes on the correct feet or turn her shirt face forward. These requests filled her with outrage. "What's the big deal?" she said. "Stupid!" she cried, pulling at her sleeves, "Stupid shirt. I'm blind! I can't see anything. I'm *blind!*"

It was an overstatement, and irrelevant, though I could imagine the sympathy Rachel got crying, "I'm *blind!*" around strangers.

Everything annoyed her. "I like sandals better!" she said on a day when she had gym and sneakers were mandatory. "Baloney! Sandals are better than sneakers. That is baloney. Sneakers are disgusting and ugly; let me tell you, Ma. Can you please pack my lunch today, please? You pain-in-the-ass sneakers. Can you please pack it, please? Can I have tea, Ma? Can you toast my sandwich? Can I have a pickle? Can I do computer?"

I tried positive reinforcements. "If you clean your room without another word, I'll give you tea." And threats: "Pick up your things by the count of three or no computer." Nothing consistently worked. On most mornings, whatever I asked was against her principles.

I tried to keep my sense of humor. Early in September, I set out the tape recorder, intrigued by her syntax, amused when she said, "I think you're a weird person, Ma, because you're helpless and don't help me when you're supposed to." Her failure to comply with everything wasn't even slightly amusing.

"Picking up my nightgown is ridiculous. I cannot pick up my nightgown. Do you hear me, scooter crunch? I cannot pick up my things." Sometimes she was frustrated. "I'm stupid, Ma. I've done my best. I'm stupid!" And sometimes deeply aggrieved: "If you come in, Ma, you're in trouble. You better cool your sheets off, Ma." And eventually: "Done! I'm done picking up! Cleaned up!" Sometimes, sung to a lively tune: "Cleaned up! Cleaned up! I am all cleaned up!"

Then seeing me in the doorway: "Will you please shut the door, please?"

It was as if she'd read and admired Raymond Carver and had adopted the language of his characters, his "please be quiet, please?" Only she asked, "Can you please find me a sweatshirt, please?"

She had to be out of the house for me to listen to the tape, because when she was with me, her arguing was oppressive. She wanted to wear a sweatshirt in the summer, and I would not let her, the way I would not let her leave the house with food on her face or her shirt on backwards or her shoes on the wrong feet, and she could not, would not understand why. She'd fight to wear flip-flops in the snow. If I tried to explain, "It's cold, your toes will freeze," the logic would not reach her. These quarrels, which were endless and futile, characterized our life together. I could not make her understand and was unable to stop trying. No matter what techniques I used, I never won.

It seemed impossible to imagine that a dog could be conditioned but not my daughter. This spurred me to try the alarm clock again. I had bought a new one with huge numbers. I put it on her night table and reminded her of the rules. When the alarm rang, she could come into my room. "If you wake me up before it goes off, you'll get toast for breakfast."

"*No!*" she cried. "No toast!"

It was as if I'd said: "If you wake me up, I'll beat you to a bloody pulp."

All day, I reminded her: "What will happen if you wake me up?"

"I'll get *toast!*"

"And what do you want?"

"Cereal!"

"So what are you going to do?"

"Not wake you up!"

Before she climbed into bed that night, I kissed her and asked, "What will you do tomorrow?"

"Wait for the alarm."

The sun came up. Rachel called, "Ma!" And the rest of it, the unbroken chain of demands, was set loose.

She got toast. There was much hysteria; there was begging and manipulation. There was pleading: "No toast!" There was bargaining; "Can I have a bagel? Can I have jelly on my toast? Can I have tea?"

Each time she woke me, she got toast, which filled her with grief and rage, and still it did not alter her behavior until one morning, for no discernible reason, she did not wake me. I praised her lavishly throughout the day, took her out for dinner, played four games of Uno with her after she showered, told her that she was good and sweet, and crooned to her at bedtime. Did she know why I was happy? Could she tell me? "Because I didn't wake you."

The next morning, she called "Ma!" in the dark and asked to come into bed with me. Though it was still dark and I said no, she ripped the comforter off my body and climbed in beside me. Her body was not just flesh (my flesh, my child) but a living package of demands; her body beside me meant being poked and elbowed, scratched by her straggly toenails. Sometimes I let her stay because there was a benevolent voice inside me, one of a chorus of so many voices that I felt like a multiple personality. This was the voice that said: *Oh, just be nice.* So I yanked the comforter back over me, let her scratch and poke at me for what felt like eternity, and then gave up and called it morning. If I had been smart the night before, her clothes had been chosen, and maybe there would be less of a struggle about dressing while I stumbled into the kitchen to make her breakfast.

If Rachel's occasional compliance was unpredictable, so was the fact that sometimes she was lovely. Sometimes, for no obvious reason, we got through the morning with a minimal amount of fuss. A day might pass, two, three. The mornings were pleasant; she returned home in the early evening mellow and cooperative, and everything was different. I felt as if the screws had been loosened and I'd slid out of a giant vise. After dinner, she would play solitaire and Free Cell on the computer, games that she had learned almost by herself. (It fascinated and tantalized me to think that, though she could not follow text across the page, she had somehow grasped that the mouse in her hand moved the cursor on the screen.) On these tranquil evenings she might play solitaire on the computer, while listening to music on her Walkman, the TV volume high. This registered as quiet.

Perhaps it's a Saturday when she's in good spirits. We'll have lunch together, Rachel "reading" the *Post-Gazette* while I look at the *Times*. Or while we're hanging out, she'll be listening to a CD, occasionally singing along. Her sweetness comes through, and I am reminded that behind the irritating nonstop talking is someone who can be cheerful, funny, happy with herself. On one of these infrequent days, I might come upon her singing in the shower, "This is the way I wash my butt, wash my butt, wash my butt. This is the way I wash my butt, so early in the morning." Or I'll come up to her room to ask her to put on her pajamas and find her naked and listening to Bob Marley. She'll ask me to dance, saying, "Come on! Take off your socks! Come on, you goober!" When I take her hands, she moves from side to side, kicking her legs in a funny, spazzy way. When I spin her, she starts to laugh in that startled way she has, eyes wide, collapsing in mirth.

These were the days that reminded me how many years had passed since I grieved over her cognitive deficits. I didn't care that she was re-tarded; it's that she was difficult—stubborn, impulsive, oppositional. No one seemed able to break her of these alienating habits, least of all me, or build on these good periods. Nothing consistently worked. I'd tried asking nothing of her, tried getting breakfast into her sooner, tried letting her wake me in the darkness, tried sitting with my head in my hands, in obvious despair, tried begging her. *Please.*

She could not empathize, not really, could not do what I asked of her out of kindness or to please me. She could not see me, would never know me. It was my misfortune to crave this connection. My problem, not hers.

My problem that I couldn't simply accept that nothing made a difference, that like it or not, in the morning, when the light was still low, she would bombard me with that "Ma!" making my head throb before I was fully awake. "Ma, I'm hungry. Ma, I want my cereal, Ma. Can I have a banana? Is the bus coming? Is it Kelly today, Ma?"

I remembered a small Scottish therapist saying, "O! the tyranny of the retarded!"

I could live with the fights, though they were constant and pointless, could live with the cursing, *stupid busted brain!* I could live with her obsessions, the notebooks, her beads, the tea she demanded but did not drink, her red sweatsuit, the hole in her underwear that drove her batty. Spying the tiniest rip between the elastic waistband and the cloth, she would demand, "You need to sew this!" Not once or twice, but all day long, the mere thought of it upsetting her. Years ago, the tags at the neck of her shirt irritated her so much that if I didn't immediately snip them out, she'd rip the entire collar off her shirt. That I understood, believing that perhaps she was tactile defensive—hypersensitive to touch—and the edge of the cloth was unbearable against her skin. The little hole in her underwear was smooth so I had to imagine that her outrage was purely on aesthetic grounds.

Still, I could live with her bringing me underwear to fix. I could live with the fact that in the morning, my daughter who could not read would quarrel with me over the newspaper, demanding I give her the one in the blue bag, the *New York Times,* and not the *Post-Gazette,* in the green. It was absurd and irritating, especially when she smuggled the sections I hadn't read into her backpack or her bed, but so what: other people had migraines or gout. I could live with the fights about soap, the fact that she unwrapped all the bars she found and stacked them on and around the sink and was unwilling to touch a bar of soap when it had shrunk to half its original size. I could live with the fact that she had the same issues with toothbrushes and toothpaste, that for all her limitations she managed to find whatever extras I'd tried to hide. She also shunned toilet paper once the roll was half used. Faced with this indignation, her strategy was simply to unroll everything from the dreaded half roll and stick it in the toilet, thus causing the toilet to overflow. I hated coming into the bathroom and finding all six new rolls decorating the vanity and sink and the toilet overflowing, but I could live with it. I also found it extremely annoying that she would not drink the last milk in the container and insisted on opening the new gallon. Fine. Other "typically developed" adults did the same. I could even live with the fact that she was too lazy to use the toilet and often held it in for so long that her clothes were damp and smelly. I hated it and despaired for her, since I didn't know who would get her to use the bathroom when I was not around. But I could live with it.

The talking was something else. The talking was flattening me.

It went far beyond the morning routine. A month or so after she had returned from camp, her incessant chatter made it hard for me to think about what was best for her or plan for her future. It made it hard for me to feel my love for her. That surfaced mostly when we were apart.

The talking wasn't new, and neither was the oppositional behavior that led to her dual diagnosis when she was ten and the behavior management services that began that year. Still, I was stunned to find in a pile of her medical and educational records that my daughter, once described by an occupational therapist as "an adorable, talkative little girl," had begun to talk so much by the age of six that I told the behavioral psychologist, "She calls my name incessantly, will continue to call, even if I tell her I'm not coming." The next year, her teacher recorded that she "frequently spoke about extraneous matters." At eleven, she was described as "very verbal . . . impulsive, intrusive, and perseverative . . ."

Reading these reports made me see the way all the years with her had worn me out. It was more than that: as Rachel had become more able, she'd also grown more difficult and demanding. Not only that, the stakes had been raised. If I wiped her face, dressed her, washed her, cleaned up her room, I was doing her a disservice. For the last ten years the message had been the same: "Train your children to be as independent as possible." It was the same with the talking. It was impossible for me to attend fully to her when she talked, or to answer all her questions when some of them didn't make sense and others she'd asked a dozen times. It would be a terrible mistake to condition her to expect that someone would be at her side responding to everything said. Already I had seen aides, counselors, and companions charmed by her for a day, and fried after a month.

These were the official reasons why I fought with Rachel at home. There was also another reason. I couldn't stand it. Especially in the morning, before I was awake.

Sometimes, bleary-eyed and half awake, I was careless. In a quiet moment, without thinking, I would open the paper and begin to read: *These are perilous times for civil liberties in the United States, according to Anthony Romero, executive director of the American Civil Liberties Union,* when suddenly: "Ma, can I have juice today? My shoes are too tight. Ma? Can I have a newspaper, Ma?"

I would slide the *Post-Gazette* to her side of the table, read, *perilous times for civil liberties in the United States, according to,* when: "Ma, I want the other paper. I want to wear sandals. Are you picking me up today? I don't want *you,* Ma. I want Kelly."

Without thinking, I'd go back to the top and read, *perilous times for civil liberties* . . . when "Ma!" like a needle.

The government must strike a . . . "The paper in the blue bag" . . . *government must strike* . . . "The other paper" . . . *perilous times* . . . "I hate this stupid paper, Ma." *These are perilous times* . . . "Can I have more cereal? Can I have some juice?" . . . *for civil liberties* . . . "Ma!"

Shut up! I'd think, straining not to scream the words at Rachel.

Shut up! I told myself, when she was gone and I could hear my own complaining. Life could get worse! You're healthy! You have friends and work you love! All this moaning and groaning and whining and bitching about your fate. You could be a leper. You could be begging in the train station in Mumbai. Shut up and get on with your own privileged life!

One might ask: Why read? If you know she's going to interrupt you, why pick up the newspaper? To which I could only respond in a helpless, stupid way: I can't help it. My eyes just go there. It could be the cereal box, with its nutritional information and free offers, or a fundraising letter from Amnesty International. I could be scrutinizing saddles in a bike catalog, eyes on the WTB Speed V Team Saddle, "loaded with all the right features to relieve pressure," quietly amused by the description of the cushioning provided by the "soft shell with love channel," when: "Ma!" Not knowing I was reading, when: "Who's picking me up today, Ma?" A question she'd asked me six times already, so that no matter what I did—ignore her or ask, "Who do you think?"—I was still completing the loop. Silence yielded another "Ma!" and my own question yielded the answer, "Kelly," which she knew all along and gave her the chance to go on. "I don't want to go to Kelly's house. Kelly's house is boring."

It was the same when I came home and had dinner with her, though she was not always as oppositional then. In the evening I could sometimes get through an entire paragraph before, "Can I have a grapefruit for dessert? Can I have Cheez-Its?"

Even when no newspaper was involved, when I was simply there, her voice had the same effect. A thought might be forming when suddenly her "Ma!" would pierce my brain. I found it harder to concentrate, harder to read these days.

In the transition report, I wrote that Rachel had fulfilled her prior year's goal of being independent for an hour. In reality, I realized in the fall of 2002, the success was mine. I learned that when I disappeared, she stopped talking. If I crept away, as long as I didn't move, she would forget me. One move—one toe on the floor, one step toward the bathroom, and "Ma?" began and would not stop. Even this small victory did little to calm my nervous system, since I kept expecting to be interrupted, kept anticipating it. The expectation of the needle made it hard for me to think. Sometimes I'd be working and have to use the bathroom. I knew if I did this, it would bring the end of the respite, so I'd resist. Then the stress of worrying how much longer I could hold it in would begin to dominate my thoughts.

So now, I had become like a dog that had been conditioned. As soon as I started to read, I'd anticipate the needle-like voice. I'd learned to take my work out of the house, to sit in coffee shops and libraries. In the summer I went to artists' colonies, serene, beautiful places, where I could lock myself away from all sound. I found that I could regain not only my ability to concentrate, but also my good humor, these two traits hopelessly intertwined. At home, I became aware of the reverse. I could not think when I was with Rachel and it put me in a bad mood. I didn't know how other people's brains were wired and what went on when they were simply *being*, only that by nature I was dreamy. Clearly, my actual dreams of finding my head separate from my body had something to do with the way I'd been made. I live in my head, write snatches in my head, hear voices, mull over conversations, recall passages from books, write letters, argue. I am always writing grand, old-fashioned letters in my head. None of this would make a difference if not for the dawning realization that we were incompatible, Rachel and I. My constant irritation affected her, I realized when I heard, stuck in the constant jackhammer talk, "Are you going to be nice to me when I come home? Are you going to love me?"

O miserable human being, bad, bad mother. I vowed to focus all of my attention on her for the next few hours. No surprise, my answers simply generated more questions. For instance, she's waiting to go outside with me and says, "Tell me when you're ready." And I say, "Okay; I'm ready."

"You're ready? You'll tell me? You'll tell me when you're ready? Okay, Ma? Okay? You're ready?"

While it was true that "mother reports that it is difficult to manage care for her daughter," and that mother wanted her to live somewhere else, of far greater interest to those in the system was Rachel's own desire, which she consistently expressed, even when I was not around. Each month when she met with Jeanette at the JCC, she said, "I want my own apartment." I knew this because I saw it in print when her "plan of care" arrived in the mail, and because I found a feature in her 2001–2 yearbook, where students in her class were asked, "If you could have one wish, what would it be?"

Dee wanted to walk on her own "without help of any kind." Adam wanted to "be a millionaire and live in a mansion." Ray's wish was for a date with Britney Spears; J.L.'s, to be a "famous rap artist." David wanted to be a security guard at a club and "check for fake ID's."

"I would wish for an apartment all my own," my daughter wrote.

"She wants to live on her own because she is an adult," Jeanette recorded.

At home Rachel was more blunt. "I want to get rid of you," she often said. Later, after Eric, a boy in her class, died in his sleep and "death" became a word she heard at school, she said, "I want you to die."

She was in a chipper, upbeat mood when she expressed this latest wish. She had been chipper when I asked her if she knew why Eric wasn't in class. "He died!" she reported cheerfully. After a while, I asked her to define the word and realized that she didn't want to see my mangled body on the side of the road. Rather, she wanted me to go far away forever, to never have to see me again.

No such luck. I was still kicking, though if her wish came true, she would get that apartment a whole lot sooner. In fact, I wouldn't even have to die for her situation to change: if I developed a chronic debilitating illness, my PUNS score would go up, and Rachel would get what she wanted. I didn't want to be tested, preferring not to go this far on behalf of my daughter.

• • • •

PUNS is the awkward acronym for a form with an even more awkward name—Prioritization of Urgency of Need for Services—designed by the Allegheny County Office of Mental Retardation and Developmental Disabilities. Jeanette produced this form annually, asking me specific questions about my life with Rachel. Because bad news is good news on this form, I let it all out. I told Jeanette that I was single (which was true); that Rachel's father saw her only a few days a year (also true); that he was in his sixties and in fragile health since his liver transplant (true, though it felt like a pathetic exaggeration). I told her I had no personal support system in Pittsburgh, no family here, apart from a mother in her eighties, devastated by my father's descent into Alzheimer's and his death in 2000. (As I recited these things, I wondered whose pathetic life I was describing; certainly not mine.) I told her I was a bad mother. It was the only thing I said easily—the only thing that actually felt true.

Every time Jeanette and I met, I was in the midst of some Rachel-related crisis. One time, my daughter's TSS had disappeared without telling anyone; on another afternoon, I had just heard that I was losing Wraparound funding; Rachel's spring break was approaching, and I didn't know who would watch her so I could teach. The first few times I deemed these crises convenient, perfectly timed, as if I'd engineered them to happen just as I was checking in with Jeanette. At some point it dawned on me that these things were regular occurrences in my life, not someone else's.

Even so, at PUNS time, the urge to put my hand over Jeanette's as she was checking off the boxes was very strong. I wanted to say, "Hey, I'm really all right," and explain the ways in which I was lucky, despite my present struggles with Rachel. I wanted to explain that my life was rich with people I loved, and my health had been excellent. Like my father (until dementia caught up with him). There were times when a sunny day or a run in the woods was enough to make me feel kissed by good fortune. I hadn't been flattened: I didn't always feel as if I had shackles around my ankles, didn't always sit cross-legged on the floor on the far side of my bed, hiding from my daughter. I could not qualify my answers, though, because the system was not subtle. There was no room for irony or embarrassment, no way for me to recite (in a guilty, grateful way) all that I had in life, while still asking for what Rachel and I both needed. My answers had to be free of shadings, the kind of simple statements that allowed Jeanette to score me in the box marked "yes" or the one marked "no."

. . . .

What else could a parent do, apart from wishing for a high score, and thus for increased hardship? Complain. This was something I learned to do, on the phone and in writing, usually after I'd lost a crucial service, access to funds, or both. On occasion, I also attended workshops and information sessions. This I did like a single person at a mixer, only I was scoping out parents instead of looking for a man, hoping to meet other families with a daughter who might want to live with Rachel.

Once in a while there were housing meetings, where I sat in a conference room with parents whose kids were in after-school programs or who attended Sunday events with Rachel. We'd been gathering sporadically for about ten years. When I first moved to Pittsburgh, the meetings were sponsored by an agency that had opened housing in Squirrel Hill for a population that fell "between the cracks," men and women with mental illness who needed some support to live independently, but who did not require twenty-four-hour staffing. That the director of this agency was interested in "assessing our needs" made me feel as if our group might be next. I saw these meetings as the first step, believed that in time—together!—we would create a place for our kids to live. It didn't happen. Our children were part of a *different* population, the director of this agency eventually explained.

Different—yes—even from each other. When I looked around the room, I was aware that no one was even vaguely compatible with Rachel. The parents at the conference table had boys, all of them young; they still talked about what they needed "some day," while I needed it now. Our kids were lumped together because of their "special needs" and hung out together, but many of them didn't actually relate. Rachel knew C. because they were in school and Sunday school together, but C. was not ambulatory and did not speak. M. she saw on the bus and after school: he had minimal language and liked to touch her, which bugged the hell out of her. S. was quiet and passive; perhaps Rachel's noisiness bothered him, not that it mattered, since his father made it clear that S. was forbidden to live in a house with girls. Perhaps S. would live with L., who had violent outbursts and thus was not good roommate material for my defenseless daughter.

Beginning in 2000, the meetings were "informational." When I attended, I learned about things that had worked in the past, when there was money in the system. In 1997, four parents had been able to buy a house themselves; they had it staffed and run by a nonprofit agency and funded by the county. We met with the head of the agency that helped these families. On another occasion, we talked about some innovative solutions for our kids—a duplex, say, with two residents in one apartment who needed eight-hour staffing, and two in the other who needed twenty-four, and the chance for them to socialize or dine together. It was a great idea, especially in Squirrel Hill, where duplexes were common.

If only there were funds. By 2002 it was fruitless to dream of such things.

Though I knew it was hopeless, I arranged to look at two of the apartments this agency staffed. Both were in Squirrel Hill, in easy walking distance of stores, movies, supermarkets, a bowling alley, and restaurants. Both were spacious and nicely furnished.

The second apartment I visited was in a long brick building, on a cul-de-sac off a busy street. A woman named Susie lived there. I knew her by sight because she and Rachel attended some of the same JCC activities. An odd little woman is how I thought of her, nearly bald, with thick glasses, hearing aids, and a squeaky voice. She was away at work when I stepped into her neat apartment, with its tidy kitchen and living room, so the staff person who'd worked with Susie for eleven years showed me around. Susie had a computer in her bedroom and shelves full of books and family photos. "So many books!" I said. "Reading is one of her favorite things," the staff person explained. "That and traveling." As she was talking, Susie was transformed for me. The person I'd carelessly dismissed as "odd" became a human being, with a home, and hobbies, and a love of books.

One night, later that year, I drove Susie home from a dance class she took with Rachel. I had parked on the other side of the busy street from her cul-de-sac, so I offered to cross with her. It was dark and rainy. She took my arm quite naturally and waited for me before stepping off the curb. When we were safely at her door, she tugged on my sleeve before I turned away, then kissed me on the lips. It made me very happy.

Of course, a life like Susie's was not possible for Rachel. It was only a dream. I knew this because of what I read in the newspaper, what Jeanette told me every month, and what this same provider who showed me Susie's apartment also said. There was no funding. No one under sixty was being placed. I should write letters; I should go to Harrisburg and complain. "It's a mess," she said. "A real crime."

. . . .

This was what our life was like when I found a flyer in Rachel's backpack, announcing a presentation at the JCC by residents and staff from a kibbutz-like community in Israel for people with developmental disabilities. It was in this period of time when it seemed as if all I did each day was fight absurd or hopeless battles, when my energy was spent trying to get Rachel to take off her sandals on a winter morning, or visiting apartments she would love but could not have. It was when she turned nineteen and then twenty, when everything I did took so much effort, I felt as if I were wearing leg irons, and the physical effort involved in walking wore me out.

It wasn't just the housing situation, since I knew that could wait, but the other cuts that occurred during these months. This is when I lost her Wraparound Services, which provided funding for behavior management therapy. Once before, I had been threatened with losing this crucial service. I'd contested the decision successfully. This time, because of even greater budget constraints, the criteria had changed. Yes, Rachel had a dual diagnosis and a well-documented history of behavior problems. But her behavior problems weren't psychiatric in origin. That she had been deemed eligible in past years was no longer relevant. According to the five-axis system of diagnosis as set out by the *Diagnostic and Statistical Manual of Mental Disorders*, fourth edition (known as DSM-IV), Rachel didn't have the necessary Axis I disorder such as autism or schizophrenia. Her service was therefore cut.

I don't recall the exact night I pulled the flyer from Rachel's backpack, only my overwhelming fatigue. Maybe I found the flyer on an uneventful day, when the only bad thing that happened was that the garbage disposal clogged and a geyser of coffee grinds and partly digested vegetables shot up from the sink. Or maybe it was the day I needed to talk to Jeanette and when I called the base service unit, I was told, "Jeanette M. is no longer an employee." Clutching the phone, I was so panicked and bereft, it was as if a lover had just dumped me. Maybe it was after Jeanette vanished, when I had called someone at the county and, getting *nothing* on the other end—no leads, no strategies, no hope—I heard myself say, at last, "If I can't get a placement for my daughter by June 2005, I'll leave her on your doorstep." Maybe it was the next day, when I followed up the phone call with a letter, stating the same thing.

Perhaps I saw the flyer when I was going through the usual stew in Rachel's backpack—water bottles, damp spiral-bound notebooks and address books, a *New Yorker* she copped, school papers with someone else's name on top, outdated schedules from the JCC, old lunch bills and playing cards. On one of those evenings, while Rachel was talking and talking, the wind knocked over a plant stand. I'd just extracted a magazine article, photocopied on pink, that the school psychologist had sent home for parents of children with special needs, and I stood amid shards of pottery and clots of dirt, reading the author's cheerful advice to "identify the stressors!" and "share with others!" and "acknowledge your positive traits!"

When I found the JCC flyer in Rachel's backpack, I smoothed the crumpled paper and tacked it onto my refrigerator. All I could think was that I *should* go to this event. I had promised Barbara Milch. I remembered her saying this community, Kishorit, was way up on top of a mountain, in a place that was beautiful and remote. To me the event was another obligation.

When the evening arrived, I dragged myself to the JCC and sat beside Rachel in the Levenson Auditorium for the video and the presentation.

It wasn't just the video that made me sit upright, though this was when I first saw the rows of yellow houses where the residents lived, and the flowers blooming everywhere, where I heard the description of Kishorit, founded by a group of parents in 1997 as a "home for life" for adults with developmental disabilities. Rather, I was transfixed by the visitors up on the stage, twelve of them, residents and staff, the way at some point they joined hands and started singing Israeli folk songs. I couldn't necessarily tell who was a staff person and who was a resident, not that it mattered. Their voices filled the auditorium. I looked around and saw that everyone in the audience had joined in. I was the only one silent, but I was electrified: a kibbutz for residents with developmental disabilities. A beautiful place to live and work.

Listening to the folk songs made me feel the weight and hopelessness of these last two years. A kibbutz—*of course*. Hadn't I been saying for years that "it takes a village to raise Rachel"? I could practically see her in a community like Kishorit, with lots of people around her, working outside, healthy. I started to wonder if she could live there.

That night, with people swaying and singing, I thought about a Fulbright fellowship in Israel that I'd been looking at in a wistful way since the mid-1990s—*Artist-in-residence. Any university*. When the fat book of Fulbright Fellowships arrived in the English Department office, I would flip through the pages and study the listings with a yearning heart, the way I imagined rural folks used to look at their Montgomery Ward catalogs. It was my wish book. I'd turn the pages and wonder how I could make it happen. Sitting in the auditorium, I wondered if it might now be possible. *If* I applied for the Fulbright in Israel, *if* it was awarded to me, *if* Rachel could live at this kibbutz . . . There were so many steps, so much uncertainty.

At the end of the presentation, I approached a man with narrow green eyes and a shaved head. Something severe in his demeanor made me feel uneasy. I put aside my usual reticence and introduced myself and Rachel. I asked him, casually, if visitors were ever accepted at Kishorit. He was a social worker and did not know. The fact that he did not utter an outright no was enough to start me off.

· · · ·

I had a lot of work to do over the next few months. First, there was the complex process of applying for the Fulbright. Then came my correspondence with the kibbutz to see if Rachel could be a guest in this community. After my initial inquiry was answered with what I took to be a maybe, I had to send Rachel's progress reports and IEPs.

In the e-mail exchanges over the next weeks, I was asked about her skills and her behavior issues. These I answered as honestly as I could. I wrote that her most serious behavior problem was excessive talking, though it seemed to me then (and still does now) that no matter how detailed my description, it always sounded lighthearted, almost laughable. *She talks too much!* Hardly in the same category as, say, self-mutilators or tantrum throwers. It seemed ridiculous except when I was living with it, or trying to hide from it.

146   During this period, I found myself dreaming for Rachel for the first time in years, not merely advocating on her behalf or fighting for her basic rights, but imagining that I might bring her to a place where she could find comfort and pleasure. The dreams were good. They brought to the fore the love and commitment that had been trampled by the sheer misery of living with her and quarreling over every single thing from sunrise, before my eyes were open, until I closed them to sleep each night.

PART 2

9

April 20, 2003

Dear Jane,

Thank you for your e-mail: In principle, we feel that Rachel would be suitable for Kishor. We would appreciate it if you could please send us her IEP from school. For your information, the monthly costs for her stay here would be $2,400.

I look forward to hearing from you.
Wishing you a Happy Passover,

Katrin

KISHORIT

Rachel and I arrived at Kishorit on a Sunday afternoon in February 2004. Though I recognized the yellow houses from the video, I was unprepared for the whole of it, the bright sun and crisp mountain air, the twittering birds, the beds of lavender and mint, the sculpture everywhere. As we trudged up a hill to the administration building to announce that we were here, I said, "This is paradise, kiddo," as if any minute she would squeeze my hand and agree that the place was awesome. I really did wish that Rachel could take in something of the loveliness here—that she might turn her pretty face to the blue sky (a relief after the ice storms in Pittsburgh) or share the sense of hope I felt. She wouldn't, of course. It was my place to remember that the environment mattered, that she deserved to live in a beautiful place, whether or not she could call it beautiful.

After all these months of dreaming, we were actually here. After all the paperwork and reports I filed on her behalf; after the long wait to find out whether she'd be accepted as the sole guest in this community designed as "a home for life"; after a period of so much violence—suicide bombings on buses, in cafés and clubs, wrenching events that filled the newspapers daily—that people no longer asked, "When are you leaving?" but said, "You're not *really* going to Israel, are you?" That decision I ended up leaving to the State Department: if travel was permitted, we would go.

At least my family understood my determination to go to Israel. Paul was intrigued by Kishorit and shared my hope that Rachel would flourish there. He had even talked about visiting us. Charlotte understood my desire to step out of my everyday life. She had spent four months in Italy as a nanny for a child with Down syndrome and was three months into a journey through India. Even my mother, whose happiest memories were of traveling with my father, seemed not to fret.

Kishorit is in a remote area, so I wasn't overly concerned about Rachel's safety. In the dreary months before our arrival, what seemed to matter more than anything was giving her a chance to be in a place where her life could radically change. A kibbutz! The mere thought of Kishorit brought to mind the hearty Eastern European pioneers who'd arrived at the turn of the twentieth century, with their agrarian, socialist ideals and their dreams of creating a better, more equitable society. Though that dream had died, and the true socialist kibbutzim—collectives—where everything is shared, including childrearing, had largely vanished from Israel, the model still existed in the more capitalistic kibbutzim that survive, and in places like Kishorit, where shared responsibility and a say in the community were seen as the means to self-sufficiency.

Sixteen months earlier, when I sat in the JCC auditorium and thought, "A kibbutz, perfect!" it was the notion of a community and equality that piqued my interest. I had a vision of Rachel living in a place where she could be herself. It was a vague and sentimental picture, admittedly, based on images of kibbutzniks working the land, eating dinner together, singing folk songs like the ones I'd heard that night.

On the long drive through the stony, mountainous Misgav region, the remoteness of Kishorit raised questions I hadn't had the energy or inclination to explore beforehand. This community (built on the grounds of a defunct kibbutz called Kishor, or "wool," where wool and lavender were sold) was beautiful and carefully planned—and separate. By sending Rachel here, I was giving up on the U.S. ideal—and my ideal—of inclusion. I kept thinking about the post–World War II "colonies" set up for children with mental retardation. Smaller communities, like the ones in Southbury, Connecticut, and Conway, Arkansas, were touted as being great improvements from the custodial institutions that were the norm, with their barracks-like living quarters and heartless warehousing of children. Although these colonies were more humane, they still advanced the theory that it was better for the child, or the family, or society itself, for a child with mental retardation to be taken from home.

There are no children at Kishorit—the minimum age is eighteen. The residents here had a range of special needs that made them dependent on support but were not necessarily mentally retarded, something that became clear on my first afternoon. Nor was this the United States; it was Israel, where the tradition of kibbutzim predated the nation by more than fifty years. I had to remind myself, too, of the reality of Rachel's American life at a time when inclusion was the ideal. My daughter had never walked down a street alone, or visited a neighbor. Paid staff were her companions, and she had no real friends. She lived with me because there was nowhere else for her to live, hating that I dominated her, railing against my rules. Despite person-centered planning that was meant to put decision making in her hands, despite legislation nominally giving her the same rights as other Americans, she was not part of my community. Rachel could not define "freedom" any more than she could describe the yellow houses, the crisp mountain air, or the scent of lavender. Still, she had been craving liberty for these past four years. Maybe here, thousands of miles from home, in this separate community, it would be hers.

For now, I was still making the decisions. I had chosen for her to live here. I was the one who spoke to the nurse and the social worker on her behalf, who described her behavior issues and strengths, and who suggested that, of all the possible jobs at Kishorit, they try her out in the dining hall. I chose this because Rachel had spent half the day in a job-training program at Goodwill until we left for Israel; her work experience there included setting and clearing tables. Although a handful of the 150 residents were from the United States, Canada, or the U.K., nearly everyone else was Israeli and spoke Hebrew; for many it was their only language. I was the one who claimed that Rachel's auditory skills were excellent, and guessed she'd pick up Hebrew quickly. I was the one who explained that she had spent summers apart from me since the age of eight and never missed me when I was gone—a statement that, even here, was greeted with the long gaze of disbelief.

Rachel wasn't purposely excluded from these discussions about her. As always, she was quiet in new surroundings. Even when she was asked a direct question, she bowed her head and mumbled, "I don't know." I knew from experience that nothing I said could prepare anyone here for her usual hyperverbal state. Not that I needed to discuss it, since I'd left five pages of notes about Rachel with her social worker, Nis, the stern, green-eyed man I had approached in Pittsburgh sixteen months before.

On our trek from the administration building to the business office, and then to see the nurse, we hardly saw a soul. In part it was because in Israel, the weekend is Friday and Saturday, and Sunday, when we arrived, was a workday. It was also a reminder that this was a community, not a camp or an institution where people do things en masse. It was more like a self-sufficient town where people lived and where they worked—on the farm, with the chickens or goats; in the kennels, where schnauzers are raised and dogs are boarded; at the stables, new that year; in the plastics factory, or the carpentry shop, where wooden toys are made (and sold internationally). If residents preferred and had the necessary skills, they could hold jobs outside Kishorit. The staff on the grounds functioned as a kind of backup corps to oversee things, but not in an intrusive, obvious way. When I was done making these decisions on Rachel's behalf, I would be leaving her with a degree of independence she'd never experienced, trusting—hoping—that she would rise to it.

Our last stop was at the apartment, which Rachel would be sharing with a woman named Ronit. Based on Kishor's principles, I assumed that Ronit had volunteered to share her apartment with the American visitor who had just arrived. It seemed that way when she opened the door to greet us, for despite her brooding expression, she took great pleasure in showing us around the bright two-bedroom apartment.

Ronit was a big woman, in her thirties perhaps, with short orange hair. She spoke solid, basic English, which impressed me greatly, and made me wonder: Why was she living at Kishorit? Would everyone here be this high-functioning? All I could intuit after a few polite questions was that she was happy here, that truly it was "better than before," as she put it. She liked her job in the plastics factory and her apartment. On weekends she often went home. Sometimes her dog stayed here—I could see his bed on the floor beside hers. She'd stocked the small refrigerator in their kitchenette with yogurt, Diet Coke, and milk, and encouraged Rachel to buy whatever she liked, too. In the bathroom, a caddy holding Ronit's toiletries took up half the shelf. She'd cleared the other half for Rachel's things.

As I unpacked Rachel's duffle bag, I found myself again reminded that my daughter had never walked alone, never decided to turn left instead of right, never poured herself a glass of juice or visited a friend. She was twenty and had done none of these simple things. I hoped she would get the chance to enjoy herself and her liberty. Certainly, she had her desires, the most fervent of which was getting me to leave.

"You can go now," she told me the moment I finished putting away her clothes. And, when I hesitated, "Go!" in no uncertain terms.

. . . .

The next morning I woke up in a small, dark bedroom, in an apartment I barely knew, in a city thousands of miles from home. I was by myself and it was very quiet. One daughter was traveling alone in India, the other living for the first time ever with minimal supervision. It was strange. In a way it was sad. It was also extraordinary. No one wanted me. No one had snapped me out of sleep with curses and incessant demands, no relentless *Ma, Mommy, Ma.* No one was arguing *stupid fat head face.*

I stayed in bed and let the sheer pleasure of the quiet flow through me. It was like warm fresh bread, the way it nourished me. From that first morning I started to regain a part of myself that I had worried no longer existed. So I had not been flattened after all—or maybe I had been, but these mornings of peace and quiet, one after another, had brought me back to life.

Peace was a word that surprised friends and family, now that I was in Israel. *Quiet* an odd way to describe an apartment that faced Hayarkon, the busy road that parallels the beach—a minor highway, the landlord called it, heavily trafficked, especially during rush hours, when the whine of motorbikes and the honking of frustrated drivers pierced the air. When I had first found this apartment on the Internet, my host at Bar-Ilan University had cautioned me about the noise, and she was right, of course; if I attuned myself to the traffic,

I could say that it was noisy; just as, if I attuned myself to the greater reality of living here, at this time when the security fence was being constructed, I could say that "peace" was a cruel, false way to describe my experience. Though the terrorist incidents had markedly declined and my neighborhood on the beach in Tel Aviv no longer showed its scars, when I began to have deeper encounters with people, their fatigue and despair were very clear.

My schedule was light for the first time in decades. My graduate fiction seminar met once a week; the students—there were eight—were a lively, interesting group, full of opinions. The oldest, Sophie, was my age and from India. Many of her stories, set in the Bene Israel community in India, were based on her father's army experience during Partition. Chana, the youngest, was from the Hasidic community in Borough Park, Brooklyn; a mother of two, she wrote about her world with rage and affection. There were seminars, and visiting writers, and Fulbright meetings where I heard about others' research projects. My unofficial Fulbright project was to *be*, to recall what it was like to wake and have the day take shape, rather than being dragged from deepest sleep into strife and obligation.

It felt like such good luck that I was here—everything, including my apartment, a kind of fluke. I had chosen to live in Tel Aviv instead of Jerusalem simply because it was closer to the university and to Kishorit. As for living on the beach—the owner of my apartment was the only one who'd responded to my Google posting.

In one of our many e-mails, the landlord described sitting on the balcony overlooking the Mediterranean. It made her think of a description of the sea in Jane Austen's *Sanditon*, "dancing and sparkling in sunshine and freshness," she'd written. She neglected to mention the excavated pit across the street, with the graffitied fence surrounding it, and she said nothing about the boulevard where the building is located, with its central promenade lined with date palms and benches. In the morning, old people sat in pairs; in the afternoon, kids on skateboards and scooters rumbled past. Falafel stands and cafés occupied nearly every corner, and on the avenue were stores displaying designer wedding gowns, one in each window, meant to be rented. I was able to take pleasure in small things, and in my neighborhood, with its beach and crowded cafés. Its secular, everyday energy gave me the chance to experience a part of Israel that was not in the news, a kind of ordinary daily life that had been scarred by the *intifada,* but went on nonetheless.

The first time I was invited to dinner, I hesitated out of habit. For the last twenty years, every moment away from Rachel had to be assessed. Was I covered? Could I fit in the pleasure of spending time with a friend when I had unfinished work, impossible to do when Rachel was around? Covered time was sacred space, saved for my most urgent priorities. If a friend said, "Let's have coffee," I had to quickly figure out how long I might spend with her, and whether I could still accomplish what I was obligated to do. The effect of this after two decades became apparent to me when I left Rachel at Kishorit: I'd fallen into a kind of madness. Don't water the plants now—you can do it when Rachel is home. Don't squander covered time by doing the laundry while Rachel is with a caregiver. To consider an evening out, I always calculated the expense—forty to sixty dollars—and the effort involved in getting coverage, especially on a weekend night. In the end, I was always weighing things, like friendship and pleasure, that should never be measured at all.

Could I have dinner with a friend? In Pittsburgh, the simple question exhausted me. It was too hard to plan. Here, after the first hesitation, it was easy. I'd love to. I could even arrive on time. If dinner was in Tel Aviv, I could probably walk. I could stay as long as I liked. I might even be able to read *and* have dinner with friends on the same day.

Of course, there was more; there were deeper, more enduring things that touched me here. Still, this peace and quiet, this chance to wake in silence and spend a day without argument, allowed me to soften, to become pliant and open, to experience the sun and light, the hopefulness of young brides, the Mediterranean that washes up and pulls back, undisturbed by the events on land.

I could have dinner with a friend. I was not in Pittsburgh. I was not living with Rachel. When I opened my eyes, this was the life before me, the life I would have until the end of June. It was a gift, something that came along and saved me from drowning.

One of my new friends dismissed the notion of luck when I explained that finding the apartment across from the beach was a stroke of good fortune. She was more inclined to think of it as *bashert,* something meant to be. Still, luck, like peace and quiet, was what I contemplated when I ran on the beach at dusk. How lucky Rachel and I were to be here. True, I asked and applied, and in that way made it happen. But the road that brought us here was so full of curves and dead ends that the mere fact of our presence here continued to amaze me.

. . . .

Rachel's transition to kibbutz life was bumpy. She irritated the other kitchen workers with her constant questions. She did not shower. More disturbing was the vomiting. Meals were served family style. Rachel piled food on her plate, shoveled everything in, and then threw up. Perhaps it was anxiety, or perhaps her enthusiastic response to plentiful food with no one limiting her portions.

I called her after the first incident to see if she was feeling better.

"*Ken*," she barked. Yes.

It lightened my mood to hear her use Hebrew without self-consciousness.

"Will you try to eat more slowly?"

"*Ken*," she repeated, in a brusque, Israeli way.

"And now? Do you still feel sick?"

"*Lo*," she barked into the phone.

Be patient, said Nis, a kind man despite the stern demeanor. Rachel had been taken away from home; she had landed in a place where she could not understand the language, where the people were new and the rules were different. "Give her time," he told me.

When I arrived for my first visit, I found Rachel sitting in the nearly empty dining room in a stained navy-blue sweatshirt. Across the table was an older woman in a crocheted cap, her attention on something in the distance. I sat beside my daughter and waited. There was no greeting or hug, not even a hello, until I prompted her. Then she simply said, "Hi, Ma," as if she'd seen me an hour before.

I convinced her to walk me to her apartment. When she did this without hesitation, I was greatly impressed. Kishorit, with its hills and curved roads and rows of yellow houses on several levels, the apartments with identical doors and nameplates in Hebrew, was a maze I was never able to negotiate well myself. Legally blind, Rachel found her apartment easily.

I was unrolling one of the movie posters I'd brought from the Jerusalem Cinematheque when Ronit came home. Hearing my voice, she lumbered into Rachel's room and began to pull at her short hair. "Anxious!" she shouted. "She is making me anxious!"

I tried to find out exactly what had happened, but Ronit's English had dissolved. Eventually, I was able to pluck a few grievances out of her raging Hebrew—a lost key, a flood on the shower floor. The rest I could only imagine.

"She's being hostile," Rachel told Nis, when we met in his office a short time later.

Nis asked her to explain.

"She's ignoring me," Rachel said.

I was moved by her clarity.

"Ronit says you confuse her with the talking. She says you wake her up. Is that true?"

"*Ken!*" Rachel said.

"You need to stop waking her up."

Nis talked to her respectfully, treating her in a way that I seldom saw. She was a person, not a baby or a pest or something less than human. He did not override her, did not direct his questions and comments to me.

"If you don't take a shower and change your clothes, people will start to complain about your smell." Even this unvarnished statement was said with respect.

When Rachel and I were outside again, I said, "You need to stop talking so much. It's upsetting people."

You would think that she would learn, after all the years of living with me, all the "no talking" times, all the nights when, in desperation, I hid from her. You would think that the years of seeing me with my hands over my ears, followed by a week of Ronit pulling at her hair, would be enough.

"People will like you better when you're quiet," I told her.

"I *like* to talk," she said.

Driving back to Tel Aviv, I remembered reading that people with Tourette's syndrome were able to repress their tics, but the urge to let them fly was sweeter and stronger than the desire to control them. For the first time, it occurred to me that Rachel's talking was like a tic. The pleasure she took in her own voice must have seemed worth incurring the wrath of everyone around her.

10

We wanted to create a different place, a framework that would really respect those in need of help and assure their human rights, rather than approaching them as one of hundreds in a pipeline who must shrink to its dimensions. This is the heart of Kishorit: Each of us arrived with an existential need dependent on the success of this project.

In those days, Kishorit had four employees, four members and five goats. The living room of one apartment was also used as the dining room, the bedroom as a laundry room. Necessity being the mother of invention, the development of the village was also born of the needs that arose. For example, what today is the toy factory started as the carpentry shop established to save on building costs and craft all the village furniture, on whose completion the factory turned to manufacturing toys.

—From www.kishorit.org

THE FOURTH VISIT

I did not miss Rachel or yearn for her company. Sometimes, in shame or surprise, I convinced myself that I never even thought about her. Of course, this wasn't true, since I called her every evening. My attentiveness did not thrill her. Though she answered her phone with a cheerful "hel-lo," as soon as she heard it was me, she said, "Call me later. I'm busy." If I stayed on the line, she would nag me about her father. She wanted Daddy to call, demanded I give her Daddy's number. She could not make outgoing calls on her bedside phone and hadn't yet learned how to dial. It didn't stop her from asking for her father's number every night.

Sometimes hearing Rachel's voice was enough, and I could get off the phone after only a few seconds. If the news from Nis had upset me, I would persist with my annoying questions, demanding more than the hollow voice on the other end of the line, with its perfect inflections, its perfect conversational placeholders and exclamations with nothing at all beneath them. If I'd never heard anything genuine from her, I would have stopped trying. But there had been times—during the meeting with Nis, for instance—when something utterly authentic shone through. I found myself prodding her, seeking a morsel, a word that reassured me, something in her tone that let me know she was all right.

Still, it was only on the drive to Kishorit that I could feel my wounded love for her, inside me like a jagged rock. As soon as I was behind the wheel of my rental car, I was aware of how eager I was to see her, that I could hardly wait to arrive. On each of these trips I found myself imagining that *this time* I'd be able to intuit from her gaze or her stance some inkling that she was happy to see me. I would picture myself walking with her, arm in arm. Then I'd try to shake these dreams from my head before I arrived.

The fourth visit was different from the start. As soon as I got into the rental car, I heard on the car radio that Sheik Yassin had just been executed in an air strike by Israeli missiles. For the next two and a half hours, I listened to the sounds of rioting Palestinians, and Hamas leaders vowing to open the gates of hell. Rachel did not come to mind. I thought only of the frail spiritual leader in his wheelchair, England censuring Israel, France condemning the attack, Hamas vowing to cut off the head of Ariel Sharon and wage holy war on the sons of Zion—all of this reported in the mellow, affectless voice of the BBC broadcaster.

The news shook me, reminding me that the sense of peace I had felt since arriving in Israel was internal; it was my peace, and I had let it shape my view of the world beyond my charming beach apartment in Tel Aviv. Listening to the roar of the Palestinian mob, I was not comforted to recall that the sheik was a man who gave his blessing to suicide attacks, and whose mosque sermons declared such aggression to be divinely inspired. I did not simply switch off the radio, which of course would have made sense. Rather, I felt compelled to listen.

At last I began the final ascent. The narrow roads curved around the mountains; the car sputtered and surged. Second left, second right; the sign for Kishor Village, the gate across the road.

The guard stepped out. In a halting, awkward way, unable to string together an actual sentence, I simply announced, *"Ema.* Rucheli Glynn."

The gate retracted. I parked my car in a small lot, beside a sculpture of singing children. The gardens were lush with lavender and mint, and the birds were twittering. There is no sky like this in Pittsburgh, cloudless and blue, no sun this bright. From where I stood, I saw the yellow houses and thought how fortunate Rachel was to live here, and how nice it would be for us to walk together, far away from the discord and misery outside the gate.

• • • •

The dining hall was empty. Earlier in the week, Nis had told me that they were trying out Rachel in the plastics factory, one floor up. I climbed the stairs, full of dread, to see if I could find her. Though Nis had not seemed discouraged by Rachel's failure in the dining hall, our conversation had come just after I'd received an upsetting evaluation from her five-month work experience at Goodwill. Rachel was "attention seeking, frequently asking others to complete work for her," I read. She often claimed she couldn't do something when it appeared she didn't want to do it. In her work-production class, when she completed a task, she always said, "I'm done" after each set, unlike the other students, who requested more supplies. I was advised to explore other options when I returned home, including day programs, where basic life skills were reinforced. The mere mention of "day programs" made my stomach twist. These programs accommodated the lowest-functioning individuals. I saw them as a dead end for Rachel. Nothing more would be asked of her.

The "plastics factory" was a big open space with several round tables. Only three people were working that afternoon. They were assembling small plastic cases for tool bits. Rachel, in her grimy blue sweatshirt and Iceland 1998 baseball cap worn backwards, was one of them. Careful to keep my distance, so she wouldn't see me, I watched her place a blue Styrofoam square in the box, then a yellow molded piece, lining up the notch in this second layer with the clasp. Rachel was working. She was fully engaged in this simple task.

I stepped closer. Her hair was matted and food was visible around the corners of her mouth. The young woman beside her whispered to Rachel. She looked up, made out that it was me, and said, "I'm working." Then she went back to her job. It was thrilling to see—proof that, in the right environment, she would be able to work.

• • • •

If I had left then, it would have been fine with Rachel, but I wasn't ready to drive back to Tel Aviv. Nor did I feel like walking around the kibbutz with her, beautiful as it was. Every time Rachel saw the shadow of a human being, she said, "Come here," and wiggled her finger. "This is my mom." People she knew, those she didn't, residents, maintenance workers, many of whom did not speak English. She was like the crassest American tourist, assuming that everyone spoke English. "Come here, come here!" When I was not around, she did this same thing, standing outside the dining hall with her water bottle, her ripped magazine, and her uncanny memory for people's names. "Tali! Sheerie! Shuki!"

When Rachel was finished working, I suggested we take a ride. She didn't particularly want to leave the kibbutz until it occurred to her that I might buy her a bottled drink, what she called, to my dismay, "a sucking bottle." As soon as I agreed that I might get her some bottled water, the negotiations began in earnest. If she wanted the bottled water, she needed to shower and change into something clean. We were right back into the life we had together, with its bargains and debates, dangled promises and stern threats. She would do nothing without this kind of coercion. Here on the kibbutz, where she had at last been granted the freedom she had craved for so long, she had stopped showering. Hygiene interested her not at all, even though Nis continued to remind her that her dirtiness antagonized the residents. At his suggestion, I'd hired an aide for an hour a day. Amy made sure Rachel showered but didn't encourage her to put on clean clothes. Every day, whatever the weather, she chose the same grimy hooded sweatshirt.

When Rachel let me into her apartment, I saw the bare mattress in the second bedroom and knew that her roommate was gone. I thought about Ronit pulling at her short hair and shouting, "Anxious! She is making me anxious!" I felt as much compassion for Ronit, driven crazy in three weeks, as I did for Rachel, who would not or could not change her behavior. But I was here, and so I helped her choose something clean and tried to coerce her into something more appropriate for the season. When she set the shower, I called out, the way I did at home, "With soap!" because otherwise she would stand under the spray with the soap in her palm, as if, miraculously, this would get her clean. "And shampoo!" I called again.

Rachel's bed was neatly made. The teddy bear she brought from home was splayed across the pillow, as if exhausted by her, like the roommate who moved out. Again I thought she is who she is, that I needed to get used to it, the way a conservative parent needed to make peace with a pink-haired, heavily tattooed daughter. I had to come to terms with what I had known for years, that living apart from me meant that she would be dirtier, heavier, and ill-dressed. For her, freedom meant wearing sweatsuits in the summer. It meant toting a backpack bulging with liters of water and Mountain Dew, with sodden rolls of toilet paper, damp magazines, and address books filled with the e-mail addresses she coerced from people she barely knew. It meant making countless cups of sugary tea (using the electric kettle in her kitchenette) and demanding the attention of strangers in elevators and in stores.

When she finished showering, I combed her hair and scrunched it with my fingers, so the curls would form and she would look like my pretty daughter, and not addled and homeless, which was how she appeared when I saw her from afar.

On the drive to Carmiel, the attractive town fifteen kilometers from the kibbutz, Rachel asked me repeatedly about the water. I tried to redirect her, as I'd learned to do fifteen years ago, by asking simple questions about her well-being, what she had for lunch, whether she had friends. She was not interested in my conversation, only the bottled water I said I'd buy. She wanted this water with a passion, the way someone else might want a baby, or a beautiful overpriced dress. The promise of bottled water was so powerful, it seemed to push out every other thought.

I found a shopping area in Carmiel and parked in a diagonal spot on a long hill with stores on either side of the street. Poor as Rachel's vision is, as soon as she stepped out of the car, she managed to see that inside the open door of the nearest shop was a refrigerator case with drinks. Her fierce desire for the bottle of water became even greater. She wanted the water, wanted it from this particular store, at that very instant.

"Let's walk first," I said.

She wanted the water.

"Come on," I said. "It's beautiful outside. Look."

I knew I should say yes. I'd driven two and a half hours to see my daughter, who had asked for nothing more than a bottle of water. I should have walked into that store instead of demanding that we stroll through town first. It was ridiculous to make her wait. I knew that my stubbornness made no sense, but I wanted her to walk, just as I wanted her to wipe the corners of her mouth when I was not there, to eat moderately, and to shower. I told myself that it was as absurd as wanting her not to be retarded, but in fact, that was at the root of it. At that moment, I wanted her not to be retarded.

Because I'm reasonably intelligent, I could juggle all these thoughts. I could know that I wanted her not to be retarded, know it was an absurd thing to want and want it just the same. I could dislike my own stubbornness, realize that it was pointless and mean-spirited, and that both of us would be happier if I simply halted right there, walked through the doorway, and bought her the bottle. I could tell myself that whatever she did in that store was irrelevant, that even if the sound of someone speaking Hebrew sent her into sputtering laughter, which it sometimes still did, it made no difference. I was in a small town in northern Israel where no one knew us, in a store where I would never return. Furthermore, the merchants of Carmiel were surely used to the residents of Kishor Village who came to shop here. Even if they weren't, I had never been stopped by anyone's disdain. If anything, it made me loop my arm through Rachel's in public places, declaring my motherhood, my connection to her, my advocacy for her right to be as she was in a world that wasn't welcoming. All this buzzed through my brain in the time it took me to lock the car.

"We're going to walk," I said.

I took a step forward, as unable in that moment to buy her the water as she was to move past her desire to possess it.

She planted herself at the top of the sloping sidewalk.

The hill was considerable, and the sidewalk was made of pale pebbles with diagonal bands of dark stone. I took a few steps downhill, away from her, then paused to look back.

Rachel made her little "come here" gesture, wiggling her finger when she saw that I had turned.

I continued down the hill, paused and turned toward her again, in part to see if she was harassing strangers, in part because, stubborn as I was, my goal was not to make her feel abandoned, but to get her to move.

She would not budge. I walked further, then turned briefly and saw the cautious way she extended her foot. I realized then that she was afraid. She could see the refrigerator case in the store, but the bands of color on the ground confused her. She could not judge the terrain, could not sense if there was a step or if she was on level ground. She brushed her foot along the sidewalk and felt that it was solid. I relented, and met her halfway.

And still I would not walk into the café, with its enticing refrigerator case. I managed to get her past it by promising that we'd go to Super-Pharm, where she could wheel a cart through the aisles and study the displays of toothpaste and soap, items she loved as much as potato chips and bottled water.

It's what we did a few minutes later. We cruised slowly down every aisle, haggling comfortably over choices. We ended up buying four bars of soap, herb-flavored toothpaste, and a six-pack of water. She was very happy with these purchases, particularly with the two-liter bottles, though they had conventional screw tops and were not sports bottles—"sucking bottles," as she had called them.

When we were back at the kibbutz, she told me not to get out of the car, that she did not need my help. "You can go, Ma." Her face was flushed, which didn't surprise me, given the sweatshirt she wore on this warm day. Still, watching her haul her packages from the car made me worry that something was wrong. Again I asked if I could help. "Just go," she said, and so I did.

As I drove back out through the gates, I was relieved at first, and then overcome with a sense of incompleteness I always felt when I visited her, an awareness that what I wanted to do—what I needed to do as a mother—was undoable. It occurred to me that I didn't buy the water right away because I had wanted to extend my time with her: the shower, the trip to town, where we might stroll arm in arm for a while. I was controlling, sure, and stubborn in ways that benefited neither of us. But I was her mother, and only attempting the familiar, rewarding, necessary tasks that mothers do: wanting to nurture, to show my love, to be loved in return. I was still seeking these things with Rachel, still trying to fix a relationship that seemed broken, though I was the only one who saw it that way.

PART 2

11

Several approaches guide daily life in the village. The first is normalization theory. It is important to note that our use of the term "normalization" does not, under any circumstances, imply mainstreaming people who are special, but to provide the opportunity for a normal life, under natural daily conditions and as part of a community to those to whom it was previously denied.

The community, similar in its basic structure to a kibbutz, provides vigor and support, and creates a routine based on work, mutual help and a common fate. Part of the "normalization" is also to learn to find a balance between the given and the desired; to find the compromise between the personal needs and wishes of each and between what the surroundings can offer and provide, and to live at peace in the gray area between the two.

—From www.kishorit.org

LOVE AND DEATH

In April, there was Dov. And there was Rachel's father, who was very ill.

Dov was Rachel's friend, or so Nis told me. What he actually said was, "She's better now. She likes to be with Dov." These were thrilling words to hear, not so much the mention of this friend, Dov, about whom I knew nothing, but that Rachel was *better,* happier, less annoying. In the conversation before this one, Nis had blurted, "She's alienating everyone!" It was the first time I'd heard him express irritation over my daughter. Though nothing he told me was new, it made my heart ache to think of her standing outside the dining hall with her water bottles and ragged magazines, calling out people's names, stopping them in mid-sentence—a pest, someone to avoid.

Now there was this friend, Dov, and a new roommate, Etti. Rachel was doing well at work, and enjoying the attention she got from Amy—supposedly there to supervise her showering, though I soon learned that Rachel had enticed Amy to soap her up and towel her dry, head to toes. (She also gained Amy's sympathy by claiming her mother never visited her.) If this wasn't exactly promoting independence and reinforcing the skills Rachel had possessed for years, it was easy for me to let it go. On her own, Rachel was waking and dressing (in dirty clothes, admittedly), making herself tea, getting herself to breakfast, working in the plastics factory. She deserved a little pampering.

Though I hadn't met Dov, and Rachel had nothing to say about him when I mentioned his name, I was beginning to know a few of the other residents. There was Clive from London, who stood on the road near the parking lot, tall and erect, the sole inhabitant of his own world. I knew his name because when I asked, he said, "I'm Clive. I'm from London," in a clipped rote recital of the facts. Ben was Rachel's neighbor. Born in Turkey and raised on Long Island, he now lived by himself in a neat apartment with an impressive collection of CDs and books. On the walls were family photos and Ben's careful line drawings of trucks. Ben was trilingual, though the reminders on the doors that said things like "Take a shower" and "Change your clothes" were in English.

I first met Etti the day Rachel and I arrived, because she was the kind of person who gravitated to strangers, eager to introduce herself. Because she worked beside Rachel in plastics, I saw her each time I visited. Rachel might be too busy to notice me, but Etti always perked up when I approached.

Etti had a clumsy gait, labored speech, and seizures, though fewer than before she was put on a new medication, she said. She was articulate and maternal, full of advice. Even before she decided to try being Rachel's roommate, Etti was looking out for her. "She needs to learn Hebrew," she told me in February. "She has to sit with her head up when she goes to the *mordone*," she explained on another visit, describing Rachel's attitude in the clubhouse. "Not like this"—head bowed. "She'll never make friends if she sits like that."

Rachel was a challenging roommate, but Etti seemed to like her. It helped that she was temperamentally different from Ronit. When she saw me, Etti didn't barrel over and start pulling at her hair and shouting in my face. Instead, she beseeched me in a long-suffering way. *Why?* she asked, as if she was trying to comprehend a destructive force of nature. "I don't mind if she wakes me during the week, but does she have to wake me on Shabbat? *Why* must she do this? It's the one morning I can sleep in."

Etti held me responsible for Rachel's behavior. "Talk to her," she said when she saw me. "You *must* tell her not to be disrespectful." I was supposed to sit Rachel down and explain that there were times when Etti wanted to be with other friends, or watch TV in peace, that it was rude to interrupt. I did talk to Rachel, and she understood what I said and promised to change and then didn't, of course. I also left money for Etti either to keep for herself or to offer as a reinforcement for Rachel, who liked taking Kishorit's bus to the mall in Carmiel, when someone was willing to accompany her. Rachel needed that spending money so she could shop. It was a powerful reinforcement I thought could possibly work.

After I finished talking to Etti, I meandered through the farm, where the vegetables grew in neat rows, then visited the chickens and schnauzers and the horses in their stalls. When I returned to the plastics factory, I asked Rachel if I should stay longer.

"Just go," she said. Now that she was doing better, it didn't hurt to be dismissed. I kissed her forehead and left.

· · · ·

Beachgoers began to arrive in my neighborhood in droves after Passover: sunbathers, swimmers, families carrying folding chairs. On Saturday mornings there was folk dancing on the promenade behind the hotels, where, earlier in the season, old men with bare bronzed chests had played *maktok,* a game with wooden paddles and a hard ball. Now so many young people played *maktok* at the surf's edge that the crisp clack of the ball, the *mak-tok* against the wooden paddles, echoed up and down the beach.

I described all this to Rachel's father when we spoke, which we often did in April. Unlike many gravely ill people, Paul was not self-centered. He remained as curious as ever about the world, and liked to hear about my visits to Kishorit, and the way I crept unseen into the factory to watch Rachel work. He liked to hear me describe my life there, my friends and students, the lively stretch of sea from Tel Aviv to Yafo, with its various beaches: family beaches, beaches with svelte young people and dogs, beaches where more Russian was heard than Hebrew (no surprise, since one out of every six Israelis is a native speaker of Russian), a beach for Orthodox swimmers, with a wall that separates men from women, and in Yafo, near the bombed husk of the Dolphinarium, a beach where kids with dreadlocks played guitar and got high.

PART 2

He was very interested in my friendship with Israel, the son of a couple whom we had met in childbirth class in New Jersey in 1983. Israel was a handsome, somber young man, almost exactly Rachel's age, whose two passions were evolutionary psychology and kickboxing. He was torn between Jerusalem (where he lived, and where, as a secular Jew, he had begun to feel excluded) and Tel Aviv (which he thought of as shallow, but where, increasingly, his friends had moved). He didn't know exactly what to do when summer came, whether to move from Jerusalem or stay, whether to continue his studies, which his parents wanted, or compete as a kickboxer, despite two serious injuries that had seemed to end his career two years before. Israel was fascinated by Rachel, though he hadn't met her yet. It seemed to give him a chill to contemplate her life, as if the closeness of their birthdays meant he had barely escaped her fate. When I told this to my former husband, his voice began to tremble, and the conversation ended. I never got to list the things Israel and Rachel had in common. Both had difficult relationships with their mothers, and uncomplicated feelings toward their fathers; both sought autonomy and were not fully independent, and both yearned for relationships, which they could not easily maintain. Both loathed their nicknames, which their troublesome mothers still accidentally used. Israel, not Solick; Rachel, not Rae.

I wished Paul wouldn't compare his daughter to Israel and judge these two by the same standards, but I could no longer say this. It was on the shorter list of things I didn't describe, like the shops on Ben Yehuda and Diezengoff Streets that rented designer wedding gowns, and the single fabulous gown showcased in each window. Paul wouldn't understand my fascination with these dresses, some sleek, others frothy and nearly edible looking, or how I liked to watch the photo shoots. Nearly every evening, a young couple dressed in gown and tux spilled out onto the sidewalk, their attendants behind them, their car waiting at the curb, wrapped like a gift with broad ribbons and bows. Paul never cared about clothes, which he bought in thrift shops, or furnishings, which he picked up at the dump.

In the winter, the idea of people marrying at such an unsettled time had touched me, since marrying (by choice, at least) meant believing in the future. Toward the end of April, when his illness worsened and the brides began showing up on the streets, it was hard not to think back to our own wedding on lower Fifth Avenue in New York, across from the dorm where I'd once lived. When I remembered my Mexican dress with its long bell sleeves, my bouquet of daisies, my husband in a fine gray suit, his long hair already turning silver, I was stunned by how confident we were, how sure that we could create the life we wanted, order it up like a delectable treat. We are laughing in all of our wedding photos—not posed and merely smiling for the camera, but truly overjoyed, ready for what seemed like the start of a long and riotous adventure.

By the end of April Paul knew that he was dying. I had never talked to someone who understood that his end was near and faced it head on. He had the same kind of curiosity about his own failing body as he had for the natural world. It chilled me to hear him talk about his death. It was also just like the man I'd known for twenty-five years, whose interest in life processes always transcended ordinary scientific curiosity about a dragonfly's eyes or the behavior of a garden slug. Degeneration and death, what inevitably occurred in "the system," had always fascinated him. At forty, he'd set up a camera on a tripod and posed against a white wall each morning, intending to capture his aging over a long period of time. A handsome man, vigorous and healthy, he looked like death in those photos, and still he persisted snapping these grim-looking self-portraits, until distracted by other projects that interested him more.

Now he spoke in a frank, dispassionate way about what had happened to his liver and what his end would be like. Listening to him describe how his kidneys would fail and he would lapse into a coma, I wanted to cry out, from my apartment in Tel Aviv, "Maybe not! Maybe you're wrong!"

I felt far away for the first time, and all alone in this, the ex-wife. When I told him I wanted to come home to see him, he said quite adamantly, "Stay where you are. It's your turn to be happy." He didn't want to see Rachel either, and asked that she not call. It's too upsetting, he told me. Of course, I did not try to change his mind, though it made me sad that this man, who could describe his failing body in heartbreaking detail, could not bear to hear his daughter's voice.

. . . .

What would she say if I dialed his number and gave her the phone? "Daddy. It's Rachel." Her usually strident voice turned velvet when she spoke his name. *Daddy.* Show her his picture and ask who it is, and she would answer in a coy way, with her eyes cast down. *Daddy.*

It didn't matter that they saw each other for short visits only three or four times a year. With Daddy, there were no limits—no behavior management, no restrictions at all. Daddy didn't curtail the endless questions or limit what she ate. Daddy took long naps and let her snuggle beside him. His love was purer than mine, more intense, full of sorrow. He looked forward to their visits, cried when he sent her back to me, and always said, "I love her, but she drives me up a wall."

Hardly a day passed in the years following our divorce when she did not ask to speak to him. Occasionally they conversed. More often, she left a message on his voice mail: "Daddy. It's Rachel. It's—what time is it, Mommy? It's 6:53 on Wednesday. Call me when you get this message and we'll make plans. I'm busy tomorrow night until 10:30, and the weekend is bad, but you can try me on Friday at eleven . . ." And on she would go, unwinding an elaborate invented schedule until, eventually, I took the phone away.

Daddy. Even his name seemed to make her happy. There was no ambivalence, the way there was with her sister, whose company she seemed to enjoy—though after the last visit, when Charlotte asked, "Are you sad to see me go?" Rachel replied, "Not even a little bit."

It was different with Daddy. At the first mention of a visit, she had her suitcase down from the closet shelf and was ready to leave forever.

Now when she asked why her father didn't call, I said, "He can't," or sometimes, "He's sick." Either way, she did not interrogate me further, could not frame the next question or did not know to ask it. Or maybe she was simply used to the fact that even when he was well, they rarely spoke.

It hurt to exclude her from all that happened in the next weeks, to keep secret the phone calls from Charlotte, begging me to fly home, and my decision, with Paul's permission, to do so. Rachel did not know that I had waited too long, and that Daddy had died before my plane had landed in New York. Nis knew the reason for my brief trip home. My own daughter did not.

Never before had I withheld something so profound from some-one. In May, when I drove to Kishorit to see her next, I felt disrespect-ful. I didn't withhold the truth because I worried that she would be upset about her father's death; I withheld it because she would be confused, and I would not be there to know if it shook her up, and to do whatever possible to soothe her. I decided instead to break the news when we were together in the States. Maybe we could be look-ing at photos in a family album. I could try to explain that she could not reach her father on the phone or sit on his lap or see him again, but we had these pictures to help us remember, and we would talk about him forever, and in this way he would stay with us. It felt lame, completely inadequate, but it was the best I could do.

My friend Mila was with me on this trip. Because it was a Saturday afternoon, I expected that Kishorit would seem emptied out and that it would be hard to find Rachel. I was not surprised that the dining room was empty, as well as the adjoining lounge that she liked to patrol. Nor was I surprised to find no one in her apartment. The sight of the stripped mattress in Etti's room stopped me, a clear sign that a second roommate had given up. I left my gifts—shampoo and batteries—on Rachel's bed and took my friend on a tour of Kishorit's grounds, hoping we'd eventually find her.

The birds were singing wildly, and everything was in bloom, the water lilies in the pond, the bougainvillea and century plants. Not a single person was outside. Even the *mordone* was completely empty. Eventually I found a staff person, who suggested that we check outside the dining room one more time. Then, as we turned, he said, "If you can't find her, come back. I think I know where she might be."

While Mila and I ambled down the sleepy paths of this commu-nity where no one seemed to live, I thought about the stripped bed in Rachel's room. Was there anyone on earth who would love Rachel the way her father had, who would ask as little of her, and make her laugh? It seemed during this fruitless walk that the answer was no.

After an hour, I gave up. I wrote a note for Rachel and started back to her apartment to leave it with her gifts.

The same staff person caught up with us. "You haven't found her yet? Come with me."

We followed him down a path to the last apartment in a row of yellow houses. He knocked on the door, then opened it with a master key and stepped inside.

A moment later Rachel appeared, attired in her grubby blue sweat-shirt and sweatpants. A young man followed—Dov, I assumed. The look on my daughter's face was serene and sleepy. "We were napping," she said. Her hair sprang out in all directions.

Dov put his arm across her shoulders. "I'm her boyfriend," he said.

He was a nice-looking young man, though very upset, and he asked a series of rapid-fire questions. Was it true that she was leaving in June? Was that really the case? Was I buying a house in New Jersey? It was what she'd said, but he wasn't sure. Sometimes she confused him. Could he have our address? He needed our address. She was his girlfriend; he needed to be able to write to her after she left.

Dov went back into his apartment to get a pencil and a pad. He gave them to me, then put his arm around Rachel again. I was surprised to see that she did not shrug it off.

Not a cloud was in the sky. Dov was agitated and intense, and Rachel was mellow. Her face was slightly swollen, as if from sleep. If her sister, as a teenager, had emerged from a room with messy hair and a boy and explained, "We were napping," I would have laughed in disbelief. Looking at Rachel, I felt certain that she had just woken. I asked Dov a few questions, mostly to hold on to this moment. He told me he was from Jerusalem. His father was a scientist at Hebrew University. Was it true I was a writer? He wanted to know because he, too, was a writer. He wrote poems. In fact, he'd invented his own language.

"I saw that Etti's bed had been stripped," I said to Rachel. "Has she moved out? Was it because you kept waking her?"

Dov interceded: Why did she do that? How would they ever be roommates if she kept waking people up? What was he going to do? She was his girlfriend; how would they live together? He wanted to know what else Rachel liked to do, because he was worried. She was his girlfriend but they didn't have a lot to talk about. "We don't have a lot in common!" he said, frantic and upset. "What does she like? How will we live together?"

The sun blazed overhead. Rachel blinked lazily. Dov held her close.

So much went through my mind. I wanted her to have a boyfriend, if it was what she desired. In an old-fashioned way—especially now, with her father gone—I wanted someone to take care of her. Unlike her sister, Rachel could not look out for herself. This boy—this man—seemed so much higher functioning that it was hard to imagine how he and Rachel related or what they did when they were together. When I thought that it couldn't be sex, that Rachel, with her septo-optic dysplasia and her history of pituitary problems, had always seemed devoid of sexuality, another thought rose up: I was denying what was before my eyes.

I looked at her sweet freckled face. She was fine. Whatever went on, she was not unhappy.

"I want you to be nice to my daughter," I said to Dov. "Do you understand? You're not to hurt her. Ever."

A few minutes later we left. Mila was surprised that I simply drove off after the encounter, without making a fuss. "About what?" I asked, explaining what I believed. She was fine. I was her mother. I could tell.

Although I appeared certain of this, and in part truly was certain, I was unsettled for the rest of the day, replaying what I saw (that she was happy and relaxed), what I wanted (for her to be loved), and what I knew about her complex hormonal deficiencies. The issues went far beyond this encounter with Dov, since, sexual drive or not, Rachel liked boys, was coy around them, sought their attention. She liked saying she had a boyfriend when people asked (which they often did), in part intuiting the status conferred by her "yes." But she had always pushed away the mildest of affections from her boyfriends of the past, even Josh, whose company I could see she enjoyed.

And how vulnerable she was! She would withdraw when someone tried to touch her, but she could be molested by someone stronger, forced to do something that frightened or hurt her, and be unable to report it. I recalled how, years before, she could not tell us who bit her or who pulled a hank of hair from her head. My concern did not vanish in more supervised situations either. I was always entrusting her care to someone—to bus drivers, aides, teachers, therapists, counselors.

For now, though, when her face and demeanor came back to mind, I returned to my initial response: Dov had not hurt her. I was still uneasy. I wanted to imagine that if a sexual relationship brought her comfort and pleasure, if she wanted a man in her bed instead of books, beads, and a stuffed gorilla, it would be something that she could have. If it wasn't, I would still want her to be cherished, to have love in whatever way she needed it. I did not know what that way was yet—apart from knowing that she needed to be around people, right in the center of things, making herself known.

"Dov is a good boy," Nis said when I discussed my concerns candidly with him. "Their friendship makes her happy." He'd been very blunt with me about Rachel's social problems at the kibbutz, so I had no reason to dispute his opinion now.

· · · ·

Seven weeks passed between her father's death and our departure. Never did I say a word to Rachel. I held onto my plan of talking to her when Charlotte was around and we had pictures. It did not work out that way. As soon as Rachel saw her sister at Newark Airport, she began to ask about Daddy, to ask and ask, until I walked them to a row of molded orange seats outside the International Arrivals terminal. There, in this awkward public space, in our separate seats that forced us forward, I said the words. "Daddy died. He was very sick."

Charlotte, raw from her father's death, began to sob. Then Rachel did. It was a contagious kind of crying, as if she had yawned in response to her sister's yawn. Tears fell from Rachel's eyes, and her sadness was real, but it had nothing to do with the loss of her father, which I assumed had not yet hit her. It would, I believed. She would miss his tactile, undemanding affection.

The words that I had planned to utter seemed foolish now, and the timing was awful. Worst of all, I had a connecting flight to catch.

I was going home alone. Charlotte was driving Rachel to camp in the Catskills. It was a last-minute plan, finalized two weeks before, when I learned that the day camp in Pittsburgh where Rachel had been guaranteed a space was suddenly deemed inappropriate for her. This change in attitude took me by surprise and reminded me that the structure of our daily lives was fragile. To bring Rachel home meant taking her to a place where she had nothing to do, no friends or activities. Fortunately, there was space for her in the overnight camp she'd attended for the last ten years.

Rachel was cheerful when I called her on Sundays. She granted
me a sentence or two, then asked if Daddy was going to pick her up

when camp was over. No, I told her each time. "Daddy can't get you
because he's dead." These cold words seemed not to distress her, nor
did they seem to stick. It was as if nothing at all had penetrated.

On visiting day, when her bunkmate saw me with a man, she said
to Rachel, "I thought your father was *dead*."

So Rachel had at least said the words to someone.

Then there was the letter she dictated to a counselor, clearly Rachel verbatim: "This coming week, I have to think of what's going
on because my sister has an application to fill out. If you can let me
know what time you are free I can talk to you then, but not until then
because I have very little writing to do myself for another person, and
it's not me, it's my sister and my dad passed away, and this is very
hard for me right now, I can't talk about it right now."

Who said, "passed away"? They were not words we ever used. Was
it the sweet counselor from Ireland? Was she also the one who told
Rachel that her dad was in heaven? What could "heaven" mean to a
person who'd never heard of this concept? Was heaven like Florida,
a place her father occasionally went? Or was it like Maine, where
he took her each summer? I had trouble imagining Rachel having a
conversation about her father, though the letter and her bunkmate's
comment made me believe she spoke of him at camp. Why then
would she never mention him to us? Nothing, even when Charlotte
cued her: "Who used to hold you in his lap? Who liked to snuggle
with you?" Had her father, a source of such pleasure, vanished completely? Or was her silence a sign of discomfort?

When she had been home for a while—unchanged by Kishorit,
impervious to everything, it seemed—I found myself wondering
whether she was ever sad about her father. I wondered if he returned
to her in her dreams—if she even had dreams, this grown-up child of
mine who said, "I had the weirdest dream," just as her sister might
say. I wondered if she still heard his voice, or his wild, unrestrained
laugh, as I often did. If his scent remained for her, the fierceness of
his love, his nicknames.

What was it like for her? Was it that she did not think of her father, or that he came to mind in dreams or images or feelings that
she could not express? It wasn't that I wanted her to weep about her

father, to rail against the world, or to puzzle over the cruel mystery of his absence. Rather, I wanted to believe that his love would last. I wanted to imagine that from time to time she might be aware of a small tender spot inside her, and that, feeling the ache, she might recall him.

· · · ·

Dov did not forget Rachel.

His letters began to arrive in July, before she was back from camp.

> Hello Rachel.
> It is Dov.
> I am still a little sick. I miss you. I want to learn literature in the university soon. Maybe in Haifa.
> I read some books. What do you do with the computer now? How do you success in computer games? Do you make beads or art? How is your family's situation? I see movies on TV. I wrote some new poems, but not much. I made a binder with important things, one of them is a philosophy passage I had written. The young girls who volunteer here will leave soon and I shall miss them. My grandfather got out of the hospital but is still ill. Bye and have a good time.

The second one arrived a week later.

> Hello Rachel.
> It is Dov.
> Today we broke from Namai a nice social worker that is leaving. Einat, a guide, came back from a birth vacation with a new baby. I wrote all my dictionary on the computer. The woman from the computer store is going to make me a CD-rom. I love you very much. What beads and art are you making? How do you succeed in Free Cell? Have a good time.

And the third, a week after that.

> Hello Rachel.
> I want to learn in university but there are problems with finding a place. I hope I will be able to learn. I got back to writing poems. I wrote a poem about wolfs, and today a poem about Don-Juan. Today I asked the pizza-seller if he had a pizza with banana, but he said there is no such thing in the world. I want to send my mom a 3-pages story I wrote once about communication. I miss you very much.

After that, every week, a letter arrived by mail or e-mail. Throughout the fall, and into the next year, Dov wrote to say what he was doing and that he missed her very much. When asked, Rachel would name Dov as her boyfriend at Kishorit, but she wasn't interested in hearing his letters read to her. Nor did she particularly want to dictate a letter for me to write, which she had loved to do when her father was alive. Dov's unanswered letters continued to arrive. The sight of them, opened or not, made me ache.

One spring day, Dov wrote that he had begun to learn literature at the university, where "most of the pupils are Arabic." That evening, I looked at footage I shot at Kishorit. Everything I remembered was there: the lush flowerbeds and noisy birds, my daughter, freckled and rosy, blinking in the sun, dressed in her grubby sweatshirt. There's footage of her in the plastics factory, pushing Styrofoam out of molds, focused and relaxed; happy, it seemed. More content than I'd seen her since we'd been home.

Dov met "a nice friend, a girl called Tehila." I found myself hoping that Tehila would remain his friend and take away his longing for my daughter, who never mentioned his name, just as she never talked about her father. I was pleased to learn that Dov saw Tehila on a day when he "ate in the university a good sendwich" and on another day when he wrote a poem "about phashicts." Later, he reported that there was "a nice teacher who loves me." Perhaps if Tehila faded, this teacher would give Dov the human connection he craved.

While I searched for a place in the United States where Rachel might live, somewhere beautiful, where people might love her, I found myself wondering what came to Dov's mind when he wrote to Rachel. I tried to convince myself that his desire to write was stronger than his need for a response, but in May, after ten months of unanswered letters, he still seemed wounded by Rachel's failure to respond. "I want us very much to keep contact," he wrote. "I am missing you very much and would like you very much to come back to Israel so we can be together." He sent "towsand" of kisses and "hot regards" across the sea, along with this final modest request. "I shall be glad if you write to me soon. I love you. Dov."

12

Rachel is 21 years old and presently functions in a Life Skills program at a level significantly below expected for chronological grade level. She requires consistent practice over time to maintain skills. . . . She names and sequences days of the week, and identifies A.M./P.M. activities with 85% accuracy. She has difficulty stating pertinent personal information. Given picture cues, she identifies products needed for grooming and demonstrates proper techniques for hand washing and tooth brushing with moderate assistance. . . . Rachel is easily distracted by noise or other environmental stimuli. She can identify and classify pictures of food, money, and commonly used signs. Rachel can identify values of coins with assistance and can match up to 7 words with corresponding pictures. . . . Rachel has difficulty focusing on and comprehending the important information in conversational speech. Cognitive/language tasks such as reasoning and problem solving are very challenging to her. Her speech is intelligible, with a consistent th/s substitution. She speaks in sentences with adequate grammatical structure. She tends to speak in a loud tone of voice. Her expressive language is abundant, but often

not related to the topic of conversation. She also tends
to repeat information over short periods of time. . . .
She has a tendency to forget or lose personal possessions
and needs to be closely monitored and reminded to
complete tasks.

—II. Student's Present Levels of Educational Performance
   IEP October 7, 2004

LIFESHARING

"Where is Rachel living now?"

This was the question everyone asked when we returned from Israel, where we had lived so well in our separate apartments, hours apart from each other.

"With me." And hating it.

She had passed her twenty-first birthday and was again living with me, in a house I had bought before we left for Israel. Only now, if anything, she was more miserable. She did not say she was lonely and bored and sick of my demands, complaining instead that I was a *b-i-t-c-h* and that her sunny new room, with its chaise and computer setup, was "stupid and ugly." She hated "the whole household," with the noisy dogs that should "just shut up"; they were morons and should "shut the f . . . up." Like the spelled-out b-i-t-c-h, the "f . . . " perhaps stood as an acknowledgment that she was on shaky grounds with her cursing.

She would not—or could not—stop. When I had enough, I'd send her—or push her—outside to wait for the bus. She was strong. It was like trying to move a fridge. My bedroom was in the front of the house. On those mornings after I'd managed to work her outside, I'd go upstairs to dress, hear the birds chirping and my daughter cursing

at full volume—"stupid moron dogs, shut the f . . . up!" Then, sometimes, silence. A neighbor had appeared, or a dog walker. I knew this
because suddenly it was "Hello! How are you? Where are you going?"
Usually I was in my underwear by then, powerless, no time to even
throw on a robe when I'd hear her say, "Come here!" and imagine
her waggling her finger. Outside a total stranger would be zipping
up her backpack or closing the front door, as she had asked.

I understood what Rachel felt. I hated my mother's telling me
what to do—controlling my life!—and had left home when I was
eighteen. Charlotte had done the same at seventeen. And here Rachel
was nearly twenty-one.

"Why doesn't she move?" people asked. "There are all these group
homes."

Everyone had examples: Houses where distant relatives or a
neighbor's grown child lived. Group homes in Erie, Pennsylvania,
or northwestern New Jersey. Did I know about places like these?
Should they send me the names of their friends? Would it help if I
had some contacts?

I didn't mean to be rabbinical, but the clearest response to this
complex question was another question: You know the debate about
cuts in Medicaid spending? I found myself asking. The money that
would allow Rachel to live in a group home—a community living arrangement, or CLA, as these smaller dwellings were now called—was
Medicaid money, and there wasn't enough of it. That's why Rachel
lacked the services she needed, why she was still living with me. It
was why there were waiting lists for all kinds of mental retardation
services. It was why, according to a *Post-Gazette* article, eight hundred
special education students had graduated in June 2004 "only to learn
that there were no jobs and services available to them." It was why
there were waiting lists in forty-six states.

I didn't elaborate on the details, unless I was asked (as I often was)
if I might be able to pay for housing myself, rather than waiting for
funding. Then I had to explain further that it wasn't simply a matter
of paying rent on an apartment for my daughter, something I could
have managed. Nor was it finding the money to pay for a day program
and her transportation, among other things. To live apart from me,
Rachel needed twenty-four-hour staffing. That was what I'd heard
called "the big ticket item." So, no. I could not afford it myself. In the

upcoming fiscal year, there was funding for sixty-two new openings in Allegheny County, and they would doubtless be offered to cases more dire than Rachel's. Apart from the new openings were those that occurred when someone died or moved from the state and therefore left the funding in place. For Rachel to be considered for one of these rare "fully funded" openings, it had to be in an apartment where the roommates were physically able young women also in need of twenty-four-hour staffing. In the meantime, the state was pushing something called "lifesharing," a program that placed "clients" into private homes. Adult foster care was how I explained it.

The part about Medicaid cuts and the waiting list was easy for people to comprehend. The part about lifesharing no one could grasp, not a single person. I would watch people try to take it in but then simply refuse to believe what I was saying. It happened each time I tried to explain. I knew why, too. Despite the budget deficits and the war in Iraq, the United States was still the richest country in the history of civilization, and this was a time of unparalleled affluence for many. It was impossible for most people to understand that there was so little money allotted for social services that the "lucky" recipients being taken off waiting lists were being offered lifesharing—adult foster care.

It stunned me, coming from Israel, where Rachel had lived in her lovely little apartment at Kishorit, to find that foster care was the American answer for disabled adults. By this time, I had learned that Kishorit was an uncommon model, even in Israel, and that advocates there were also struggling to get people with mental retardation out of institutions and into their communities. If anything, Israeli policy was two decades behind U.S. policy, with more funding available for institutional care and 60 percent of this population still institutionalized. Still, our economy, alarming budget deficit notwithstanding, was far more sound than theirs. And the United States stood as the bastion of democracy, or so our government claimed.

Sometimes, even months after having been told about lifesharing, I would start to explain it to someone and have trouble believing my own words. When that happened, all I had to do was open a Pennsylvania Department of Public Welfare bulletin from February 2005 that vigorously promoted this option. Lifesharing, defined as "living with and sharing life experience with supportive persons who form a caring household," offered more individualized attention for the client, and more consistency than in group homes, where the staff was often paid minimum wage and the turnover rate was high. It was also "more cost effective for the system."

· · · ·

Why should I have expected anyone else to grasp lifesharing when I had difficulty comprehending it myself? I first heard the term on a mid-August morning in 2004, several days after Rachel and I had returned to Pittsburgh. We were sitting in a chilly conference room with Michele, who'd been assigned Rachel's case after Jeanette disappeared. Both of us were feeling mellow. Rachel was freckled and serene after her happy stay in camp, and I was still cushioned by my time in Israel. In our bad-news-is-good-news world, the death of Rachel's father had elevated our PUNS score, bumping Rachel from the "critical" category into "emergency." Officially she was classified—along with 2,046 others—as "needing services immediately," so we were in a better position than before we left for Israel.

Michele was upbeat, too, full of reassurances that things would work out well for Rachel, and that we'd find her a place to live by the following June. She'd heard rumors about possible openings on the South Side, and near the airport in Moon Township. People had been waiting for us to return, eager to meet Rachel. Already Michele had two interviews lined up for her, one with an agency that was anticipating a fully funded opening in a house in Penn Hills, and another with an agency that had a lot of success with lifesharing, where the client lived in someone's home.

I was nodding and yessing, hugging myself to keep warm, absorbing Michele's optimism. Even so, I failed to take in the detail about the client's *living in someone's home.* True, I was busy decoding all the new acronyms that had replaced the familiar ones, and trying to take in the complex details about funding streams and types of waivers. I was distracted, perhaps, my thoughts darting back to the unpacked cartons all over my new house, and ahead to the time line itself—by June 2005—that I'd held onto, like a dog with a bone. Sitting in the conference room with Rachel and Michele, I could feel the imminence of that dreaded "someday," its hot breath coming closer.

I had readied myself for what lay ahead. The move to a different house, my decision to get a dog and to clear my life of all unessential commitments until Rachel was placed—these were things I did to prepare myself for this last difficult stretch, during which we had to find (and fund) a place for her to live, find (and fund) meaningful daytime activities. *We*, because although I knew that all my effort had to be devoted to getting Rachel settled, I also understood that my diligence alone was useless and that I had to depend on the supports coordinator who managed her case. I liked Michele and was grateful that she was energetic and upbeat. If she wasn't the first person to work hard on Rachel's behalf—Katie had obtained Rachel's funding for summer camp; Janet, another supports coordinator, had gotten Rachel into Title XIX before I fully understood how limited the slots were or that it was a prerequisite for any residential placement—she was the most attentive, calling every day or two to update me on leads she was pursuing and conversations she'd had on our behalf.

Michele was a former nun who lived with her partner and their two dogs. She never complained about her job, despite the long hours and a salary that was about one-third of what a New York City sanitation worker earned, after the same number of years on the job. In this era of tax cuts and slashed social service budgets, it was not easy for her to find adequate services for the eighty-five clients in her caseload. While I understood why so many supports coordinators left after a short time to find better paying or more rewarding positions in and out of the system, I was counting on Michele to stay with us through this period. At the same time I was aware that one day I might call her office and hear the receptionist say, "Michele K. is no longer an employee"—just as had happened with Jeanette.

I put Michele's contact information under "temporary numbers" in the memo section of my Palm Pilot. It was a ridiculous and superstitious maneuver that would not protect me or make me feel less lost, less alone, less frantic, if she left. Still, it was all I could do, and so I did it.

In every other aspect of my life, I was inclined to grit my teeth and push on alone, but it was impossible to plan Rachel's future by myself. Michele held the key. I needed to depend on her to think of Rachel when there was an opening in a CLA that might be appropriate, a rare house where the roommates were women, close to Rachel's age, ambulatory, not medically fragile, roughly at her cognitive level. I needed to trust that Michele would "put her up" for that spot. When the day came that supports coordinators from all the agencies "presented" the clients they deemed suitable for the opening, I had to trust that Michele would make Rachel's case in such a way that she would be chosen. If the coveted space went to someone else, I needed to trust that Michele would keep on making Rachel's case. It wasn't only housing. I also needed to trust that Michele was familiar with the different kinds of day programs in the area and could find ones with available spaces and show them to us. I needed to trust that she would be able to secure the funding necessary for Rachel to attend. I could make phone calls (and did), could advocate (and did). I could visit work sites and tell other people that Rachel was graduating, and that I needed to find her a place to live and activities for day and night. I did this, too, and was always asked, "Who's your ISC?" I needed to depend on Michele, needed to count on her to stay; I needed to push without alienating her. I had no other choice.

In this anxious state, with so much rocketing through my brain, I found myself processing information slowly on that August afternoon, then racing to catch up. Michele had finished her cheerful description of lifesharing when I started to take in what she had already said. Rachel living in someone else's house? Like a foster child? It was so far from what I had imagined as her next step—especially after Kishorit, where she had gained such independence. It would be moving backward for her to live like a child in someone else's family.

Michele tried to reassure me that it wouldn't have to be that way. Rachel would still have responsibilities in the host home. She'd have to get herself up in the morning and go to school or work, just as she was doing while living with me. She'd continue with her activities, only the host family would be responsible, instead of Mom. Michele had been in touch with an agency that had set up a lot of these host homes, and she was thinking of arranging an interview for us in a week or two.

A host home? It felt utterly wrong to me, a kind of stopgap solution for incompetent parents. Most troubling was that it subverted every goal we had set for Rachel, every plan we'd made. Rachel's outbursts reminded me that she needed peers—not another mommy setting the rules. If she'd been able, I was certain she would have said so herself.

I didn't want to consider this option, even for a minute.

"Sure," I said, because I had to. "All right. Fine. Set up the interviews."

Take Rachel to every interview and look at everything that's offered, I'd been told. Do what it takes to get her into the system. You can move her after she's in. Then there were the instructions I gave myself: Rely on Michele, trust her instincts, trust that she'll stay, that she'll keep working on Rachel's behalf, that she'll think of us and advocate for us until Rachel is happily settled.

I put my trust in Michele.

At night I dreamt that I had lost my arms; in their place, useless rubber prostheses dangled from my shoulders. The situation didn't particularly stress me at first. It was only as time passed, in this dream that seemed to last for weeks, that I began to come up against all that I could no longer do: Write without dictating to someone. Wash my hair. Make dinner by myself.

Find a place for Rachel to live without Michele's help.

So "yes" was where I felt I had to begin, no matter what I felt in my bones.

• • • •

"No," Charlotte said, when we spoke by phone. "Don't even *go* for the interview. It's just *wrong*."

This was before she'd moved home and immersed herself in this world, before she had a second role, as a filmmaker, working on a documentary about Rachel's transitional year. Charlotte's "no" felt like the response of a sister whose complex feelings had taken a turn in the months since her father's death. Though I'd never said, "Now you are the only one left," she had, without discussion, begun to shoulder some of the responsibility for her sister's well-being. When she returned to Pittsburgh in late September to start shooting the film, she became an equal partner in our search to find Rachel a place to live and a life she would enjoy, my confidante in these matters, my ally and sounding board.

My praise annoyed her. She was making this film because it was the natural thing to do. It didn't make her a good person. "Stop thinking I'm this great sister to Rachel, because I'm not," she told me.

Maybe she was right, and making the film was simply a natural

thing to do—the way, for me, writing about Rachel was natural, inevitable. Even so, her powerful "no" was one of the many things that
made my head pound during the drive to one of the interviews Michele had set up. I felt in that "no" the response of someone who was
a generation younger than I, more idealistic, more easily outraged. I
also felt that it was the response of someone with nothing to lose if no
placement was found. Still, seeing Rachel beside me, with her stormy
expression, and her explosion of uncombed curls, I was humbled by
the passion of Charlotte's "no"—and by its stark contrast to my own
feeling of having useless rubber arms.

Glancing at Rachel, I wished I could discern the reason for the
belligerent look on her face. Was it PMS, a bad night's sleep, or a
grudge she could not articulate? If I was going to reach her, it had
to be right then in the car, because as soon as we walked into that
conference room, it was over for me. Even if Rachel said she had a
cat, that her favorite movie was *The Mask*, that she loved to eat at
Bob Evans, and that she was best at word searches and crossword
puzzles—information that had been dutifully recorded, though none
of it was true—I had to keep silent. Knowing these trivial pieces of
fiction had been accepted as fact didn't matter as much as the overall
way the search for what Rachel wanted was conducted. She'd been
asked, for instance, if she was satisfied with the services she was
receiving. And where did she hope to go after graduation? When
Rachel said Monroeville was where she wanted to work, her request
was written down. Monroeville is a suburb, not particularly close to
where we live, not a town where we have connections. Perhaps it was
a place name that Rachel liked, the way I liked Moon and Plum. It
made me think that if she had answered, "the moon," her ISC would
have written, "Client wishes to live on the moon."

Add to this the fact that I had no idea what might constitute a successful interview. Would she get points for seeming more mentally
retarded than she was? Or less? Would it benefit her to be cute and
charming and seemingly shy? Or was it better if she exhibited one
of the behaviors that made her so difficult to parent, proving to the
interviewer that "what mother reports" was reliable? Even if I'd possessed an official list of do's and don'ts, it's hard to imagine I would
have been able to coach her in any way.

That morning, after we parked the car, I said, "We're going to a meeting. We're going to talk about your getting an apartment. When the people you meet ask you where you want to live, what will you tell them?"

"With *you.*"

Before I could call out, "You don't!" she had pushed inside the building ahead of me, snagged a pencil from the receptionist, and from the waiting area grabbed a magazine with Oprah smiling on the cover. Trailing behind, I envisioned "Client wants to live with her mother" recorded in her file.

Michele was already in the conference room. Beside her, waiting to meet Rachel, was Christy, a dark-haired and dimpled young woman who radiated such good cheer it was as if she had been untouched by misery of any kind. She shared some glowing reports about the clients her agency had placed in people's homes, then turned her attention to Rachel.

"I hear you're a very active young lady."

Rachel sat with her chin lowered, clutching the pencil and magazine.

"Mom says you like bowling."

"Idon'tknow," she mumbled.

"And basketball. You play on Sundays, don't you?"

"Idon'tknow."

"You're a great swimmer, too, I hear. I bet you swam a lot at camp, didn't you?"

Rachel sat with her eyes averted, hanging onto her booty. The questions would go nowhere, I knew, as Christy went on, calling out each activity that Michele had recorded—Special Olympics! Music! Dancing! Walking on the track! Pool!

To every enthusiastic mention, "Idon'tknow."

Christy was indefatigable. "Mom says you're a vegetarian. What kinds of things do you like to eat?"

Unable to bear another "I don't know," I said, "Do you eat hamburgers, Rachel?"

"*No.*"

"Then tell Christy what you like best for dinner."

"Salad."

"What else?"

"Pizza."

Christy dimpled. "Sounds just like a teenager."

On it went—Christy's chipper questions, Rachel pleading the fifth, until, without warning, the big one was popped.

"So Rachel, where do you want to live?"

Rachel pointed her pencil at me.

I held my breath.

"Far away from *her*."

"*Not* far?" Christy asked.

Michele started to laugh.

I simply exhaled, for one small moment full of relief.

· · · ·

I began to do some lifesharing of my own. Barrington was his name. I'd found his photo on the Internet; I saw his warm dark eyes and nicely trimmed goatee and knew at first glance he was the one for me.

Barrington was a year-old miniature schnauzer, housebroken, good with kids and other dogs, who'd been left for unknown reasons at a shelter an hour north of the city. That's all it said in the Petfinder description beside the winsome photo. It was all I knew—all anyone knew. Even so, the competition to adopt him was fierce. I called the shelter the afternoon his listing was posted and was told that dozens of people had already requested an application.

I labored over the questions on that form. Not so much the easy ones about my prior experience with dogs or the kind of home environment I would provide, but the ones that asked me to write about training and discipline and the theories I followed. What would make me return a dog to a shelter? "Unprovoked biting" was my answer to that one.

Afterward, when it was too late to change, I regretted my hasty response. *Nothing,* I should have written. Nothing could wrench him away. Maybe it was a sign of my weakness to confess, once again, that I was the kind of person who could give up. During the wait to hear from the shelter, I wondered if I'd been damaged by my struggles with Rachel. Maybe I'd be unable to take care of anything, even a dog.

When the call came, I drove to the shelter to meet him, still troubled by these thoughts. Then he was brought from the kennel, shivering and unsure, with an awkward orphanage cut and a bow tied to his collar. I kneeled down and said, "Hello, Barrington."

The sound of my own voice surprised me—its softness and warmth. It was the voice that had been released when I first became a mother. I'd forgotten it was still inside me—hadn't known, until that moment, that it had been killing me to sound so harsh.

I expected that he would have problems. Why else would his original family give him up after a year? The dog trainer I had consulted grimly warned me to prepare for the worst: You don't know who this dog is, and you won't know for months. His good behavior is temporary. He could become aggressive, could turn into a beast that froths at the mouth, could maul your neighbor's child and eat your shoes. You never knew with these shelter dogs.

Barry—what we called him from the start—didn't morph into a vicious monster. As he grew more comfortable, he became mellower and sweeter, responsive to everyone. When we ran in Frick Park, he turned back if he got too far ahead, making sure I stayed in his sight. When I called his name, he raced toward me, kicking up his rear legs, bunny style. More important was the simple pleasure of taking care of a creature that liked me. He wanted breakfast the very instant he woke, just like Rachel—but his tail wagged, and he twirled, sat obediently, and twirled again. He did not call me a bitch (though I assume if he'd been able it would've been a term of endearment or a simple fact). Nor did I care if I was pathetic for enjoying an allegiance that some claimed was based solely on my role as food provider. I had needed this simple exchange badly without knowing it, had missed the fussing and tending that once, long ago, I was able to do.

I liked this dog. I liked the sound of my own voice, free of irritation, when I called him. Even Rachel enjoyed him, perhaps because he always listened when she called his name, no matter how many times he heard it.

· · · ·

It was when I returned from running Barry in the park that I found a breathless message from Michele on my voice mail. "You know that opening in Penn Hills?" she said when I reached her. "Rachel has been chosen. They're really excited to meet her."

"Wow," I said, a little stunned.

Charlotte was puzzled when I phoned her with the update. For months I'd been sending her news clips, information about federal programs and county agencies, links for sites that gave the details about slashed budgets and waiting lists, all so she would see that my struggle to help Rachel find a life after school was not unique, but part of a national crisis. I'd claimed that it would take a year of relentless work if anything was going to happen. And now this, so soon.

"It's only an interview," I told her, embarrassed yet hopeful. "Whatever happens, it's only the start. And nothing may happen. You never know."

Driving to the house with Rachel a few days later, I found it hard to act as cool as I'd sounded with Charlotte. I couldn't help thinking what a nice transition it would be, if Rachel could move from my house while she was still in school. The CLA was less than twenty minutes away; already I imagined taking her to dinner once a week, having her stay over if she liked, picking her up on Sundays for her activities at the JCC. Without the nagging and bickering and morning warfare, I could repair our relationship, become the treat-giver and source of fun.

It was a nice house, a tidy ranch, set at the top of a steep, winding road in Penn Hills, a hilly suburban neighborhood. Built as a group home in 1989, it was pristine inside and out, with sturdy furniture and inoffensive hotel-style décor. The house manager had worked here for over a decade. The other staff—two obese women flipping through magazines at the table—had also been here for years. In this way, it was everything I wanted for Rachel: a clean, pleasant house, close to where I lived, with a staff that was not transient.

In the bright living room, one resident was curled on a couch, face in the cushions. Another sat with a diaper in her hand, spitting and rocking vigorously. Every so often, one of the aides looked up from her magazine, said, "No spitting!" and praised that client for using the diaper to wipe her face. There were two other residents: a young woman with shiny curls framing a pretty face, devoid of expression, and a thin man with one ear and a lobster-claw hand. No one approached Rachel as the house manager showed us the bedrooms, the kitchen and laundry area, the yard, where we saw the van they used for trips. No one smiled or touched our arms. No one noticed that we were there.

No, I thought, trying to squelch it. Don't turn down anything. Get her in the system and you can move her later. Nothing can be done until she is in the system. Just get her in.

She'd be safe if she lived in this nice, clean house. The staff would get to know her. There'd be school and Goodwill and JCC; on the weekends, she'd have Special Olympics and time with me. It wasn't as if she'd be here for that many hours. I'd be close and see her often. It wouldn't be terrible.

"No," I said when I was outside with Michele.

She nodded. "It wouldn't harm her being there, but she wouldn't get anything out of it."

As soon as I drove off, I felt a chill of fear. Maybe I had made a huge mistake. Maybe nothing else would come up in the little time we had or Michele would quit. Maybe my "no" stemmed from a kind of vanity that Rachel, herself, did not possess, and I was still struggling foolishly to make her more like me. Maybe my "no" came from the surprise of seeing her with the spitter and the man with the lobster-claw hand. Maybe . . . Still, no one had looked up when she walked in. No one noticed her. She could make no friends here, could find no community. It was away from me, but nothing more.

"People model," Jezelle, Rachel's longtime companion, reminded me when I told her what I had seen. Rachel, in particular, absorbed others' habits: her grandmother's throat-clearing, one friend's habit of asking people for their e-mail addresses, another friend's squeak, her father in the midst of a phone call saying, "Let me switch ears."

I knew Rachel better than anyone else did, and I trusted my answers more than I trusted hers. Still, I was only guessing when I tried to figure out what she'd like best, and my guesses were shaped by my own biases and observations, by what I saw in her, what I imagined for her, what I believed was important. When I turned down the house in Penn Hills, I was reminded that despite all my scrutiny, Rachel remained a puzzle. I could never really know for sure.

• • • •

Observing Rachel at Goodwill, where she went every weekday afternoon, I was tormented by these same questions. She'd been placed in the production area, a large, open loft-like space, where her job was to gather garments from a box and put them on hangers. The present goal was for her to start by independently gathering five to six items in an hour, and then to work her way up to twenty.

As soon as I was on the floor, I could see that the job wasn't right for her; she would never succeed. In this noisy, echoey place, full of distractions, she was supposed to choose a hanger of an appropriate size and get the garment to fit on it properly. The task clearly frustrated her. Even as I was telling Rachel's supervisor about her success at Kishorit, how there, she was seated, with her work in easy reach—even as I was describing that task as satisfying, the way beading had been, even as I was joking that maybe it helped that in Israel not everyone spoke English—I was wondering. Maybe I was wrong about this, too. Maybe it was foolish holding onto this last dream I had for Rachel—that she would work. I remembered the Goodwill evaluation from the year before, suggesting that we look at day programs, and my firm rejection of that advice.

Now, as I was reiterating what I wanted for Rachel and why it was important, as I was explaining why she needed structure, why she needed the same sequence of activities, as I described how she thrived this way—even as I was endlessly advocating on her behalf—I was thinking of the house in Penn Hills, of the empty bedroom in Rachel's kibbutz apartment, of my own fatigue.

· · · ·

A woman named Karen, with seventeen years of experience in various capacities "in the field," wanted to open her home to a person with mental retardation as part of the lifesharing program. Michele thought Rachel might be a good match, so on a cool, sunny afternoon, we drove to Karen's house.

"We" by then included Charlotte and her cinematographer, Eddie. They'd arrived in time for a dance party we hosted for Rachel's twenty-first birthday, with pizza and cake, and salsa lessons from Carmen, her favorite teacher. Along with them came Becky, another Petfinder match, rescued from the streets of Puerto Rico, with a dachshund's winsome face and short legs, and a muscular shepherd's body. Her gangrenous tail had been amputated, and she wiggled her whole hindquarters in tentative greeting.

When they arrived, the house came alive with noise and conversation. There was the dogs' constant rough-and-tumble play and the

fun of meeting Eddie. It was an adjustment going from three crea-
tures to six, and there were times when I couldn't stop myself from
worrying about sheets and clean towels and what everyone would
eat. There was the awkwardness of a camera in the kitchen at 7:00
A.M. when I was barely dressed and already quarreling with Rachel.
Even this was offset by a kind of relief. Let someone else see what
happens. Let them see that sometimes it was my own bad mood that
triggered Rachel's outburst, and other times it was her frustration at
having put her shirt on backwards or losing her shoes. Often, though,
the rage ignited for no obvious reasons. It was hard to see myself on
video, to see on my blank face the look of someone who has departed
her own body, who is there and not there. I knew it was from the
effort of forbearing, of holding everything in check. But to see that
everything had been leached out of me, all my laughter and sorrow,
stunned me. Still, having witnesses eased my guilt about being a bad
mother, a whiner and selfish betrayer, the kind of person who could
tend to a dog but was abandoning her daughter, feelings that ran
parallel to the voice that said, "No one could do these twenty-one
years much better."

Rachel was the star of the documentary and the complex, demanding center of everything we did. "The family business," we called
her, only partly in jest. After all, we lived with her, wrote about her,
captured her on film, talked about her constantly, shared documents
and information, repeated the details from phone calls. All night long,
I heard that strident *Ma!* Sometimes the call came from Rachel in the
flesh. Other times, I replied to a taped Rachel, replaying on TV.

Though the neighborhood where Karen lived was rundown, her
house was spotless. Karen was a single woman, tall and handsome,
with stylishly cut hair and a pressed denim shirt. She had no children, only the exuberant dachshund that twirled at our feet. The
TV was chattering away in the living room, where Michele, Christy,
and Larry (a man from Christy's agency) sat. After a few minutes of
forced conversation, and lots of questions Rachel could not answer,
Karen left the room. She returned a moment later with a doll in a
clear plastic storage case, which she held for Rachel to see.

"This doll is something like forty-one years old, and look what
good shape she's in! That shows you how good I take care of things.
Come on, let me show you around."

She took Rachel to see the empty bedroom on the ground floor. "There's a room upstairs, too, but look what this has. Come here; look, there's room for all your things."

The closet was empty, and the adjoining bathroom gleamed. Karen opened the medicine cabinet to show its bare shelves.

"You can bring whatever you want. You like to bowl? I'll take you bowling. You want to bring friends here? You can bring all the friends you want. I'm good people. Mom says you like popcorn," she said, climbing the stairs to the second floor. "We can make popcorn in the microwave."

The doll, the empty rooms that seemed to be waiting for someone to fill them, her openness—these things tugged at me. I could sense her loneliness, could feel how eager she was to have company. Rachel could never be the companion Karen was looking to have, I thought. Then I stopped myself and changed course, imagining them sitting together, eating popcorn and watching TV. Maybe if Rachel had all the attention she needed, in a house where there were few distractions, where people weren't rushed, where there were no pressing obligations, maybe she could be that companion. Christy had said that people interested in lifesharing had "caring hearts." Maybe it wasn't a village Rachel needed as much as the steady attention of a single, willing soul with a caring heart.

It was strange imagining her living with someone else, like a confession of my incompetence. Yet it felt better imagining her here than in the house in Penn Hills.

Karen and I exchanged phone numbers and arranged for Rachel to visit for a few hours the following Saturday.

All week I thought about the doll in the plastic case, and the bare rooms in Karen's immaculate house. If Rachel lived with Karen, would she be coddled and cosseted, allowed to revert to total dependence? Would that kind of attention allow her to retain the behaviors that drove other people crazy? I knew there were serious problems with finding and retaining reliable staff to fill the minimum-wage positions at CLAs. But there were other roommates, potential friends, with their own quirks and demands, who would tolerate only so much annoying behavior. And there was companionship.

I imagined Karen giving Rachel absolute free rein to wear what she wanted, eat what she wanted, to use the bathroom when she wanted;

I imagined her retrieving every tissue Rachel dropped, pouring every glass of water. Would my daughter then be a more pleasant person? And the quality of her life, would it be better or worse? Would it be harder for her to cooperate at work—to hold any kind of job? Would she wear out Karen, the way she had quickly exhausted one roommate after another at Kishorit?

And what if Karen agreed with me that Rachel had to pitch in and help with the chores she was capable of doing, if she had to wake to an alarm and go to whatever activity was planned for her during the day? What if she pushed Rachel to dress in clean clothes, appropriate for the weather, to leave the house with her face wiped and teeth brushed? What if Rachel had to wash her dish or put it in the dishwasher, use a teaspoon of sugar in her tea and not a half a cup—my desires, not hers. If Karen agreed with this, though Rachel herself did not, *then* what? Would she enjoy Rachel after the honeymoon phase? Was there another mother who would not mind being followed around the house, who would not be made loopy by Rachel's barrage of questions?

Maybe yes. Maybe Karen would enjoy it and Rachel could live there, and see me for dinner, and hang out with me on the weekends. Maybe I would build a different kind of relationship with her, a better one, with less strife. Maybe it would work.

On Saturday morning I called Karen's number to confirm our date. A drawling male answering-machine voice told me no one was home. Later that day, I heard the same lifeless voice. Christy confirmed the number. Still, I was never able to reach Karen.

"A miscommunication," Michele called it, when I spoke to her on Monday. Karen had thought we had decided upon Sunday.

I called to apologize and reschedule. The machine man picked up again. No one could tell me what had happen to Karen, least of all "him."

At our next meeting, three months after Rachel's return from camp, Michele was less buoyant. The rumored openings were in fact rumors; the only actual news she heard about housing concerned further cuts. There was another family interested in lifesharing, though, a couple on the North Side with two small children. I shouldn't panic. On account of the letter I wrote before I went to Israel, Michele's boss understood the urgency of finding Rachel a place to live.

I was surprised. "The letter was taken seriously?"

It was. Around the time I sent it, a mother had left her twenty-two-year-old daughter at a police station. The daughter remained in respite care, still awaiting permanent placement.

I wanted more details, yet, in truth, I really didn't need them. I could not imagine leaving my daughter at a police station. Despite my threat, I knew I never would. At the same time, I fully understand it. There is a point when you reach the end, and it can come out of nowhere. You do, you do, you do, you bear up, you get on with things, you live around the edges, you skitter in the corners, away from this tyrannical person, this daughter, this overwhelming, beloved, impossible being. And finally, one day, you can't.

I could imagine the reasons. Maybe this other daughter screamed day after day or smeared shit on the walls or knocked her mother down. Or maybe she was medically fragile, with gastric tubes and catheters, and when the nurses quit without notice, the mother could not cope. Maybe this daughter's needs were unquenchable and her ability to give in return nonexistent. Years may have passed this way. Ten and then twenty.

It was somebody else's life, not mine. Some callow, helpless person, not me. The stuff you read in the newspaper—distant, and easily forgotten.

I was all right, I really was. There were the dogs, and the pleasure of Charlotte's company. But I wouldn't be all right in June, and I knew it.

PART 2

13

Jane [reading e-mail from Dov]: "I miss you so much tonight. I dreamed about you. I'm having a literature seminar in college. I took an English lesson and we read scientific articles in English. Two days ago I had a small English test and today I'm having a bigger English test. Bye and have a good time. I really hope to see you soon." It makes my heart ache; it really makes my heart ache.

Charlotte: Why not just e-mail him back?

Jane: And say what?

Charlotte: My name is Rachel and I'm a big bitch. I'm really, really mean to my mom, my sister's making a movie about me, and I'm going to live with strangers in the middle of nowhere.

—From a taped conversation, March 2005

AT EMILIA'S

Her name was Emilia, and she lived with her husband and two little boys in a townhouse on a highway north of Pittsburgh. To me, it was a distressing nowhere kind of place, off a busy road dotted with stores, but Emilia, who was reserved and said little, told me she was happy there. She liked the trees and the playground behind the houses. She was less certain about why she wanted to have Rachel live with her family or what it would be like. When I asked her, she said, "I'm home with my boys anyhow." It was the kind of answer I had hated hearing when I interviewed caregivers for Charlotte, many years back. Weren't you supposed to love babies, if you were looking to care for one? And if your reasons were less pure, shouldn't you be clever enough to claim you adored babies anyway?

Emilia continued. Her sister did this—"this," meaning lifesharing—in Ohio, where Emilia and her family had lived when they first came to the United States eight years earlier. Emilia sometimes helped out, providing respite or backup care when her sister was unavailable.

It was early December 2004 when I sat in Emilia's long, narrow living room, where the TV chattered away like an oblivious guest. It was six months until Rachel's graduation. After the opening in Penn Hills and the disappearance of Karen, there had been nothing. No openings, rumored or actual. The funds allotted to take sixty-two people off the waiting list had, indeed, gone to the most desperate people, those whose parents had died, who had nowhere at all to live. For Rachel, there was only Emilia—or perhaps there was Kishorit. I'd looked at the footage I'd shot while I was there, and once more saw the sun and flowers, the bright apartment with the kitchenette, where she made herself tea each morning. I hadn't forgotten the roommate's bedroom with the empty bed, or Rachel standing outside the dining room, calling out to other residents. Still, it seemed better than anything Michele had shown me.

I felt in my heart that lifesharing was not the right next step for my daughter. She needed a push into adulthood, not another family. Yet, out of desperation, I kept moving forward, hoping I might be proven wrong, or that something better would turn up. As Emilia's little boys, aged three and five, spied on us from around the corner, then quickly retreated, I found myself wishing that it could work, thinking that maybe other people in another family could give Rachel something I was no longer able to provide for her.

"She can be difficult," I said.

Emilia laughed. She was a pretty young woman, with a lovely lilting voice. "Oh, she can't be more difficult than my own."

Yes, she can, I thought. With her own, there was the usual arsenal of rewards and punishments. They might not always work, but they worked often enough. She could build toward something with these two little boys, who kept peeping and disappearing in giggles. She could see them change and grow, learn social skills, gain independence.

I said none of this, because it seemed cumbersome and heavy-handed for a first meeting. Instead I asked a few more questions and found myself wondering what she thought of me for placing my own daughter with strangers, for giving her up. It was a strange dynamic. What rights did I have at this point? Why should Emilia bother listening to anything I had to say?

• • • •

Winter arrived early, with an inch or two of snow falling every day for nearly two weeks. In the park, where I walked the dogs in the morning, it was beautiful to see the new snow covering the boughs of the trees and the trails—soft, white, untrammeled. But the snow was often slick, which made the workaday world hard. Waking up each morning, I never knew if the school bus would come or if Rachel's afternoon companion, very pregnant, would be able to drive. I didn't know how I would marshal the energy to find—and train, and trust—someone new after this companion's baby was born. It was the winter when flu shots were carefully rationed. I didn't know how I'd work if Rachel got the flu and had to stay home from school.

Worst of all was the prospect that, after graduation, Rachel would live with another family, instead of in her own apartment. I couldn't believe it was the only thing out there for her. Knowing that it was, I pushed on, arranging for her to visit Emilia's house twice more—once for a day, and the second time with an overnight stay. Both times, when I arrived to bring her home, I paused in Emilia's foyer, hungry for details. When I asked how things had gone, Emilia said, "Oh, she was fine!" in a kind, rather surprised way. "She was no problem at all!"

Did Emilia have *any* questions? Any concerns?

"No, nothing. Not yet. Everything's been good."

It wasn't that I wanted Emilia to have problems as much as I was hoping she would ask me about Rachel. How much can she see? Does she get anything out of watching TV? Can she read? How much does she understand? These were the kinds of questions that the best of her staff asked from the very beginning. Can she walk for a half hour? Is she okay in the bathroom alone? Does she know how to use a knife?

Emilia asked nothing. Perhaps she was shy. Perhaps I was being insensitive to someone whose culture was different from mine, who might not feel comfortable asking me direct questions, or who did not think in an analytical, questioning way. Still, how would I know what was really going on when everything was simply "Fine." How could I trust this woman—this stranger—if she could not tell me a single detail about the day's events?

Christy wanted me to trust Emilia. "She likes Rachel a lot, and the boys are really excited about her visits. They fight over who's going to be with her. 'My Rachel.' 'No, she's *my* Rachel.'"

I was pleased that Emilia seemed genuinely to like Rachel, and I thought perhaps that in Emilia's house, where people were more relaxed, Rachel might become more easygoing. Maybe she did like being in a family, albeit not mine. Maybe she was like the people in the stories I had read on Web sites or in the newspapers, stories that bore out the state's claim that "individual satisfaction and positive service outcomes" were higher for people in lifesharing than in other living situations. Without exception, the people in the Web site photos were middle-aged. It was easy to imagine that they had been in institutions most of their lives and had no families of their own. Perhaps when they were babies, their parents had been pressured to give them up. Not so long ago, the advice was to institutionalize children with disabilities. Parents were encouraged not to visit or to look back. Stories were beginning to surface of middle-aged siblings finding their never-mentioned brothers and sisters who had been sent away, excised from the family as if they had never been born. In an earlier time, that had been the system, too, the expert advice, the right thing, better for the marriage and for the other children.

Now the "right thing" was lifesharing.

I could see it working for people who had been deprived of family life and possessed the capacity to enjoy it. I could imagine it as *one of many* options, rather than *the answer*.

Though Emilia didn't waver in her interest—or so we'd been told—the holidays arrived, and with them, school vacations and out-of-town trips. It grew difficult to plan the next step. December passed, and then January. If it was a relief not to be preoccupied with lifesharing, this break still brought us closer to Rachel's graduation. Time was ticking away, while I stood around, with no clear direction, only the knowledge that I had to keep pushing. Rubber-armed or not, I had to make something happen. I couldn't slack, couldn't afford to lie down on the job, certainly couldn't get sick.

Never in Rachel's lifetime had I been sick in bed—until that January, when I got the flu. She didn't like it either. One feverish memory: the *feeling* that Rachel was standing in the doorway of my bedroom, studying me. I thought I conjured this up until I felt someone yanking the comforter off me and demanding, "Get your lazy butt out of bed!"

What would I have done if Charlotte hadn't been there?

Restless in bed, I kept turning over the options. I fell into sweaty sleep, mind buzzing with anxiety, and woke shivering to think: if Emilia didn't come through, *then* what?

The number-one alternative, proposed by many well-meaning

friends, was what I thought of as the benevolent-dictator solution. It went like this: "Suppose you hire one person whose full-time job is to be with Rachel—one *really good* person . . ."

This meant trusting that I might find the elusive Really Good Person. And that this person would become a slave to Rachel and me, and never leave. And that she would have limitless patience, while somehow giving Rachel the autonomy she craved and the life she deserved.

Or was it the job of the Really Good Person to keep Rachel chained, as if under house arrest? To let her out only for approved activities, while I stood in the background, monitoring her food intake, her grammar, her choice of attire?

There was also the issue of paying for this Really Good Person. Even if I could, I kept rejecting this idea. History and common sense had shown that there was no such thing as a benevolent dictator.

Second only to the benevolent-dictator solution was this: "Send her back to Israel."

This was assuming that Kishorit would even take an American resident, given the waiting list of Israelis. It was assuming, too, that each year I could come up with the "tuition" and airfare.

Another family in Pittsburgh was also thinking seriously about Kishorit. The father, Avri, was Israeli and had relatives near Carmiel. One night, while Rachel and their son, Josh, played Uno in the next room, Avri asked what I thought about sending Rachel to Kishorit along with Josh. The two of them had known each other for years and got on so well. Rachel seemed to delight Josh—even her nonstop talking amused him.

Things had not gone so well for Josh since he'd graduated the previous June. In the beginning he stayed home, with nothing to do. After weeks of delays, his parents were finally able to find funding for him to enroll in a work-training program. The goal was for him to start at a hospital, wheeling patients or working in the records room. Despite the glowing reports about Josh's abilities, the placement had never come through. Avri dropped by the program unannounced and hated what he saw: so many people in his son's class just sitting, doing nothing. He'd given up on the United States, he said. Their son wasn't going to live in someone else's house. As for those group homes: did I *know* the kind of people who worked in those places?

Yes. I knew about the abuses and the high turnover, common in minimum-wage positions. I'd heard about insensitive, ill-educated staff. But there were also dedicated, caring people. You had to stay close to your own child's situation. As a parent, it was simply what you had to do.

If I sent Rachel to Kishorit with Josh, Avri's family would visit every week. They'd make her one of their own. He wanted to know if I'd consider it.

"Yes," I said, feeling something clench inside me.

"Pretend she's going to college," said the mother of a high school senior. "People send their kids to school in L.A. or overseas and see them four times a year. It's not that unusual."

A wise friend agreed. Wasn't this the time when I was supposed to be focusing on Rachel's adult life, thinking about what would be best for her? "Everything you've said points to the kibbutz."

Even Charlotte, looking at the footage from Kishorit, said, "Send her to Israel."

It wasn't the separation; we were both ready for that. It was that if I sent her to live many thousands of miles away, she would lose her place in our family, no longer be one of us. I would be giving up on my staunch insistence that she was ours. More than that, though, was the memory of our phone calls. If we were apart, I could call her every night, just as I had done in Israel, hear her voice, and never have a sense of how she was. I would be thousands of miles away, unable to intuit whether she was sick or well, happy or badly treated.

I said yes because I was supposed to be thinking about her life, not mine. I would send her back to Israel if I had to. It didn't feel right, but neither did any other option: not keeping her home, not having her move in with another family, not sending her thousands of miles away. I felt this when I was feverish with the flu. When I was back on my feet, my mind once again clear, the choices seemed no better.

• • • •

On a snowy, sleety day in February 2005, four months before Rachel's graduation, a group of us met in the conference room at the not-for-profit agency where Christy worked. Seth, the agency's director of rehabilitation, was at the table, and I had asked Rachel's longtime companion, Jezelle, to come to the meeting, too. If lifesharing was the only option for the present, maybe Jezelle could serve as the respite person, as Emilia had done with her sister.

Seth talked first. He was a great believer in lifesharing. If it was up to him, he'd close all the CLA's immediately and move everyone into lifesharing, except for maybe one or two clients with medical issues.

And someone like Rachel? Since she wasn't with us, I tried to be candid about the behavior issues that didn't show up during short "interviews": the talking, the manipulation, the oppositional behavior.

I was describing the mornings in our house, how sometimes simply trying to get her to dress was a struggle, when Seth began to laugh. Maybe it was a little further out on the continuum, but he had a three-year-old and a five-year-old and what I described sounded just like the scene at his house every morning.

No. It was different. "You can't use reason with her."

"Like my wife," he said.

It was *not* like his wife, I said, with obvious irritation.

"Don't take it personally, but when it's mom and her daughter, you know, those buttons get pushed."

Again I tried to explain that Rachel had a history of behavior problems.

"I have no doubt there are other pieces, but moms tend to lose perspective."

I could feel the room divide just then: on one side those of us who knew Rachel, and on the other side the providers, trying to jolly us out of our concerns.

"Has she had any behavior management?" he asked.

"Many years of it," I said. "Until her funds were cut."

"What strategies work with her?"

"Nothing works consistently."

"You just never know with Rachel," Jezelle added. "Some mornings, nothing can get her going, and then other times—I can never figure out why—she's just the most cooperative."

I could weep, hearing someone else say it.

Seth again, with that unctuous smile: "My wife is like that."

Christy, sunny as always, explained that the agency worked with families when problems arose. They had behavior management specialists who stepped in, and there was monthly monitoring. "And I always have my phone with me, if there's a problem."

If I had worried that Karen would simply grow tired of Rachel, my worries about Emilia were more complex. She seemed good-hearted but naïve, and the boys were so young. Rachel would chew them up. "She can be very challenging," I said. "And with two small children on top of it . . ."

"Emilia thinks she can manage it."

"What do you know about her?" Charlotte asked.

"She's very enthusiastic, and her children love Rachel. They're really excited about her visit."

Later, Jezelle said, "They just don't understand. This Emilia has two small children; it'll be so much easier for her to just do things for Rachel. I hate to see what's going to happen to Rachel after all the gains she's made."

For all the gains, yes; because, despite all the cursing and the irritating habits, she *had* made gains. Beneath the layer of annoying behavior, we had glimpsed a layer of ability. Fight to get her out of the house, fight to focus her, fight to make her do the things she did not want to do, and ultimately she did them happily. Who would do the job when I was not on top of her?

• • • •

A cluster of little Esthers, in tiaras and sparkly dresses, stood outside the JCC when I pulled up to the entrance with Rachel. It was Purim, a festive holiday commemorating the triumph of the bold Queen Esther and her Uncle Mordechai and the downfall of the evil Haman, a day for costumes, noisemakers, and fun. On one side of the gym, tables were set up with games of chance. Across the room were inflatable play areas, where little kings in capes and crowns tumbled down slides, and superheroes and ballerinas bounced in plastic balls.

I gave Rachel seven dollars for tickets for the games and left her to meet up with her group.

It was April, sixty-seven days before graduation. All we had in place was a worksite for Rachel, a big warehouse, where the workers seemed old and unkempt. Since August, no one had asked to interview Rachel about any living arrangement. Michele no longer mentioned openings or rumors. I had called the Department of Human Services deputy director; the county liaison; the representative from an advocacy organization put in place by the federal government to oversee county services; and the president of Achieva, a major Pittsburgh advocacy group for individuals with developmental disabilities. Yes, it certainly was a bad situation, everyone agreed. "Hold on to what you have." "If you intend to make that deadline, lifesharing is your only option."

Maybe I really would send Rachel to Kishorit; I let Avri push forward on that.

Meanwhile, I had agreed to a monthlong trial period at Emilia's that would begin after the Purim carnival. We had chosen April as the trial month despite—or because of—Rachel's long spring break, ten days without her usual routine. Let Emilia experience a long stretch of time with Rachel when she had no programming, I was told. That was as much a part of the reality of living with Rachel as the "covered days," when she had school, work, and the JCC.

Charlotte was angry with me for buckling, and while I agreed with all her objections, I found myself packing Rachel's big duffel bag with clothes, medications, and instructions, replaying what I had been told on those phone calls: there's no money in the system. People sometimes waited years for family members to be placed. Lifesharing is cheaper.

When I returned to the JCC three hours later, I found Rachel in a balloon hat that looked like a chicken. She'd put all the money I'd given her into vending machines and bought too many bottles of soda to hold. One bottle slid from her grasp; a second fell when she tried to get the first; a third began to slip. The chicken hat was askew. She was squealing with fury when the bottles slid, when she couldn't jam them in her pockets, when they fell and fizzed at her feet.

All the way to the North Hills she fixated on the soda bottles, enraged that I wouldn't let her take them into Emilia's.

"Maybe there is no right place for her," I told a friend later that night, after I'd dropped Rachel off.

I'd never uttered anything like this before—never allowed myself to think it possible. Always I had believed that her capacity for happiness was her greatest attribute, that she would be content if we could help her fit into the right kind of life.

Maybe I'd been deluded and it was all downhill from here.

It was the lowest I'd ever felt.

That night, I could hardly sleep. When at last I drifted off, Emilia was screaming at me: Emilia in a dream, saying Rachel couldn't stay with her anymore, not for another day; she was kicking her out for having spilled a glass of juice at dinner. And I was arguing, furious: *That's* why she can't stay with you, because she spilled her *juice?* That's nothing! If you think that's bad behavior, you don't have a clue.

The next day, on the phone, Emilia said, "Everything is fine! No problems at all!"

. . . .

What did happen at Emilia's that month? Rachel was in good spirits when I took her to dinner four nights after she had moved in. During our short meal, she kept asking, "Am I going back to Emilia's?" She was eager to leave me and return to the North Hills. It buoyed my spirits, seeing her this way.

I had arranged with Emilia that I would pick up Rachel at nine on Sunday morning. When I arrived, everyone in the house was asleep, including Rachel and a woman I'd never met, who occupied the bed beside hers. I had to wake my daughter, root in her open suitcase for something clean to wear, and haul her into the car without medication or breakfast. It was unsettling that she was sleeping so late, and that Emilia hadn't bothered to get her up, even though I had asked that she be ready. It wasn't a major infraction, though it was troubling that during this trial period, when most people tried their hardest, Emilia was so lax. Still, Rachel seemed happy. I reminded myself that wherever Rachel lived, her life would be different. She would adapt to someone else's rules and culture and ways of living.

Let it go, I thought, when I was home again. *You have to let it go.* I didn't yet know what "it" was exactly, or how much of what I wanted for her I needed to give up. Too little time had passed, and anyhow, she was so eager to finish with me and return to Emilia's.

I had to attend a conference in Vancouver several days later. Charlotte had arranged to film some of Rachel's time at Emilia's while I was gone, simply to document this experience, not to spy or report back to me.

On my second night away from home, she called me at the hotel, crying. "Mom, you *cannot* leave her there. It's horrible. They do nothing. They stay home all day long, watching the country music channel. They never went out, not once, even to the store. The kids have no toys, and they're rough with her. She says she has to cover her chest because they touch her. And no one talks. No one said a word to her at dinner."

"No, no problems at all!" Emilia said when I called that night to ask how things were going. "Everything is great."

"No problems" had begun to feel like a blackout. It meant no information, no sense of things. "Everything is great!" became a wall I could not scale.

Emilia saying, "Everything is great," Charlotte saying, "You cannot let her stay here." Rachel, the most unreliable source of information, capable of giving me five different responses to the same question, telling me she was happy there and wanted to stay.

What if I agreed to this? She'd be at work during the day, wouldn't she? Work, then social activities. I'd be part of her life, and so would Jezelle. Emilia's would be a base, a starting point for now, not forever. There'd be no other nine-day periods spent sitting in front of the TV tuned to the country music channel.

"This is what Americans do," said a scornful friend. "They watch TV. Not everyone talks as much as you do."

Different. A different culture. Was it a crime if this family slept in on a Sunday, or if sometimes she had cereal for dinner, as she had told Charlotte. Was that even true? And if she was happy and safe, did it make a difference? Could I still complain?

Maybe we were scrutinizing Emilia too closely—a whole gang of us judging her unfairly by our standards. But we weren't the only ones: Marissa, who ran the teen program at the JCC, complained that Rachel was dressed inappropriately for the weather, and that her hair was greasy. When Marissa told her to wash it, Rachel said she couldn't, because I hadn't given Emilia any money for shampoo.

Of all the hearsay and allegations, this disturbed me the most. I couldn't imagine Rachel inventing this detail about money for shampoo, or overhearing it in another context and taking it for her own.

• • • •

At the midmonth meeting, we piled into Emilia's living room, the system on one side, the family on the other. Emilia sat between us, curled on her recliner, hugging a pillow, quiet, young, uncomfortable. Officially, this was a time to talk candidly about Rachel's stay thus far, to air whatever problems might have surfaced. Seeing Emilia in the recliner, hugging the pillow, I knew it would be hard to elicit information from her; I'd have to be careful not to start out with accusations or third-hand information.

That wasn't all I was trying to manage. We were losing Michele. It wasn't the same as in the past, when Jeanette, an earlier supports coordinator, had vanished without warning; this time, the whole unit was closing. The hospital that operated it also provided services and was therefore in competition with itself, which was against the law. Supervisors at the base service unit (Michele's boss, for instance) had long known about the upcoming closing, but others—including supports coordinators and families—did not.

The change was handled in a way that felt awkward and heartless, with families being asked to choose new providers before they knew where or whether their current supports coordinators would be hired. Days before we received the official letter explaining the changes, Michele had called to warn us about what was happening. In the midst of her explanation, she began to cry. We were the family she had worked hardest with, her number-one priority. She wanted everything in place before the unit closed. She was also worried about herself. She and her partner had just bought a house. She didn't know how she would make the mortgage payments without a job.

The rupture was painful and frightening—especially now, with so little time until Rachel's graduation. When I left this meeting, I had to take our complex history somewhere else. It was like beginning a serious romantic relationship in middle age. All this baggage—the details, the time lines, the personalities.

Meanwhile, we sat awkwardly at the midmonth meeting, exchanging niceties. Emilia, barefoot, hugging the pillow; Christy, starry-eyed and full of optimism. Charlotte was glowering, though perhaps not noticeably. Only I had seen the veneer of the detached filmmaker crack, revealing underneath that she was a fierce defender of her sister's well-being. It had always been this way: even during times when she ignored Rachel, or was ashamed of her, or hated Rachel for spurning her affection, when she felt cheated that Rachel was her only sibling, still she would knock to the ground anyone who mocked her sister or threatened harm.

Rachel was elusive, impenetrable. It was disrespectful to speak about her, as if she was made of wood; foolish to expect, as Christy did, that her answers truly indicated what she wanted.

"It's been *good,*" Emilia said, in that soft, lilting voice. I believed it was the truth as she saw it.

It was not enough. I asked what her mornings had been like.

"Good. She gets up without any trouble."

And after school?

"She's been fine." Again, the slight surprise at my question.

Had she been cooperative about using the bathroom and showering?

"Yes."

Was she washing her hair?

"Yes."

"Marissa said her hair looked greasy."

"It was the shampoo we were using. I bought her something else, and her hair looks much better now."

"And the boys? What do they feel about having someone new in the house?"

"They like her a lot. They fight to be with her. *My Rachel,* they call her."

"Are they rough with her?"

"No."

"What about her talking? Has it been a problem?"

"No."

It was pointless. I looked around the room at Christy's dimples and Michele's hopeful face, and Charlotte, rigid with anger. This wouldn't be the way I would get information. It wasn't going to happen in this room, with these people all saying, *Fine! No problem at all!* I would get nowhere here. I felt foolish, ungrateful, insensitive—and ashamed in front of Charlotte.

"You cannot consider this an option," she said when we were leaving. "It's horrible."

What about the fact that Rachel seemed to be happy there? If she hadn't, it would be different—if she asked to go home with me; if she cried when I pulled up in front of Emilia's, or if she showed some sign of unhappiness. She had complained before—about Kelly and Jezelle. She screamed and resisted when she didn't want to go somewhere.

"It's what she says now because it's new. You know the way she is. Ask her when she's been home for a while."

. . . .

It was true, of course. On her first night home, six weeks before graduation, I asked Rachel if she wanted to go back to Emilia's.

"Yes," she said.

At breakfast the next morning, I asked again. "Would you like to stay with Emilia?"

This time, "No."

"Why not? You liked it there!"

"The boys are too rough."

"Do you want to go back to Emilia's?" I asked the next day.

"No."

"Just to visit. For an afternoon."

"No."

"Are you sure?" I asked another time. "Even for an hour?"

"No."

We drove to Emilia's the following week to retrieve some of the clothes we'd left there. Rachel would not get out of the car. Even so, it was hard to trust what she said, hard to know for certain what she felt.

. . . .

Later, after so much had changed for Rachel and for me, I watched some of the footage Charlotte had shot while I was in Vancouver. Emilia is at the computer; Rachel sits on the couch two feet away, the little boys bouncing beside her. In the background, country music plays on TV. The kids are whacking each other with a stuffed animal, their only toy. They throw the stuffed animal at Rachel and bop her on the head. Then she bops them. The giggling and screeching escalates steadily. "Gabby, stop," Rachel complains. "Gabby, quit it." Emilia never looks up.

Rachel tries to hoist herself off the couch. The boys push her down. "Gabby, get off!" she yells. At last she manages to stand. She is huge and bulky compared to Emilia's wiry little sons, and strangely docile. The boys keep hitting her with the stuffed toy. It's the play of very restless little boys. Rachel doesn't seem afraid or upset as much as defenseless, standing there with her shoulder raised.

Later, Emilia is upstairs. You can hear the drone of the vacuum over Rachel's plaintive "Gabby, get off." She is standing in the corner of the living room, and the boys, giggling and full of energy, try to climb on her back. They knock her against the wall and jump again, one and then another. It's as if they're in a playground, and my daughter is the only piece of equipment there.

14

Virtually the day a student graduates—the day, the moment—all of his educational entitlements end. . . . My measure of a successful transition plan is that that person's not sitting home on the couch, but that person can wake up the next morning and have a job, have a volunteer position, whatever that particular student wants to do. . . . School districts by law have to provide information on transition, so there's a lot of information out there. The impediment that creates the most problems for families, though, is that there's no funding. So you can have the best plan in the world, but funding is critical in order to implement that transition plan following graduation.

—Nancy Murray, former president of Achieva

COMMENCEMENT

On commencement day, sixteen graduates walked or rolled up the aisle in emerald-green mortarboards and flowing academic gowns. Beneath Rachel's shiny gown was an open-backed dress we'd bought for the occasion, navy blue cotton with tiny appliquéd whales. The dress was nothing to her. She didn't care about the dress or the pink T-shirt with the New York skyline in sparkles, or the pink linen skirt with the ruffled bottom. She didn't care that her sister had pushed for her to have these new outfits (and others). She didn't care about the sandals with metallic green straps that we picked out for her, the purple polish for her nails, the hair clips or the bracelet studded with rhinestones. What thrilled her was the strapless bra she got that day. The bra, the "high heels" with the ankle straps, the beaded prom dress. These she loved. The prom itself, which she attended with her old friend Josh, was nothing compared to these items. They took hold in her mind, and for the next few months they became the only things she wanted to wear, no matter the weather or the occasion.

On commencement morning, she'd been unhappy that I would not let her wear the heels, but I agreed to the strapless bra, necessary beneath the open-backed dress, and that was enough to help her move past her disappointment with little fuss. That afternoon, when I saw her in line with her classmates, her face was glowing, and I could see that graduation meant something to her, though what, I could not guess. Watching her march in with her classmates, I was impressed by how focused she was, by the way she took note of us sitting in the audience, then continued up the narrow aisle onto the ramp, finding her seat on the dais with ease, and waiting with great poise during the introductions.

Prior to this modest ceremony, held in the multipurpose room on the lower level of Rachel's school, I had been apt to complain about graduation exercises, with their long, banal speeches about the meaning of success, the facile parsing of commencement—"noun; a beginning"— and the tedium of sitting as hundreds of graduates took and shook. I had feared that this graduation, too, would be saccharine. A month earlier, families had been asked to send in photos for a PowerPoint presentation along with a few words that described our daughters or sons. I had fretted some about how this material would be used.

That afternoon, as each graduate received a diploma, those photos were projected onto the screen, along with a sentence or two about future plans, and I saw that my concerns were groundless. What a range of abilities and personalities there were among these young men and women who made their way up the ramp, who spoke clearly or with difficulty, who signed or used a language board, whose plans included entering a therapeutic day program, training for supported employment, or staying home; whose aspirations included working at a home-improvement store, taking classes at community college, or simply having fun; whose hobbies included playing with the dog, watching wrestling on TV, or going to the airport to see planes take off and land. Graduates were described by family members as "outgoing and kind," as "unique, good looking, and honest," as "stubborn, funny, and persistent," "a real character," "friendly, talkative, and lively." These last words were my description for my graduate, sitting with her hands folded on her lap, looking lovely and serene.

All of the "scrapbooks" projected onto the screen started at the beginning. Baby beside the family dog, or posed on Santa's lap; baby on a fuzzy rug; at a birthday party; on a couch between siblings. Some of the parents sitting with me in the audience had been unaware of their child's disability when those photos had been snapped. Others,

I supposed, had been told the kinds of things we had heard: *She will be blind. There is a high probability she will be intellectually impaired.* Looking at the pictures of the graduates as babies, I remembered the first weeks after the diagnosis, when I cried so hard I thought the force of my grief would turn me inside out. So much could set off my sadness in those days: teddy bears, flattened squirrels in the road, frail old people, photos of injured dogs, sunny days, rainy nights. Sometimes the whole world was a minefield. The years of worry came back just then, different from the ordinary anxiety forever entwined with love: years of wondering if "intellectual impairment" was a euphemism for "retarded" or if it would be something milder, of worrying whether Rachel's failure to meet a certain milestone was a sure sign of this kind of impairment, and, if so, how impaired she would be.

Still, for all the grief, all the dashed dreams, all the concrete pronouncements every parent in the room had surely heard (he will not walk; she might not speak; she will be blind; he might not use his hands), the soft, sweet nature of babies allows parents to hope. We believed that the diagnosis was wrong, or the prognosis would be better than expected. We trusted that the world would be kinder, that there were strategies yet to try, revolutionary treatments just around the corner. Some of us believed in miracles or answered prayers. They were babies, adorable, every one.

Like Rachel, with her curls and porcelain skin, standing, reaching for her diploma.

Charlotte and I had chosen the photos projected onto the screen because they were favorites. Still, it was wrenching to see these pictures from a time when the four of us were a family. The young mother in those photos was weary now; the vibrant father was dead; the big sister with the long hair and round glasses who had *lived* Rachel's story had stepped in, shouldering so much responsibility for someone her age.

In the early days, I could hear awful news, stumble in despair, get up and find something I believed was still possible for my daughter. A psychologist could say, "It's going to be devastating," and I would believe his prophecy for one blazing moment, feel the truth of it, and then forget, the words extinguished, as if incinerated in the heat of that moment's grief. Gone, forgotten. I was too busy working with my daughter. No matter how accepting I was of the news, something remained possible. The walls were not up, the complex picture not yet fully observed. She will not care about her sister's fierce protection of her, will not care about the shopping trip or the backless dress, but she will love beyond reason the strapless bra. Who could have predicted this? She will need in a heartless way, unable to give back. She will talk and not stop.

During the ceremony, one of the graduates, a tiny, slender girl with curly hair and big teeth, kept calling, "Ma? Mommy?" and rising from her seat. My heart jumped the first time I heard that. It took a moment for me to see that my own curly-haired daughter was quiet and composed, the mortarboard perfectly balanced on her head. Another girl was calling "Ma?" Another mother darted forward to coax her back into her seat. The woman was small, like me, and single, I assumed, because in the next part of the ceremony, when the graduates, one by one, presented a rose to their parents, she ascended alone, as I did.

I cried throughout the short, sweet ceremony, salty tears streaming down my face, chest aching, as if my heart was still bruised. I was not sad, though—not entirely. Sitting on a folding chair up front, I couldn't name all the complex emotions I felt, but I knew that hope was one.

We had seen a house that we loved. A place for Rachel.

It was a homey ranch on a long, hilly street in a town near the airport. This house on Sycamore Street had a warm, lived-in look, and a deck out back, with a glider and grill. The house manager, an energetic woman named Nina, talked with affection about the "ladies" who lived there, about their swimming nights and bowling league and their trips to the ballpark to see the Pirates suiting up. While Nina was telling us these things, one of the residents sat beside her, eager to be part of the conversation. Each time she interrupted, Nina said, "Not yet. You'll get your turn." I liked the firm, pleasant way she related to this woman.

After the visit, I stood on the sidewalk outside the house with Charlotte, taking in the sweet smell of freshly mown grass. When Wendy, our new supports coordinator, caught up, she waited for my response.

"Wow," I said. It was all I could manage.

"As her sister, I'd be proud to visit her here," Charlotte said next.

A broad slow smile crossed Wendy's face. She knew it was a great house, had predicted we would respond the way we did, and had waited for our reactions before letting us see her own.

· · · ·

I didn't believe that someone like Wendy existed when I attended a "fair" to meet staff from the three remaining providers eight weeks before graduation. (A "fair" instead of an "information session," I guessed, because along with the literature at each table were souvenir pens and flashlights, Band-Aid dispensers, and key chains.) It wasn't a very festive event—Charlotte and I were the only ones pocketing the goodies—and I wasn't a particularly cheerful "consumer of services." I dreaded losing Michele and starting all over, with new people at a new agency. Though I continued to push hard for Rachel's move, I no longer believed that anything good would come of it. I thought about her move as a way to get in the system. A necessary first step. I didn't allow myself to imagine there might be a house like the one on Sycamore Street, where she could have the kind of life she deserved.

I recognized a man standing at the middle table, so I approached him first. With so little time, I had no choice but to be blunt. My daughter was graduating in June and needed an immediate placement, I said. All we'd been shown these last months was lifesharing, something that wasn't right for her. What about *your* agency? Was lifesharing the only housing option you're offering clients at this time? What do *you* think about the statement from the state's Office of Mental Retardation claiming lifesharing was superior to other residential options? What's *your* personal opinion? What's your agency's stance? How do you handle clients on the emergency list?

I listened to the responses this man (the director of mental retardation services for his agency) and a coworker gave—listened, then realized that I actually understood what I was hearing. I wasn't simply standing there, bleary-eyed, distracted, and confused. Something in their crisp replies made it clear that these people knew the system and understood our particular objections to lifesharing for Rachel. There were no sweet, vague descriptions of loving families opening their homes and of happy clients fitting right in. No, lifesharing was an option; it was being pushed hard for the reasons we already understood. At this agency, they'd seen successful lifesharing arrangements and dreadful ones. Same with community living arrangements—CLAs—where some houses were run exceptionally well and others were so substandard the agency would show vacancies to no one. Without question there were serious budgetary constraints and very few openings, and people sometimes languished on waiting lists for years. But the people from this agency said they'd support our desire to see Rachel in a placement we deemed appropriate. They promised to do everything possible to make it happen by June.

I decided to transfer Rachel's case immediately, rather than waiting until June, when our base service unit officially closed. The day after the fair, I called to set up a meeting. When we convened the next week—without Rachel—the supervisor we'd met at the fair brought along a supports coordinator she believed would work best with us. Her name was Wendy. Reserved is how I would have described her at the time. Later in the week, she would visit Rachel at work. In the meantime, Charlotte and I were trusted to represent Rachel and to respond in her behalf. Instead of the flawed, laborious, literal process of staff questioning Rachel and recording her responses verbatim, we got to talk about Rachel's likes and dislikes in a candid, detailed way, to convey as clearly as possible who she was and what might work best for her.

Our plan was to find a CLA for Rachel—not simply a place where she could move, but a perfect place. It was April 26 by then, so we agreed on a backup plan: respite. A temporary placement in a CLA would be preferable; if that was unavailable, and it was absolutely necessary, then respite in lifesharing.

After we'd settled on this, Wendy asked if we'd chosen a worksite for Rachel. We had. The last thing Michele had done was secure the funding that would make it possible for Rachel to start in a supported employment program, since a day program of this type would cost roughly fifty dollars a day. "Okay" was how I described the site to Wendy in an offhanded way: a big, noisy warehouse, where the workers were old. Michele had liked it a lot because the site had a steady contract to do packaging for a local brewery; at other places, there wasn't enough work coming in and the workers were sent home for weeks at a time. With graduation looming, it didn't seem like a priority to change what was acceptable, especially given Michele's caution about getting budget approval for Rachel to enter a work program. Only Charlotte knew that it made me sad to imagine Rachel in this dark place, among this group of unkempt, unloved-looking workers, more my age than hers. This is how it is, I'd been told, a fact of life that the workforce at these sites was largely middle-aged. It was why I hadn't visited another worksite, why I had said little of what I'd felt.

This team agreed that it was crucial to have the funding for this program in place by graduation. The difference was that they encouraged me to look at more worksites.

"You don't have to compromise," Wendy said.

The next day, Wendy made arrangements for us to visit four other worksites. A day later, the details arrived in the mail: time, contact information, driving instructions.

How profoundly different one place was from the next. At one site, the workers were kept busy with major contracts from the federal government to manufacture desk calendars and other office forms. They used equipment that cut large sheets of paper and shrink-wrapped the final product. The workers included able people who'd struggled with substance abuse or mental illness or chronic unemployment. On a tour of a second site, we heard about the workers putting price tags on sunglasses and sizes on hangers, but we saw them sitting idly at long tables. The room was grim; the lunch area smelled of sour milk. When Wendy asked, "What do people do when there isn't enough work?" she was told, "They stay at home."

"You can never ask, 'Is there enough work,'" she told us afterward. "People will always say yes."

Wendy knew what to ask and how to ask it. When she heard, at another site, that the staff-to-worker ratio was one to sixteen, she said, "I don't like that. It's also against the law."

One site, then, would have been dangerous place for Rachel. At another, she might have been idle for long stretches of time. At the third she might not receive the training and support she certainly would need.

We saw something else, though: a bright, cheerful worksite with a quiet room, and an adjoining room where the radio was tuned to an oldies station. The fifty-five workers, busy on that day with various assembly jobs, were of different ages and abilities (one woman had been trained to use her feet), and the ratio of staff to workers was one to eight, far lower than the mandated ratio of one staff member to fifteen workers.

I didn't despair that I would be leaving my daughter to sit idly in a gloomy warehouse. I could imagine her here, learning a job she could enjoy and making friends. It gave me a good feeling about her future. And so, even before we saw the CLA in Sycamore Street with the awesome house manager and the glider out back, I had begun to see what the future could be for Rachel. I could dare to imagine a better, more fulfilling life.

Wendy's attitude—her determination not to settle—helped me overcome the sense I'd had of myself as a beggar, on the dole. Her persistence had a contagious quality that let me silence the inner voice that said, *just be grateful we're giving you anything at all.* Michele and Christy believed in the fundamental goodness of people and institutions; they viewed Rachel as malleable and sweet, or so it seemed. Wendy's optimism was different. It served as the engine behind her drive to find a day program and a residential placement that would be perfect for Rachel, rather than grabbing whatever was available and trusting that it would work.

When Wendy took on Rachel's case she did something else that changed my daughter's fate: she looked at houses where there was no funding in place. The house on Sycamore Street was one such place. Whoever had vacated had taken her funding with her. Michele would not have pursued the opening because Rachel didn't have nearly enough money in her budget to cover the expenses. Wendy's strategy was different. She visited all the houses with openings that seemed appropriate, and when she saw one she liked, she invited us to look next. That was the first step. We shared her enthusiasm, and the staff who met Rachel thought she might fit in well with the women who were already there. Two more visits had to be scheduled next: the first for dinner, the second for a full day's visit. If those get-togethers went well and Rachel still seemed compatible, Wendy would ask the agency to submit a budget. If the budget was reasonable, she would petition the county for the necessary funds that would enable Rachel to move.

On commencement day, all of those ifs remained. Money was tight. Wendy couldn't guarantee that our petition would be approved. If the budget was reasonable, she thought our chances for approval would be very good. In the meantime, she continued looking for other openings that seemed promising, and she sought out lifesharing providers, in case no CLA came through.

Christy's agency recommended a woman who was interested in lifesharing and also willing to drive Rachel each morning to the new worksite we'd chosen. (The Americans with Disabilities Act of 1990 guaranteed equal access to transportation, so paratransit was available to Rachel. However, there was no route between this woman's house and Rachel's job.) Five days before commencement, Charlotte and I took Rachel to meet her.

I was taken by this woman's warmth at first, the way she closed her hands over mine to say hello, by the display of trophies and photos of her kids that dominated her crowded house. Now it was Christy and Wendy on one side of the living room and Charlotte, Rachel, and I on the other, and the same stilted conversation, slightly less awkward because this woman was especially garrulous and kept things going, chatting about her kids and their accomplishments, the empty room in her house, the fun she would have with Rachel, the trips they'd take to the amusement park, the snacks they'd eat, the job she loved, despite its 7:30 start time.

I interrupted, puzzled. If she had to be at work by 7:30, who would drive Rachel to her job?

"Oh, my boyfriend said he could take her. And my friend Joyce, up the street, said she'd pitch in."

I looked at Rachel sitting quietly, at her soft, sweet, freckled face.

Christy did, too. "They have all their clearances," she said, ever cheerful.

I knew that anyone wanting to work with Rachel had to submit to a criminal background check and a child abuse history clearance first. But it was not enough.

When I phoned Christy a few days later, I asked how she felt about Rachel moving into this house, where a boyfriend I'd never met and an unknown neighbor would be responsible for her care.

"They have their clearances," she said again.

"So you think that situation is okay."

"Lifesharing is being part of a family, and families are part of a community where everyone pitches in."

I remembered her telling me in the fall that lifesharing providers were "people with that special caring heart." At that moment, her description felt reckless and naïve.

Nor was I alone in feeling this.

After that visit, Wendy was determined to find Rachel a CLA. "I could not imagine her living there," she told me some time later. "I remember thinking, 'Over my dead body . . .'"

All I knew, sitting on the folding chair at Rachel's commencement, was that Wendy had encouraged us not to settle for a worksite and we had searched until we found something we loved. Wendy had encouraged us not to settle for lifesharing, so we pushed on, taking risks I would never have attempted without her support. Nothing was in place when Rachel stood to receive her diploma; nothing would be in place for another two months. I was nervous, without question. It was a different kind of nervousness, though. Even if I had known on commencement day that Rachel would never live in the house on Sycamore Street, I would have believed that we would find her a place to live. Not any place. Not just a bed in someone's house. Someplace that would be perfect.

15

Wendy: Do you want to live in an apartment or a house?

Rachel: Both.

Wendy: Doesn't matter?

Rachel: No.

Wendy: And you want one or two or three female roommates?

Rachel: I don't care.

Wendy: Or four or five?

Rachel: Let's try to go up to ten, as many as possible.

Wendy: So you want to live in a sorority house!

Rachel: No, like ten roommates, that's what I'm saying.
As many as ten roommates. You know what I mean?

Wendy: All right, so you want a whole bunch of female
roommates around your age. And do you want to be
close to where your mom lives?

Rachel: No.

Wendy: You want to be far away from where your mom
lives?

Rachel: Yeah.

—From a taped conversation, April 2005

HOW IT HAPPENED

All through June and into July, the house on Sycamore Street was everything I wanted for Rachel. Each morning I woke, seized with the determination to get her into that empty bedroom, with Wendy's help.

In reality, there was nothing I could do apart from dreaming about the long, hilly street lined with neat houses, and it was killing me. "I know it has been hard for you to manage the uncertainty surrounding Rachel's residential placement," Wendy wrote in an e-mail on July 6. "I know that you have an intense desire to actively do something to improve Rachel's chances," she wrote the next day. "I know it's maddening to sit and wait for a response that determines so much about Rachel's life and future, but it's what we need to do."

I waited for a second visit to be arranged. Then I waited while Rachel spent the afternoon with the other women on Sycamore Street. I waited to hear if that visit went well, and when she was still deemed compatible, I waited for the budget to be drawn up. Two years before, when there had last been a vacancy in this house, the budget had been $58,000, a figure Wendy thought was quite reasonable. While I was reminded of the great expense involved in supporting those who are less able, that sum was far less than the average annual cost of care for a resident in a public institution in Pennsylvania, which in 2002 was $157,656.

When the new budget for this vacancy was at last presented, it was $71,000, a figure that panicked me but seemed to dishearten Wendy only slightly. She had in hand budgets from two other agencies that managed CLAs twice as expensive. Wendy planned to include this information with Rachel's request so that people at the county level would see that the Sycamore Street house, "where Rachel could be happy and grow as a person and have all her needs met," was also the most fiscally reasonable option.

So I held onto the dream of Sycamore Street and let myself hear Nina say once more, "These ladies *love* to go out."

· · · ·

While I was trying to figure out what to do in Rachel's behalf— and doing nothing beyond obsessing—Wendy continued to look for backup housing. That summer, she presented Rachel for four fully funded openings. In three situations the roommates were significantly older and nonverbal, and placement wasn't really appropriate. Wendy had thought of them as possible "starter houses," where, if all else failed, Rachel could live for six months or so, eventually "trading up," this time with the budget attached, money she could take with her when she looked for a more suitable place to live.

The fourth opening was different. The roommates were Rachel's age and, on paper at least, seemed compatible with her. Though Wendy hadn't yet seen the townhouse apartment, she'd heard it was particularly nice. The providers were eager to meet Rachel. She wasn't the only contender: three other young women were also invited to visit the house. Even so, it was a fully funded opening, something we could not afford to let pass.

Wendy didn't need to remind me how rare this kind of opening was. Ten months had passed since Rachel had been asked to visit the house in Penn Hills. Ten months since I'd turned down that placement, believing my decision was right, though I was tormented just the same.

Of course we would visit the house, I said.

My heart was not in it. It was as if I was betrothed, as if, having found the one I loved, I did not really want to look so closely at the others. During the short car ride, I kept recalling the small, ordinary things about the house on Sycamore Street that had charmed me, the glider on the back deck, and Nina's cheerful energy. It made me eager to find fault with this new house, whatever its value. On the drive past strip clubs and bars, on the outskirts of a town that had once bustled with manufacturing and now looked bleak and abandoned, it was easy to hold on to my loyalty.

The apartment—the last in a row of five attached units in a handsome beige brick structure—was on a busy road beside a car repair shop, in an area with undeveloped land and the remnants of industry. Inside, the unit, "Ehle A," was airy and starkly new. It had an open kitchen–living room area that was supersized in that uniquely American way that made the furniture, itself outsized, seem tiny. One of the roommates had just returned home from the worksite where Rachel would go in August. She was an outgoing young woman whose desires were close to the surface. Within a few minutes we learned that she intended to move from the supported workshop to competitive employment, to lose weight, to learn to cook healthy food. She escorted us past the carefully lettered "do not enter" sign she'd posted on her door to show us her room, with its knickknacks and diplomas, photos of her boyfriend tucked into the edges of her mirror. The second roommate returned a few minutes later—the curly-haired graduate who had called "Ma!" during commencement. She greeted us by saying, "I hate you," and flapping her arms. A staff person redirected her in a coolly efficient way, saying, "No you don't," but she kept wheeling around to say, "I hate you!"

Once again, at the end of our visit, we stood outside with Wendy and shared our reactions. As I was explaining why I liked the Sycamore house better, I kept thinking how astounding it was to be able to say, "The other house seems homier." I knew even then that this house had some assets. It was closer to my home. The workshop we'd chosen for Rachel was only a few minutes away and run by the same nonprofit provider as the house—a good omen, since I had such positive feelings about the worksite. We wouldn't need to arrange for paratransit to get her to work and back, either. Staff could drive her and her roommate to work.

Only a short time ago, the options for Rachel—at home or with Emilia—had seemed so cruel. Now I was saying, "She would be fine here, but the roommates at the other house seem a better match." I could imagine Rachel hanging out with the women in the Sycamore house, while here, I had no feeling at all.

· · · ·

It's true that love is blind. In its first mad flush, we tend to push away whatever troubling glimpses we have of the loved one. When I left to drive Rachel to the Catskills, a week late for camp, with nothing yet decided about her housing, I knew that the house on Sycamore Street wasn't utter perfection, knew and chose to ignore it.

The first hint had come early on, when I had taken Rachel for her second visit. A stranger answered the door, a woman who seemed puzzled to see us, as if no one had told her that Rachel would be staying for the day.

"I'm sure it's in the log," she said. I invited myself in while she perused the logbook and, finding nothing, made a few calls.

Without Nina's exuberant presence, the house had lost some of its glow. I waited for the confusion to be resolved and for the day's plans to be settled. Then I walked back to my car alone. The houses on the long, hilly street were still neat, and the air fresh-smelling from newly mowed grass.

Of course, I knew that Nina was only one staff person in this house, that if Rachel lived here, I would need to trust several others. *This is what parents mean when they talk about problems with staff,* I thought, a little shaken; it's what proponents of lifesharing were fond of pointing out. It was the first reminder that "perfect" was ephemeral at best, that even after Rachel had a place to live, I could never turn too far away.

It wasn't as if I'd had positive feelings about her dinner date at Ehle House, the fully funded apartment. A familiar face appeared after we rang the bell, and Rachel walked inside. "Pick her up in two hours," I was told. Then the door closed and I was left on the doorstep—confused, shut out.

Wendy had hoped we would stay in Pittsburgh to see things through, but when June drew to an end, nothing had yet been decided. At Sycamore Street, there was the matter of the budget. As for Ehle House, the providers wanted to see Rachel for a third visit, this time with a sleepover. When that would be scheduled no one could say, since not all of the other candidates had yet come by for dinner. Given all this, I drove Rachel to her Catskill camp, promising I would drive her back to Pittsburgh for the sleepover if necessary. "If necessary," because my heart remained set on Sycamore Street.

· · · ·

By the time Rachel had become reacquainted with her camp bunkmates from past years and was swimming in the pool, conning, charming, and frustrating her counselors, Allegheny County had received the budget request for the Sycamore Street house. By law, the county staff were to respond within ten days. I tried simply to wait things out. If at times my own privileged position made me feel uncomfortable, it was hard not to recall that much of what Rachel had gotten over the years came from some unusual push. She had started on growth hormone, enabling her to achieve her full adult height, because of the prodding of the neighbor who was a pediatric endocrinologist. She had Wraparound Services, years of behavior management, because our other neighbor, the child psychiatry chief, had urged us to apply, then made a call for us, saying, "See this child now." And she had gotten Title XIX funding before the gate closed because our supports coordinator understood before I did just how crucial it was.

"Of course you can't sit around doing nothing," said a friend in New York. "Call the mayor. Call the president of your university."

"In Russia, they give gifts," said a friend who'd grown up in Siberia.

Gifts, an Israeli friend agreed.

What about a letter from your therapist, saying you're no longer able to take care of Rachel, someone else suggested.

"Call *everyone* you know," I was told at Achieva. "Your state representative, your congressman, anyone you know at the county level."

"Legislators are the most important group," Nancy Murray, then president of Achieva, had told Charlotte in an interview about the waiting list. "No elected official, even the best of the best, could possibly address every issue or know every issue. But when an elected official starts to get a lot of phone calls . . . that's when they become more knowledgeable and take a stand."

I thought about Murray's words, took a deep breath, and called my state senator, introducing myself as the mother of a twenty-two-year-old daughter with mental retardation (still, after all these years, finding it awkward to say those words). I reminded him of the numbers of people on waiting lists for mental retardation services in Pennsylvania, then compressed Rachel's history, slowing down only when I came to the present situation—the house on Sycamore Street, with the roommates whose company she could enjoy, and the budget that needed county approval . . .

When I told Wendy about the phone call and the state senator's polite questions, she responded in a respectful way, trying not to let her feelings show. From her viewpoint, the process was already working for Rachel. The request for the unfunded vacancy on Sycamore Street had been submitted. Rachel was eligible for four funded vacancies as well. Wendy didn't know for sure whether my call would help or hurt, only that *she* didn't like to be pressured and neither did I. So it was hard to say what effect pressure would have at this point.

"Behind a system that is inundated with paperwork, complicated processes, and funding hurdles, there are people who are working hard to make sure that everyone's needs are met," she wrote in an e-mail. "When we talk about the 'County,' it often sounds as if it is some inhuman, robotic unit with metal-edged gears that slowly turn. There are so many people at the County level who truly want to see every individual safe and happy, just as we do."

• • • •

Late in July, just as I had promised, I picked up Rachel from camp and took her to Pittsburgh for a couple of days. Many things had changed by the time I made that long drive. Rachel had been turned down for two of the funded vacancies in houses we'd viewed as backups. As for the Sycamore Street house, Wendy hadn't yet received word from the county. She felt it was important to tell me she'd heard some disturbing things about the house, first from another supports coordinator with a client there, who'd been visiting the CLA monthly to check the medication chart, monitor the socialization, and make sure the services were all in place. The log was a mess; the house was poorly run. The vacancy had arisen because a family had moved out their daughter. Another roommate's family was contemplating the same thing. It was possible that Nina had been brought in to take charge of things and the situation would improve. Even so, Wendy wanted me to know what she had heard. This was important especially because of a phone call she had just gotten: the providers at Ehle House had liked all four of the women who had visited. All of them seemed perfect for the house. Two men were living in a three-bedroom apartment in the same unit. The providers had decided to move the men and start another apartment for the women.

I was confused at first. "*All* of the women have been chosen?"

"*All* of them," Wendy said.

I saw something that hadn't existed before: six women in two neighboring apartments. Neither of the women I'd met seemed compatible with Rachel. Now Wendy was saying there would be three more. Five possible friends. In an apartment that was close to her worksite. Five possible friends, and a mere half hour from me.

And it was definite? I didn't understand how this agency could suddenly offer four openings. All I knew was that I wasn't driving Rachel back to Pittsburgh to see if she'd "win" the coveted spot. Instead, I was driving her there to see which of two apartments would be preferable for her.

· · · ·

When the summer had drawn to an end, and I was washing and folding the clothes Rachel had brought home from camp, I started thinking what good luck it had been to find Wendy. Luck. That's what it was. Our base service unit had closed, forcing me to move to another agency. I'd tried hard to hold on to Michele and been unable. With great reluctance, I'd attended that fair. (And if the base service unit hadn't closed? If I'd been able to keep Michele as Rachel's supports coordinator? If I had skipped the fair, the way I'd ignored so many information sessions these last few years?) True, I had been pushing to make the system work for Rachel for the last seven years, and at the fair, I had stepped up to that table and asked for something a dozen professionals at every level in the field had called impossible: *In the next two months find a place for my daughter to live.* These people, strangers to us, accepted that challenge. Wendy heard about our case and took it on. She was still fairly new on the job, with only eight months of experience. How could I have known, when we first met in the conference room that April morning, that the young woman with the cropped hair and ramrod posture, the face that betrayed no emotion at all, was "stubborn to the point of being obsessive"? We didn't know that she sought out big challenges and didn't easily accept no for an answer, that despite being a rookie at this particular job, she had been working with kids and adults with developmental disabilities ever since she was a fifteen-year-old camp counselor.

"I do this because I care," Wendy said, reminding me that caring was a necessary quality and something easily lost, given the demands of the job and the shortcomings of the system. Wendy did more than simply care. She also thought, "Over my dead body." That's the kind of person you need on your side. My hard work wouldn't have amounted to a thing if Wendy hadn't come along, hadn't thought *over my dead body.*

Still, there had been one fully funded vacancy when Rachel first visited the house. How could I explain the fact that shortly after Rachel moved into the apartment, two other roommates arrived? I haven't the heart to say that it was good fortune or a lucky break.

Someone had died. That was why, instead of putting everything back into Rachel's bureau drawers at summer's end, I was packing her clothes into thirty-gallon plastic bags.

The person who died was a man who'd been living with a roommate two doors down from the apartment we had seen. After his death, the provider moved the surviving roommate to a different CLA. This left the unit—a big three-bedroom apartment—available. It also created a second fully funded opening.

16

Jane: What's the best part of your apartment?

Rachel: Everything.

Jane: Oh, come on. Tell me what you like best.

Rachel: When the roommates are here.

Jane: Which roommate?

Rachel: Every one of them.

—February 2006

A PERFECT PLACE

I didn't truly believe that Rachel was moving until the morning of August 23, 2005, when I sat in the bright, open kitchen of the apartment that would be her home and helped to plan her new life. I had announced to family and friends that we'd finally found a place for her to live, taking pleasure in hearing my own words. I had packed up her clothes and possessions in bags and loaded them into the car. I'd shopped with Charlotte and Rachel, choosing new linens and towels and pretty things for her room. I had set up meetings with my students for the following day without first making any plans for Rachel's care. The whole time, though, there was a little worm of doubt in my mind, as if I expected that any minute I'd get a call saying the move wouldn't happen after all. It was only when I was sitting in the kitchen of Ehle C with the people who would be responsible for her well-being, when I was answering questions about her self-care and safety skills, her interests, habits, and behaviors, when I was describing her food issues and excessive talking and the abilities she possessed but would not necessarily reveal, that I began to believe that we really had found an apartment for Rachel, and that it wasn't just any apartment.

When I had finished sharing everything I believed was important and true about Rachel, the program manager, Betty Jean, slid a document in front of my daughter with a bold header that said "Statement of Individual's Rights." She waited until Rachel seemed to be paying attention and then said, "I'm going to read you your rights, so you'll know what they are."

Then she began. "I understand that I and everyone else have the right to be treated with dignity and respect . . . to be free from neglect, abuse, mistreatment, and corporal punishment . . . to refuse to be part of any proposed research project . . . to privacy, including in my bathroom and my bedroom, at all times . . . to receive, purchase, have and use personal property . . . to buy what I want, keep it where I want, and use it whenever I want . . . to receive visitors at any reasonable time . . . to meet with my visitors privately and say whatever I want . . . "

Rachel was picking at her nails, listening or not, understanding none or some or perhaps, in her own way, everything. My eyes welled with tears as Betty Jean read aloud, just as at graduation, when I had been overcome by hope and desire. Each right, spelled out on that paper, reminded me of everything I wanted for my daughter and of all of the ways she could be exploited when my back was turned. Her right to be treated "with dignity and respect" reminded me of the long history of those with developmental disabilities being treated as subhuman. Her right "to use the telephone to call someone or have someone call me . . . to . . . make phone calls in private and . . . get help if I want help," to use the phone, send and receive mail "without anyone reading it," to be "free from excessive medication, so much medication that I don't feel like 'myself' . . . " reminded me of all the ways she could be abused, conned, drugged, raped, or cheated once I walked out her front door. When Betty Jean read that Rachel was protected, "as are all U.S. Citizens, by the Bill of Rights/Constitution, the 1964 Civil Rights Act, the 1990 Americans with Disabilities Act, the PA Human Relations Act, the Universal Declaration of Human Rights of the United Nations," I stopped thinking of these rights as obstacles, as I had for so long, instead understanding them as fundamental rights, wrongly withheld for generations. I was grateful that wiser people than I had fought hard to have them protected by law.

Rachel would not sign the paper. "You do it," she said to me.

I knew she was capable of holding a pencil and making a spidery approximation of an "R." She could also be coaxed to write the "a" and sometimes the letters that followed. She was unwilling at this moment—might be unwilling forever—since it was hard for her and made her uncomfortable. The nature of that document was such that I could not possibly sign on her behalf. Betty Jean seemed to know this and inquired again, gently. Rachel still could not be shaken from her desire to have someone else write her name. Betty Jean asked her permission to do hand over hand. When Rachel agreed, Betty Jean put her hand over my daughter's hand and helped her leave on paper a pale, shaky signature that I recognized as her own.

During all this, and for the rest of the day, while Charlotte and I emptied the car and helped Rachel settle into her room, I forgot about the tension between these perfect, necessary laws and the nature of my daughter's desires. It was so thrilling to choose which of the three empty rooms seemed best, and to make up the bed with the new red duvet cover and matching shams. We assembled the red desk and wheeled desk chair, connected her cordless phone and programmed it for speed dialing, tacked the family photos on the bulletin board we'd brought, chose a place to hang the huge schoolroom clock and the poster of Rosie the Riveter, arm flexed, saying, "We can do it!" We unpacked her toiletries, her new towels and washcloths, put her clothes on hangers and in drawers. We set the stuffed frog on the bed beside the turtle, the crab, and the teddy bear that had traveled everywhere with her and seemed limp and exhausted from the effort.

"Just go," she said, when our work was done. We hesitated. Her other roommates had not moved in. When we went home, we would be leaving Rachel in this big, nearly empty apartment with a staff person whom neither of us knew, and then at four o'clock with another staff person, and at midnight with a third. Yet, as always, she was eager for us to go and turned her face away when I tried to kiss her good-bye.

I went home and puttered around for a while, opening mail that had piled up over the last frenetic few days and tidying the mess we'd made while packing. I went into Rachel's room—a nice room, with a black chaise, a setup for her computer, a fireplace with a broad white mantel—and thought about how much she hated it, how she preferred to sleep on an air mattress in a closet-sized room instead. Then I stripped the rumpled sheets from the bed and went to sleep.

PART 2

In the morning, I woke of my own accord. I let the dog out back, retrieved the papers from the front, ground the beans for coffee. While it brewed, I stood in the kitchen and slowly, peacefully entered the day.

Rachel woke in the dark on her first morning in her new house (so I heard) and asked to have coffee with cream and two sugars. When it was time for her to dress for work, she chose her beaded prom dress and heels. Had she been at home, I would have said, "Go back to bed. It isn't morning." I would have said, "You don't *like* coffee." I would have been peevish and abrupt. "*Forget* the prom gown," I would have snapped. "You can't wear a prom gown to work."

She wasn't at home. She was in her own apartment, where her rights were protected by the law, and the staff was prohibited from saying no. It was still dark when the first flurry of phone calls occurred—the staff person calling the house manager calling the program manager. I was in the deep well of sleep while this problem was discussed and a strategy devised to get her out the door in pants instead of her beaded gown without employing the blunt, effective no that was legal under my domain but not theirs.

I laughed when I heard this. *That is so Rachel,* I thought, reminding myself that no matter how perfect the house might be, when she moved, she took her own self along.

• • • •

I didn't laugh at all when Rachel decided she wanted to be incontinent.

She had been living at Ehle C for a month by then and at last had the company of the first of her roommates. This delightful woman, calm and good-humored, possessed a sparkling personality and an ability, in short order, to erect some boundaries and ignore my daughter's relentless demands. *Perfect,* I thought, when I spent time with her. She was a perfect roommate, much the same way that Ehle C was the perfect house.

There were issues, of course—there would always be issues. What made it perfect was how much happier Rachel was than at home. I could hear it when she called, as she did six or seven times a day, ignoring the speed dial we'd set up, able after years of futile attempts to remember phone numbers and dial them whenever she wanted, leaving messages that perfectly evoked her mood. There was the cheerful, half-sung, "Hi, Mom! It's your daughter Rachel! I want to talk to you! Bye," and the gloomy hoarse-voiced, run-on: "It's Rachel I need to talk to you bye." Sometimes, especially in the first weeks, when she was getting up in the middle of the night and was chronically sleep deprived, the calls would start at six in the morning. When I complained that she had woken me up, she would tell me to get my lazy butt out of bed, or cry about her stupid shoes that were ugly as a b-i-t-c-h. There were fewer of these bad mornings after we moved her from the front bedroom we'd initially chosen to the back one, where she was less apt to wake when the staff changed at midnight.

Before Rachel decided she wanted to be incontinent, I dealt with the issues coolly as they arose. There were the sleep disturbances that affected her moods and that the psychiatrist had wanted to medicate, and the assessments sheet I received in the mail that stated that Rachel needed help to brush her teeth, wash, shower, use the toilet, choose her clothes, and handle clothing fastenings—because she had reported being unable to do these things, though she'd been proficient at these tasks for the last ten to fifteen years. After my input, new assessments were drawn up that restated her abilities, bringing her closer to what she was able to do—closer, but not fully, since she knew how to feign incompetence and get her *staff* to do the work. "My staff," she took to saying, early on, as if she was royalty, out on the town.

I trusted that even without the ability to say no, her staff wasn't going to send her to work in her beaded dress and heels. And my own no to a diet of junk food was backed up by a letter from her physician, stating the necessity for her to maintain a low-fat, low-calorie diet and to lose the weight she'd gained over the summer that had put her just on the edge of being clinically obese.

It was harder to convince the staff of how important it was for Rachel to be kept busy, especially when she said no to every activity they suggested. No, she didn't want to swim, or bowl, or go to a dance. I knew that, after the honeymoon period, the long stretch of time between her three o'clock dismissal from work and her bedtime was going to be a problem and that it was important for staff to learn to move her beyond that no. "You'll see how happy she is doing these things once you get her going," I kept saying, to no avail. I had already seen my daughter badger a staff person with her constant questions and relentless need for attention. This woman, unable to redirect Rachel or set limits, cringed at the sound of my daughter's voice, hating her, I could tell.

I was struggling with these issues and believing they would be resolved when a staff person called to ask if Rachel needed a pad at night. Her roommate had bladder control problems and used one on her bed. Rachel wanted one, too.

"No!" I thundered. "Absolutely not! Under no circumstances!" She hadn't wet her bed since she was ten, and she wasn't going to start now. Everyone in that house, including Rachel, needed to know that.

Ooh, I thought, when I hung up. *Overreacted to that.*

The next day, Rachel called, crying, to tell me that she had "wet herself accidentally." I didn't care what Rachel wanted then, had no interest in hearing that "No" was forbidden. Maybe it was Rachel's right to become incontinent, but it wasn't going to happen. Someone was going to figure out what word to use in place of "No," to let my daughter know that she would no sooner become incontinent than get behind the wheel of my car and drive me straight to Mars.

. . . .

Why then, given these snags and many others, did I persist in thinking of Ehle C as perfect? Because when I stopped by one Saturday night without much notice, Rachel was busy getting ready for a dance. Five women were living in the two apartments by then, and four of them were buzzing around. The whole time I was there, the phone kept ringing. Rachel and her roommates were scurrying from apartment to apartment, giggling, worrying about what to wear, calling each other on the phone. It was like stepping into a dorm room on a weekend night, and my daughter was part of this, laughing into the receiver, rushing next door.

I sat on Rachel's bed that night, listening to her giggles. I looked at her corner étagère, with her books, games, and knickknacks, at the lava lamp the dead man had left behind, and Rosie on the wall. I thought of her room at my house, of how it had been a place of banishment in her eyes, *away* from the life that went on in other rooms. I thought of her fervent desire to be part of the fun and conversation when she lived with me, and of the inevitable bad behavior that arose from her frustration at being unable to join in. It wasn't her fault, or mine. I couldn't be expected to keep living a life dominated by her demands, and she couldn't be expected to conform to my ways. Here, though, she had the chance to be herself—and often was, in every way. I knew she was sometimes obnoxious here, as she'd been at home—impulsive, stubborn, unstoppable. She still risked alienating peers, staff, and strangers, still needed to have her behavior managed. It was different, though. Here she could live in her own skin, without the constant, grating reminder of all she could not do.

Sometimes her behavior in the morning shocked the staff. Sometimes, though, she and her roommate started the day by tickling each other's feet, then sitting across the table from each other, eating their breakfast together, comparing the lunches they'd packed, getting into the van to go to work. Sometimes she screamed and cursed, but not always. Once I arrived at her apartment for a morning meeting while she was getting ready for work and I heard her call Joan, the morning staff person, "Turkey Head," and Joan retorting with "Chicken Face." I was touched and pleased to see that Rachel had taken the game we invented to her new house. She had found someone who knew how to play it, and did so with humor and affection.

I called the house perfect because, after two months, the house manager said in passing, "She really *is* much happier when she's busy," at last believing what I had claimed was true. "We've started to see that even though she always says no, when you watch her, like at basketball, she's in there with the others, doing all the exercises, having a really great time."

I called it perfect because after breakfast, Rachel got into the van and a few minutes later walked through the door of TOC, the Training and Outsourcing Center, managed by the same private not-for-profit corporation that supervised her apartment. At this worksite there was no risk that expensive job coaching would fade before Rachel's skills were intact because it was the job coaches who stayed in place. The employees who gained independence were the ones who moved away from them. That meant less anxiety in the early months, when the staff struggled with Rachel's attention seeking and her constant requests for help. At TOC, she was given a training goal that took advantage of her interest in being with staff, the job of putting paper in the fax machine and printer as soon as she walked in the door. Eventually her desk was positioned so that she faced the corner instead of the other workers. This simple adaptation helped her concentrate on her job. After eight months, she was described as a good worker, who'd mastered the skills needed to do packaging and mailing. She'd really found her niche, I was told. She was sunny and popular, with lots of friends. "Everyone wants to sit next to her at lunch. And the guys? I don't know if she's told you, but they all want to ask her out. She says she's not ready to date yet."

I have to imagine that someone helped my daughter phrase that answer. Perhaps it was someone in her perfect house.

. . . .

In October, I made arrangements for Access, the county paratransit system, to take Rachel from her worksite to the JCC twice a week so she could meet up with her old friends in the after-school program. Early in the summer, when I'd initially asked if Rachel could rejoin the group come fall, there was some hesitation. Officially, it is an after-school program for teens, I was told. Rachel wouldn't still be in school by then, and wasn't even a teen. Even I had some second thoughts, worrying that I foolishly clung to this program because she was with kids here and could still be a kid herself. After I obtained the approval for her to attend, I remembered the other reasons I'd wanted her to return. The JCC had been in Rachel's life for fourteen years. It was a place where the desk attendants, maintenance crews, and security force knew her name and watched out for her when there was a transportation snag or a miscommunication. Neighbors and people I knew from school often saw Rachel when they were at the JCC, which made me feel as if she was still part of my community, not some shameful hidden daughter. It was also near my house and gave me a chance to pick her up once a week and drive her home.

A parent meeting had been scheduled for six o'clock on the day she rejoined the program. As soon as I entered the teen lounge and saw the parents already seated around the table, I could tell a crisis was brewing. Parents had received letters from their base service units saying they could no longer use waiver money to cover the cost of this JCC program because it was "recreational" in nature. One of the parents had drafted a letter of complaint to the head of her base service unit; another had begun calling people at the county level.

I took an empty seat. Though the problem was no longer mine, I felt a familiar tightening in my gut and found myself thinking: *This is what it's like.* Funds cut, every time you turned around. Programs necessary for our children or for our families curtailed with scant notice, and parents scrambling to have them reinstated or replaced. Teenagers were especially in a void. This particular program had initially been developed in collaboration with Western Psychiatric Institute as a therapeutic after-school program and run that way until the rules changed and several of us lost the trained support staff, who came through Wraparound to implement behavior management strategies. The JCC program coordinators responded to that crisis by redesigning the program and making it recreational instead of therapeutic, though the "structured setting" remained, and it was still described in the catalog as a place where teens could "build life skills, express themselves in creative ways, gain confidence to interact with the community and their peer group."

How ironic that after adjusting to these changes, parents were now being told that the program wasn't therapeutic enough and would therefore not be covered. Waiver money could be used for in-home services instead, one parent was told: for caregivers, in other words—a costly, cruelly isolating "solution." Teenagers at home with caregivers lack the chance to interact with peers; they can't simply have fun with friends, something they did in this group.

Sitting silently while the other parents talked about their strategies to deal with this latest crisis, I thought about the afternoon in late August 1999, when I had tried to register Rachel for the after-school program and was told by the director, "Didn't we decide she was too old for this program?" The question shocked me even though it was utterly reasonable, since the cutoff age in the program was eleven and Rachel was then sixteen. I thought about the teen after-school program that was started that fall and about Barbara Milch's telling me not to worry, that the JCC would always be there for Rachel. I had believed her until one year, after she herself had left, a parent phoned me to say that this after-school program was being canceled because not enough kids had registered to make it financially viable.

During the next days of furious phone calls, when I wondered what Rachel would do after school and how I would teach my classes if we failed to get the program reinstated, I saw myself asking the parent of a "typically developed" child to picture what it was like for us. Imagine sitting at your desk in August and hearing that your child would not have school in the fall. Now imagine living with that kind of uncertainty not for one year, or two, but for fifteen years, or twenty. Or more.

One of the mothers approached me after the parent meeting in October 2005 and asked how things were going with Rachel.

"She's so happy," I said. "The house is just perfect."

This mother, an attorney with a sixteen-year-old son, told me she was planning to get the families together and to sue the state. I listened, wished her luck, and offered to share everything I'd learned, though it seemed just then that I could summarize it all in five seconds: I pushed hard. I had a supports coordinator who wouldn't take no. I got lucky. A man died.

I was standing in the lobby for a moment after she left when the impact hit me, like a physical force: What a long time I'd been in this world, dependent on luck and on the goodwill of strangers, buffeted by political decisions enacted far from my home, made useless as a mother. *That was hard,* I thought, as if for the first time. *That was really hard.*

. . . .

Not that it is over. You love someone and it's never over. Now, though, Rachel is in the system. Her funding is *attached* and the two of us are unchained. I've been freed from Rachel's unquenchable needs, and she's been released from my domination. When I said, "She's so happy. The house is just perfect," I meant it fully, never for an instant forgetting that "happy" is a land with peaks and valleys, and "perfect" a place with uncertain terrain, never free of hazards.

That was why I could still say the house was perfect when a new staff person, a fluttery, anxious woman, told me of her own accord that she did exactly what was in the log, followed the menu, played by all the rules—and then, that very day, gave Rachel French toast and cereal for breakfast, and decided to forgo taking her to the JCC for basketball, though it was written in the log. It gave me the chills to realize I knew these things only because Charlotte, who'd moved back to New York by then, happened to be visiting and had seen them herself. Trivial incidents, but a reminder that I had entrusted the care of my daughter to many people, not all of them honorable.

It is why many parents chose to keep their developmentally disabled sons and daughters home, why many of those "children" who reached their thirties and forties were still cared for by aging parents. Oh, the awful things that could happen, the parents say. They were right, of course: awful things did happen, under their watchful eyes and not, as I well knew. It was why a mother whose daughter also lived in a CLA took me aside one day and said, "No one can take care of our children like we can."

She was also right. No one would ever be as invested in Rachel as I had been since the day of her birth. No one would scrutinize her language as carefully, or listen as closely, transcribing each word, aching to wrest meaning from her utterances, to find the subtext beneath her convoluted sentences. No one would dress her as well or worry as much as I did about the kind of food she ate and whether she got exercise. No one would check the crevices of her arms and the backs of her ears to see if she had a rash, or chase her around the house when she had a blemish, trying to put astringent on her face. No one would fret over her dry skin and put lotion on her legs or kiss her funny feet—not as often as I did, at least.

No one would ever search as hard as I'd been searching to find her soul.

It mattered. I know it did. I know it still does.

It hurt when I saw her with food around her mouth, dressed in clothes that were wrong for the season. It hurt when she said, "She don't come in till four," and "I don't got no money." I could still say, "*What?*" and she would correct herself, but not for long. When she moved into Ehle House, she entered a world where the influence of others took hold, and where soon I would become distant to her. It hurt, but it was the worthwhile price of letting her have the life she had wanted for years, in her own apartment, with her own phone and computer, with roommates and staff and the freedom to wake at six for coffee with cream and sugar, whether she drank it or not.

The other mother was right: no one would love Rachel as much as I did. But to keep her beside me in the name of love would be to bind and gag her.

My daughter, my Rachel, funny, unruly, mysterious—she's all grown up now, living and working on her own. As for me, I'm like a giant, unseen bird, circling above her perfect house, eager for a glimpse inside, swooping low sometimes, hoping now and again she'll hear my flapping wings, look up, and think of me.

ACKNOWLEDGMENTS

This book would not exist if Ann Lowry hadn't asked in the late 1990s if I would consider writing a "successor/companion" to *Loving Rachel,* then asked again several years later. Thank you, Ann. Thanks also to the hardworking, book-loving people at the University of Illinois Press.

I am grateful to Jane McCafferty, Lee Gutkind, and Eileen Stukane for being my trusted readers; to my colleagues in the English Department at Carnegie Mellon University for helping create a home for writers; and to our department head, David Kaufer, for his unwavering professional and personal support. Thanks also to Kari Lundgren and Kira Dreher.

By necessity, more gets left out of a story than gets told. Nowhere in this book do I mention the Harveys, the Haskells, or the Siddalls, who made Rachel part of their families. Thanks to them, and to Warren Siddall for his enduring affection for Rachel; to Edwin Martinez, cinematographer and cake-maker extraordinaire, for brightening our lives; to Lilly Halperin for taking care of me in Israel; to Loren Fishman and Carol Ardman for taking care of me in New York; to Dr. Cynthia Johnson for being a friend and stellar professional; and to Dr. Martin Lubetsky for his wisdom and dedication.

Thanks to the Blue Mountain Center, where I was nurtured, fed, and given the silence I desperately needed, and to the Pennsylvania Council on the Arts for awarding me a Fellowship in Creative Writing.

266

At the reception after Rachel's commencement ceremony, a cafeteria worker shyly approached to offer her congratulations. "I'll really miss you, Rachel," she said. That was when I learned that for thirteen years she had been preparing Rachel's lunch—and more. A belated thank you to this woman and to all the teachers, therapists, psychologists, social workers, bus drivers, supports coordinators, counselors, and staff who have worked with and for Rachel. The list is so long. Thank you Barbara Milch, Marissa Fogel, Angelica Miskanin, Jezelle Stiggers, Chrissy Voos, Kelly Jane Walker, and Wendy Parkin. To those of you I have not acknowledged by name and those whose names I never learned, thank you for feeding my daughter, watching out for her, worrying about her, and helping her find her way. My gratitude is beyond words.

PART 2

JANE BERNSTEIN is a professor of English and creative writing at Carnegie Mellon University. She is the author of *Departures; Bereft—A Sister's Story; Seven Minutes in Heaven;* and *Loving Rachel.* Her numerous essays and articles have appeared in publications such as the *New York Times Magazine, Prairie Schooner,* and the *Massachusetts Review.* For more information see www.janebernstein.net.

The University of Illinois Press
is a founding member of the
Association of American University Presses.

———————————————————————

Composed in 11/14 Cycles
with Bell Gothic display
by Jim Proefrock
at the University of Illinois Press
Designed by Dennis Roberts
Manufactured by Sheridan Books, Inc.

University of Illinois Press
1325 South Oak Street
Champaign, IL 61820-6903
www.press.uillinois.edu